(Un)Becoming

(Un)Becoming

Darla Peters

Elm Hill

A Division of
HarperCollins Christian Publishing

www.elmhillbooks.com

(Un)Becoming

Published in Nashville, Tennessee, by Elm Hill, an imprint of Thomas Nelson. Elm Hill and Thomas Nelson are registered trademarks of HarperCollins Christian Publishing, Inc.

Elm Hill titles may be purchased in bulk for educational, business, fund-raising, or sales promotional use. For information, please e-mail SpecialMarkets@ThomasNelson.com.

Scripture quotations marked AMP are from the Amplified˚ Bible. Copyright © 1954, 1958, 1962, 1964, 1965, 1987 by The Lockman Foundation. Used by permission. (www.Lockman.org)

Scripture quotations marked ESV are from the ESV˚ Bible (The Holy Bible, English Standard Version˚). Copyright © 2001 by Crossway, a publishing ministry of Good News Publishers. Used by permission. All rights reserved.

Scripture quotations marked KJV are from the King James Version. Public domain.

Scripture quotations marked THE MESSAGE are from *The Message*. Copyright © by Eugene H. Peterson 1993, 1994, 1995, 1996, 2000, 2001, 2002. Used by permission of NavPress. All rights reserved. Represented by Tyndale House Publishers, Inc.

Scripture quotations marked NIV are from the Holy Bible, New International Version˚, NIV˚. Copyright © 1973, 1978, 1984, 2011 by Biblica, Inc.˚ Used by permission of Zondervan. All rights reserved worldwide. www.Zondervan.com. The "NIV" and "New International Version" are trademarks registered in the United States Patent and Trademark Office by Biblica, Inc.˚

Scripture quotations marked NKJV are from the New King James Version˚. © 1982 by Thomas Nelson. Used by permission. All rights reserved.

Scripture quotations marked NLT are from the Holy Bible, New Living Translation. © 1996, 2004, 2007, 2013, 2015 by Tyndale House Foundation. Used by permission of Tyndale House Publishers, Inc., Carol Stream, Illinois 60188. All rights reserved.

Library of Congress Cataloging-in-Publication Data

Library of Congress Control Number: 2020901331

ISBN 978-1-400332809 (Paperback)
ISBN 978-1-400332816 (eBook)

TABLE OF CONTENTS

PREFACE

*O*kay, God, I'll write...but you have to give me the words. This was the (reluctant) agreement I whispered just moments ago on this ~~snowy~~ rainy February morning as I tossed a load of the girls' dirty clothes into the washer, eyes blurred with unreleased tears. Even now as I begin to type, I'm fighting the strong desire to back out of the deal. Maybe it's not too late. (*Mostly* kidding.)

Sure, my flesh would rather not tackle this perceivably daunting endeavor; I've never considered myself a budding author, nor aspired to be one. Yet my spirit knows that where the Father leads, He also forges a way. And not just *any* way, but one marked with sufficient grace and unforeseen joys.

Thy will be done.

I can hear it now: *It's about time, Darla!* Yes, there are several of you who have served as God's megaphones, gently (yet persistently) nudging me in the way of writing. While obedience to the Father is my first priority, I also feel I owe this book to those who have faithfully followed our story.

So without further ado (and before I conjure up a legitimate excuse not to do this), let's start where any good story should...the beginning.

"Faith must be tried, and seeming desertion is the furnace, heated seven times, into which it might be thrust. Blest the man who can endure the ordeal!"

(C.H. Spurgeon)

CHAPTER 1

UNKNOWN

It was the spring of 2017. We had just enjoyed a wonderful Mother's Day weekend camping trip with friends at a nearby state park. There's something so refreshing and freeing about being immersed in God's creation—not to mention adventurous. Still, as we tore down our tent and packed up our stuff, there was an excitement about returning home to a warm shower and comfy bed. I felt tired, maybe even a little rundown. Though, who isn't after days of outdoor activity with two young girls, followed by nights of tent-floor sleeping? We drove home, unpacked, and cleaned up before heading to my in-laws' home for a Mother's Day dinner.

Sitting on the back patio next to my sister-in-law, she asked how our camping trip was. I can't recall my exact response, but I do remember somewhere in the midst of the conversation mentioning how I felt especially worn down. Again, nothing a good night's sleep in my own bed wouldn't fix, I was convinced.

Little did I know that this was actually the *best* I would feel for a very long time.

I woke up Monday morning with a slight sore throat. *Ugh!* I must've picked something up while we were camping. *Oh well!* I was sure it would soon progress into a cold, and life would return to normal shortly thereafter. But when I woke up the following day, the throat pain was no longer *slight* but *strong*. My husband, Brian, suggested I head to urgent care before dropping Wendy (our youngest) off at preschool. *Great* idea! I gently woke her up from her peaceful slumber, explaining that Mommy was sick and needed to get to a doctor before school. She looked up at me half awake and said, "Oh, good, because my ears hurt!"

We walked away from the clinic with two new diagnoses—double ear infection for Wendy and strep throat for me. Walgreens was our next stop to pick up our prescriptions and then back home to rest and recover.

As it usually goes with strep throat, the uncomfortable symptoms began to mostly ease up twenty-four hours after my first round of antibiotics. *Perfect* timing! I had Wendy's preschool "Picnic with Mom" to attend that week, not to mention her end-of-the-school-year program. The following day, I was a chaperone for Clara's (our oldest) kindergarten zoo field trip; and on Saturday, I was leaving for a weekend women's retreat where I was helping lead worship. *Phew!* No room in the schedule for sickness.

While the retreat was spiritually and emotionally refreshing, late-night talks and early-morning risings left me physically drained. One of these days, I was going to feel rested, I was sure of it! But instead of getting better with time (as I expected), new frailties seemed to rise to the surface. Intermittent chest pains, lower back aches, and a fever sent me once again to urgent care one evening late in May. They ran an EKG and chest x-ray, which thankfully both turned out fine. The urine sample they collected was iffy, so they prescribed an antibiotic to treat what appeared to be another infection.

Memorial Day weekend was just two days away, and the whole family was getting together to celebrate my mom's sixty-fifth birthday. With food to prep and people to visit, I certainly didn't prefer to be sick. And thankfully, in God's grace, I sensed His covering during that time. While I wasn't fully "myself" (mainly due to a strange fullness in my upper right abdomen, resulting in a lack of appetite), I was well enough to enjoy everyone's company. We even came away with a new family photo. And though I didn't vocalize it at the time, I had an uncomfortable (almost eerie) thought that there was more significance to this all-family picture than we could fathom in the moment. *Would it be the last?* Of course, I couldn't answer this question either way with full assurance, nor did I want to. What I *did* know was that something was up...and it didn't seem right.

From there, things took a steady decline. Everyday activities—once thoughtless and effortless—took on new challenges. Walking up the stairs left me breathless; crossing the parking lot to watch the girls play soccer felt like the last stretch of a marathon (not that I've ever run one, but it's what I imagine it to be like). One evening, as I lay in bed struggling to fall asleep, the sound of the bathroom clock demanded my attention. Pressing my fingers against the side of my neck, I began to count beats against the ticks and tocks. Was my heart rate—my *resting* heart rate—*really* 100 beats (maybe more) per minute?! This would explain my frequent short-windedness, but why?

Summer break had officially begun, and I wanted to soak up as much time with the girls as I could. Maybe it would help take my mind off the physical anomalies as well. We spent time outside, visited nearby museums, got together with friends, ran through the sprinkler in the backyard, played at the park, splashed in the splash pad, enjoyed outdoor picnic dinners, and worked on crafts. Still, I recognized my growing limitations, and more often than I desired, found myself telling the girls, "We're going to have to go home soon; Mommy isn't feeling well." Looking back, I'm especially grateful for how patient and understanding they were. I don't remember them ever complaining but were compassionate and loving. "Okay, Mommy!" What a gift.

Speaking of gifts, Brian surprised me with a long weekend away to celebrate our eleventh anniversary at the beginning of June. He'd arranged for the girls to stay at his parents' house, made reservations at a hotel for two nights in a nearby larger city, and even packed my suitcase without me knowing. *Impressive!* (Not to mention incredibly sweet.) I was hesitant to go at first because of my recent health (or lack thereof), but once again—like Memorial Day weekend with extended family—God's grace blanketed that specific pocket of time together; my ailments mostly remained on the backburner for those couple of days, and we enjoyed an overall wonderful getaway. It was difficult, however, to silence the same thoughts that haunted me before: *Would this be the last?* I felt strange keeping private these wonderings from Brian; then again, I couldn't see how sharing them would in any way be beneficial. Why spoil the moment?

While we had planned to stay two nights, God had a different idea. Walking out to the parking lot the next morning, we realized our car (along with several others in the hotel lot) had been broken into. Thankfully, we didn't have much left in the car, and even less that would be considered valuable; all that went missing was a cheap cellphone car charger. (Quick tangent: That coming Sunday morning, we would be leading the two-and three-year-old class at church. A folder with the teaching material was in the car, and it was obvious, *Someone's been rummaging through my folder!* The Goldilocks bandit must have been desperate!) Still, it altered what the rest of our time would look like. Our first priority was finding a company that could clean out the glass in our car and cover the window with a temporary sheet of plastic. After that, we enjoyed a few more sites in the area and then both agreed we'd prefer to head back home for the night. I wonder if even that was an act of the Father's love as things would soon be taking a rapid turn for the worse.

My sore throat was back! At first I suspected a recurrence of strep, but unlike last time, my tonsils and soft palate were noticeably swollen. Thankfully, there was an opening with my usual family practice doctor; no urgent care this time. Even though both the strep and mono tests she ordered came back negative, she still had concerns. I left the clinic with a five-day Z-PAK prescription, as well as a follow-up appointment the next week. The doctor knew enough to know something wasn't quite right.

Things progressed at warp speed. While the sore throat was slightly improving, my lymph nodes were increasingly swollen. And not just the lymph nodes in my neck, but ones in various locations of the body—places I didn't even know they *existed* until then. More and more bruises were showing up, large and unexplainable. In fact, simply carrying a bag over my shoulder from the grocery store to the car left immediate streaks of bruising. My rib cage was in chronic pain, and inhaling triggered a strange stabbing effect in my upper torso that forced me into a partially doubled-over stance; this, of course, encouraged shallow breathing, which I didn't prefer. My heart rate remained at a constant elevated state, leaving me easily winded. I also began having daily fevers. *What was going on?*

While I know it's not always the most reliable source (or even the wisest of decisions), I consulted *Dr. Google*. Typing out each of my symptoms as one long thread in the search bar, "leukemia" resulted as the closest match. *Leukemia?* Surely not. Then again, except for two ailments—petechiae and bleeding gums—my symptom list was spot on with leukemia's. I'd never even heard of *petechiae* , but after looking it up realized I indeed had these clusters of tiny purple and red spots on my skin in various places. Still, I didn't foresee issues with my gums anytime soon. Being an avid flosser and a DK (Dentist's Kid) the likelihood that my gums would suddenly start to bleed seemed slim-to-none. Holding onto this *one* unmatched symptom out of the *many* matches seemed like a nice buffer. Well, wouldn't you know, in the next day or two, my gums started bleeding during a routine floss. Looking more closely in the mirror, I noticed they were quite red and swollen. *Hmm.* This whole leukemia thing didn't seem so far-fetched a diagnosis after all. In fact, it seemed like the only sensible explanation at this point.

In the midst of all this, I was scheduled to help lead worship that Sunday, June 11th. With how I was feeling—especially the jabbing pains I experienced when taking a deep breath—I wasn't sure it was feasible. But before texting the worship leader that morning with my final decision, I knelt with my head on the bathroom floor and asked the Lord one simple question: *Should I follow through with my commitment, or bail this time?* God's response wasn't immediate; it took several minutes of watchful waiting before He answered. But in the stillness and solitude, I eventually heard His answer, thanks to the songbird outside the window who was incessantly tweeting. *How Can I Keep from Singing?* are the words He put in my mind, and which I repeated with my mouth. Some of you may recognize the title of the old hymn, and in *Googling* the lyrics, I heard an even clearer answer from the Lord: "No storm can shake my inmost calm, while to that rock I'm clinging." Translation: *Darla, I'm not promising you complete health this morning, but let Me be the Rock to Whom you cling.*

While there was a bit of discomfort from time to time that morning, God sustained me. It was obvious that it was *His* strength—not my own—playing those notes on the keys and singing each lyric on the page. One of the songs we sang that particular morning was one by Hillsong Worship called *Cornerstone*, which became even more meaningful and significant as time went on. The Lord would be my firm foundation, despite the storm surrounding me.

That final stretch before my follow-up appointment tested every ounce of endurance left in me. I wasn't scheduled until Thursday afternoon to see the doctor again, and quite honestly, I didn't know if I could wait even those few more days leading up to it. Symptoms were multiplying, and on top of it, my monthly cycle began. I was losing so much blood I didn't know how to manage it, especially through the night. I've never been one to rely on medicine, but I began taking regular doses of ibuprofen around the clock. Still, it seemed to be doing *nothing* for the pain I was experiencing. It's like it was in my bones, which later I'd find out it was! Sleep was nearly impossible in my bed, so I found a way to slightly prop myself up on the couch downstairs. It wasn't ideal, but I managed to get a little rest that way. Uncharacteristically, I called the clinic every day that week leading up to my appointment, asking if my doctor happened to have any sooner openings pop up. Unfortunately, she didn't, so we would just have to wait it out a few more days. Here's hoping (and praying) I could.

Thursday, June 15th, had *finally* arrived. The girls and I made some homemade playdough that morning before heading to the church to clean the nursery toys. Our next stop was a local cultural center the girls (and I) enjoy visiting. But by the time we got there, I had very little left to offer. Simply walking up the long set of stairs to the exhibit felt like an accomplishment. When we got to a room set up with fun mazes and life-size building blocks, I set the expectation from the beginning: "Girls, I'm going to sit here and watch you play." Five minutes into this much-needed rest, in walked someone from our church. Looking back, I wish that my pride wouldn't have gotten the best of me. For fear of seeming like *"that mom"*—disengaged, checked-out, perhaps even lazy—I picked myself up off the floor (where I was sitting), and proceeded to walk through the maze with Wendy and build blocks with Clara. I left the place dragging, and couldn't be more thankful the time of my appointment was nearly here.

After having a quick bite for lunch, Bapa and Nana (Brian's parents) came to the house to watch the girls. Brian arrived shortly thereafter, because he wanted to go to the appointment with me. At the time, I wasn't sure it was necessary for him to come, but I'd soon find out his presence was crucial! In the car on the way to the clinic, we were praying that God would provide the physician with the wisdom to properly diagnose and the discernment to accurately treat whatever my body was trying (and failing) to fight. Or, at the very least, that she would refer us to someone who could. When the doctor walked into the exam room, she looked dressed for war. Not literally, of course—she still wore her usual white lab coat—but her expression and posture were focused, strong, and determined. After listening to my list of ailments (which had only grown since the week prior) and examining the areas that concerned me, she spoke firmly and directly: "We need to get a chest x-ray and blood work from you today, and I need you to stay here until we get results."

The doctor settled us into a different room once my tests were done. I lay flat on a hard exam room table (not designed with comfort or longevity in mind) with my feet dangling off the edge for three hours while they pumped bag after bag (three in all) of fluids through my IV. Apparently, I was dehydrated. It was evening by the time the doctor walked in the door with my results. It wasn't good. Even before uttering a word, the stern look on her face gave it away. My platelets and hemoglobin were dangerously low, and my white blood cells were uncommonly high. She'd already called our local hospital and gotten us admitted to a room in the ER. She was short and to the point. There was no time for more.

Since we were very close to home, Brian advised we swing by so that we could both change into comfier clothes—he was still in his work attire (shirt and tie), and I was ready to swap out my jeans for something less constraining. Walking up the stairs to our bedroom about did me in; I crashed on the bed and told Brian, "I don't know if I can make it to the ER." Thankfully, he wouldn't allow me to settle for defeat and encouraged me to my feet. Toothbrushes, extra clothes, and supplies needed to take care of this continued menstrual cycle were quickly packed. Back in the car we went, *this* time, on our way to the emergency room.

I don't remember much about that initial entry into the ER. Vaguely, I recall plopping myself down in the nearest available chair as soon as we walked in the door. Even sitting seemed like too much effort at this point, so I attempted (awkwardly, mind you) to somehow lay my head down on the arm rest, letting my arms spill over into the chair next to me. It's funny what you'll do (and the dignity you're willing to compromise) when you're feeling downright lousy. I couldn't have cared less how strange I may have appeared to the public in that moment, nor was I well enough to notice.

Once we were settled in the ER, the doctor had reserved for us, I came to realize just how much that long stretch on the exam table did me in. The achiness I was experiencing in my back was unavoidable, and no matter which way I turned or lay or sat, it wouldn't ease up. Meanwhile, several attempts were being made (by multiple people) to get an IV started; finally, it was in, and they were able to collect blood for more tests. And since the three bags of fluids weren't enough (I guess), a fourth bag was started here. Next, I was led to a room to have a CT scan done. I still remember how difficult and excruciating it was to take the deep breaths and hold them for the scan because of those stabbing pains I experienced whenever I did.

When I got back to the room, it was time to wait for the results of all these various tests. In the meantime, they brought in a bag of blood for a transfusion (because of the low hemoglobin) as well as platelets—as it turned out, the first of *many* (of each of these) I would receive that month. A group of friends who normally met on Thursday evenings to pray at the church came to my hospital room instead. Forming a big circle around my bed, heartfelt petitions were lifted up through tears. Not much sooner had they left than the on-call doctor made his way into our room with an official update. Professionally, yet compassionately he broke the news: "Well, it looks like you either have some sort of rare virus we aren't sure of, or you have leukemia...it's probably leukemia."

Honestly, I can't say we were surprised by the announcement. In fact, the doctor was more surprised by our calm reaction than we were by his news. God had so kindly been preparing our hearts and minds along the way. If anything, I felt a sense of *relief* that there was now a diagnosis, which meant a plan (though one I was certain I wouldn't particularly enjoy). And truthfully, "leukemia" sounded more appealing than "some sort of rare virus" (which may or may not have had a known cure). While they worked to prepare a room on the fourth floor for us to stay the night, a friend of ours who was also on-call in the ER that evening stopped by. He wiped away tears, expressed his genuine sympathy, and prayed for us.

Once we had a moment to ourselves, we held each other (avoiding the IV and various tubing as best we could) and prayed. No doubt there were tears, but there was also an inexplicable peace that invaded our hearts. Sure, we didn't know all that was ahead (And thank God for that!), but we knew the One who did and who was going on this journey with us. He hadn't abandoned us, and we were grateful for His willingness to walk alongside us on this hard road.

As I lay in the hospital bed, I turned to look at Brian through my tear-stained eyes and said, "God sure does love us." I didn't speak these words facetiously; there was no hint of sarcasm or cynicism in my tone. It was a sincere declaration of how I felt—and what I knew to be true—in the moment. I didn't feel angry, but *honored*. I didn't feel scared, but *relieved*. Without getting into a theological debate, I believed that if God chose us for this trial—if He allowed it in His sovereignty—He knew we could "handle it" *with* HIS strength and *with* HIS grace. What a privilege! It was as if He had handed us a gift—one not necessarily packaged in pretty paper—and it was up to us to decide what we did with it. From day one, I was determined that no matter *what* this journey held..."I'm not dragging God through the mud!" That HE would be glorified...that HE would be magnified...this was (and is) my desire and prayer.

By this point, it was late, so we sent emails to many and phone calls to few for the latest update. That may have been the hardest part. Then it was time to settle in to our new location...

For now.

CHAPTER 2

UNCOVERED

All things considered, we had a fairly restful night's sleep that first evening on Ball Hospital's fourth floor. (It wasn't until now—upon revisiting Brian's first journal entries on my *CaringBridge* site—that I realized I was placed in the Medical Telemetry Unit, which specializes in critical care. Oh, the things from which I was shielded...thankfully!) Was it *really* only the 16th of June? How *full* the previous day had been! It makes me especially grateful for our naïveté at that time. If we had known how long and bumpy the road ahead of us was, we may have crumbled under the weight of it.

We were visited by a hematologist that morning who was both personable and informative, though I have little to no recollection of what he shared with us. Funny how that goes. It must not have been terribly profound; either that or the pain meds I was on dulled my coherency. I *think* he mainly shared a broad overview of what leukemia is and what to expect in the next few days: biopsy, staying put for a few days, and eventually being transferred to another hospital.

In order to confirm my diagnosis and gather crucial details surrounding it (what specific form of leukemia I have, etc.), I was scheduled for a bone marrow biopsy (which became my first of many) that afternoon. The normal protocol in this particular hospital for the procedure is to put the patient fully "under"—I was okay with that! Once I was wheeled off to surgery and the medicine was administered through my IV, I don't remember anything until I woke up to a completed biopsy. *Wonderful!* Proving true once again that sometimes ignorance really is bliss.

A brief medical sidenote*:

*Warning: If you have an especially weak stomach, skip ahead to the paragraph that begins, "The rest of the day..."

Now that I've experienced a whopping *ten* of these bad boys, I realize why most hospitals simply do local numbing (sedation at most) for a bone marrow biopsy. It's not a long procedure (*usually*), and while they're far from pleasant, they *are* tolerable. For those who haven't already paused to *Google* for more information, I will do my best to explain: Lying on your side or stomach (whichever the person performing the procedure prefers), the skin around the hip bone (either your left or right side) is numbed using a local anesthetic (shots of novocaine). A wide needle is then inserted and pushed deep into the spongy part of the bone to aspirate some of the marrow. After that, back in the needle goes, this time fishing for an actual piece of the bone. Twist, pull, and *voila!* The treasure (bone) has been found!

Probably not best if you're reading this before dinner. My apologies if you were.

The rest of the day was surprisingly nice...even somewhat restful. We were visited by my parents, our pastor, and several friends (both from church and college). How sweet of them all to show up; it meant a great deal to us. When people asked for updates, we shared only what we knew up to that point: We would be at this hospital until the results of the biopsy were back (which they said would take several days), and after that we'd be transferred to a hospital in Indianapolis. The thought of being able to "stay put" for a few days sounded good to me.

Between procedures and visits (both from medical staff and outside visitors), my mind was captivated anew by the incredible reality of Jesus' *spotless* blood. Untainted by sin or sickness, this faultless Lamb of God sacrificed His very *life* for the sake of the world...for the sake of *me*. To think that my blood—now marred with a grave disease—has been (in a spiritual sense) washed clean by Jesus' blood! *Astounding*. Despite what happened to my physical body—even if it would be an early death—I knew that His blood was pumping within my veins, breathing life that would live beyond my earthly tent. Even in the days of animal sacrifices, it was clear: "for the life of the body is in its blood" (Lev. 17:11 NLT).

That evening, Brian was asked to visit the nurse's station to take a call. In his very own words: *It might have been, literally, one of the hardest to hear phone calls I've ever taken. First of all, there's just a lot of background noise at a nurse's station with all of the people milling about. Secondly, there was a little desk fan blowing in my face making noise. Lastly, it sounded like the doctor was talking on a cell phone while driving a speedboat with horrible reception. As I struggled to comprehend what the doctor was saying, one part that came across crystal clear was that some other test results came back and confirmed it was leukemia; officially...100%. Because the leukemia was now confirmed, the doctor on the speedboat mentioned we would get transferred to Indy either tonight or tomorrow.*

Not understanding how severe my disease actually was at this point, we were annoyed. Things were starting to feel more comfortable, almost "homey" in this place, and now we had to leave *"tonight* or *tomorrow"*?

Our fleshly thoughts started taking over, so we stopped to pray—even asking God to spare us from having to be transferred that night. We were longing for a moment of stability, not to mention a decent night of sleep.

It's a good thing we serve a sovereign, omniscient God who *did* recognize the severity of my condition. About an hour after dozing off (11:30 that night), the nurse turned on the lights and greeted us with a rather unpleasant (not to mention loud) wake-up call: *Rise and shine!* (Added for dramatic flair.) "The ambulance will be here soon. Pack your bags, because you're heading to Indy tonight." (Man, I can't believe I'm saying this, but I'd *much* rather be woken up by an alarm clock—even one of those *really* obnoxious ones. Just sayin'.) The initial thoughts upon awakening were, *Is this real life?* and *Do I have to?*

As I slowly sat up and got myself out of bed, more questions came to me: *Was an ambulance necessary? Couldn't I just ride with my husband in our little silver Civic?* There was no room for budging. The nurses made it clear: *You're going in the ambulance.* Final answer. What little we brought with us was quickly and easily packed. They brought the stretcher and strapped me securely in it while Brian made his way to the parking lot to locate the car.

"Riding in an ambulance" added to my growing list of "firsts" just from these past couple days. Good thing the hospital they were transferring me to was only an hour or so away. I wouldn't call being immobilized in the back of a truck with a male stranger exactly comfortable. I probably sounded like a broken record to God, as I was mouthing all sorts of repeated prayers. Things like, *Keep us safe on the roads. Keep Brian alert as he follows behind us. Help me know what to say to this guy. Shine through me.* My eyes scanned my surroundings, and I couldn't help but notice the EMT's arm tattoo. *There's a place to start,* I thought. So I asked the man if there was significance (I mean, I assumed so, given they were written in permanent ink on his body!) to the two names on his arm, and he said, "Yeah, they're my kids." That seemed to open the door to a whole lot more about this man's life—his ex-wife, his second job, 100-hour work weeks, and his battle with Parkinson's. The conversation helped pass the time, and once they figured out *which* hospital we were going to (yes, there was some confusion), we meandered the dark, abandoned lobby (places like this are a bit creepy at nearly 2:00 a.m.) in search of the right elevator. We did meet up with one other person roaming the halls...Brian! Man, was it good to see him.

It required some major navigational skills to figure out exactly where we were going; good thing no one was relying on me for directions—not my forte. Finally, we had arrived! Simon Cancer Center, third floor, Room C22. There was a very sweet night nurse to welcome us and ask a slew of questions for their standard check-in process. The exhaustion finally caught up with me, and I fell asleep in the middle of answering her inquiries. Brian was able to take over for me—*tag team!* He journaled, *The head nurse took me on a quick tour of the floor, which was quite sprawling. She showed me the showers, family lounge area, laundry facilities, and kitchen/ microwave area. At the time, I thought, "Laundry? That's nice but we won't be needing it."* It wouldn't be long before he understood the significance of the tour—laundry room included.

The first thing I noticed upon waking that Saturday morning was a significant pain in my right side, which became progressively worse as the day wore on. I tried to ignore it as much as I could while we had our first meeting and introduction with the doctor. We found out it was his last day on call, so we actually wouldn't have further interaction with him after this. Giving us more specific details about my bone marrow biopsy, he uncovered that I had what's called acute myeloid leukemia, better known as *AML*. Later in the week, we would find out that—because of a "deleted seventh gene," which was also revealed from the biopsy—my full disease is *MLL-AML*. I was starting to sound like a really prestigious doctor with all these letters after my name!

Darla J. Peters, MLL-AML

You can certainly do your own further research if you're interested, but in a nutshell, *AML* is an aggressive, rapidly progressing cancer of the blood and bone marrow. The specific form I have affects a group of white blood cells called myeloid cells, hence the name. These are the cells that should (and in a healthy individual they do) develop into red blood cells, platelets, and white blood cells. When you have AML, however, their growth is stunted which leaves you with immature cells that mutate and form leukemic blasts.

Now, what I didn't know at the time (but found out *much* later through a search on my online health records) was that my initial blood work showed 76% leukemic blast cells swirling around in my marrow, crowding out space for the "good stuff" in my blood. In less than twenty-four hours this number had jumped to a whopping 93%! (No wonder they shuttled me off in an ambulance when they did!). To put it in perspective, healthy marrow should have no more than 5% blasts, and to qualify for *AML* only requires 20%. *Yikes!* I guess you could say I was very nearly "done for" upon entering the hospital scene. Thank God He got us where we needed to be when He did! A Father—especially a heavenly One—certainly knows best!

The doctor went on to explain the roadmap for my stay. First of all, we would be there for approximately thirty days (yes, as in three-zero), which made sense of the whole "laundry room" business. That evening, we would begin what the doctor referred to as the "7+3 chemo plan"—seven consecutive days of a twenty-four-hour continuous drip, along with three bags of another chemo drug that would run alongside the other for the first three days. This just goes to show my ignorance in the overall world of cancer, because I had no idea (until then) that there were multiple variations of "chemo." Up to that point, I thought "chemo" was "chemo"—who knew there was such a vast variety of formulas depending on what was being targeted?! (Okay, I'm guessing lots of people knew—and you may be one of them—but I was clueless.) After the chemotherapy phase would come a period of rest, tests, another bone marrow biopsy on the fourteenth day, and then more tests. He started discussing long-term treatment options, but there was nothing to decide just yet—we still needed to wait for the full report from my biopsy to help guide our next steps.

Before the chemo could begin that day, there was work to be done. I still had IV lines in both arms from the ER two nights ago, and one of those needed to be swapped out with a PICC line. *What in the world is a PICC line?* Basically, it's similar to an IV except a catheter runs up the vein to deposit medicine closer to the heart, getting it into the bloodstream that much faster. Being blessed with small veins (both ER IVs were a struggle to thread), I anticipated this whole PICC line placement to be a challenging (and, therefore, unpleasant) procedure...both for them *and* for me.

Two younger-ish fellows came in the room to try out their traditional methods of locating veins, but eventually needed an ultrasound machine to locate and verify that mine were even big enough to accommodate a PICC line. They determined it could still work, but they stepped out to gather different (smaller) tools. Upon returning, they kicked Brian out of the room to minimize the risk of infection (since they considered it similar to surgery), had me put on a mask, and raised my bed to its highest capacity. While they attended to a less than routine PICC line placement, they also kept the conversation lighthearted and downright funny. What a hilarious duo these two made! Between their distracting humor and my nearly constant prayers to the Father for strength and shielding, He carried me through the entire experience. What was estimated to be a half-hour-long procedure ended up taking closer to an hour. Oh, how thankful I was for God providing a big enough vein and a small enough tool for the PICC line to be placed.

By afternoon, the sharp and shooting rib cage pain was *excruciating*. It had become so miserable that it belabored my breathing (even with the oxygen I was on) and made it difficult to change positions. Deep breaths were out of the question, normal breaths were unbearable, and shallow breaths (though the pain was still extreme) were going to have to do. Unfortunately, it wasn't an option to stop breathing. The doctor was concerned too, especially because this could be a blood clot in my lungs. In order to confirm or dismiss this suspicion, he ordered a CT scan. *Wowzers.* This was probably one of the most agonizing procedures I'd ever done up to that point. All the movement (being transferred from my hospital bed to the transportation bed to the CT bed), plus all those deep breaths I had to take and hold. *Ouch!* Apparently I remained still enough for them to get the pictures they needed. Thank you, God!

We were grateful to hear there was no blood clot (we knew the implications of that could have proven fatal), but the CT scan did reveal extra fluid around my lungs. *Some* fluid around the lungs is normal, but the extra accumulation in my case was not. In meeting with the doctor a second time that afternoon (around 2:00 p.m.), he talked about draining the cavity around the lungs to relieve pressure. If we were going to go through with this, however, I would need an infusion of platelets first. As mine stood, they were way too low to be able to handle a puncture for the draining; in other words, my blood wouldn't be able to properly clot to stop the bleeding.

I honestly couldn't tell you what happened between that conversation and the rest of the afternoon and evening. *Are we doing this draining? Where are the platelets they talked about?* My poor sister-in-law was witness to the whole scene. I was a pitiful mess, gasping for each breath and writhing in pain every time I inhaled. At one point, hearing me faintly mouth words, she came over to the bed. I was simply crying out to God—"Be merciful, O Father! Breathe your breath through my lungs." I couldn't seem to form actual tears, so seeing some stream down my sister-in-law's face was strangely therapeutic. I'd lost track of time, but I knew that I'd been in this state of severe chronic pain for hours upon hours. When the nurse came in, I barely could choke out the question between all the shallow breaths: "Are...there any...pain med...options?" She looked at Brian and said, "Is she a wimp when it comes to pain?" That may have stung more than the pain in my ribs. The fact that I hadn't been offered anything seemed pretty callous to me, but this was downright insulting. Still, by nothing short of a miracle, I managed to bite my lip and proceed in this grueling test of endurance. God would either get me through it or I would round my final lap toward the finish line. If I'm being honest, the latter sounded preferable.

With all the rib cage excitement, I was nearly oblivious to the fact that my chemo began that night as well. Here's what Brian wrote: *It was a surreal moment when the nurses came in at 6:00 p.m. and hung the two biohazard chemical bags on the IV pole. It's a weird feeling to look at something that is so toxic and so dangerous, yet is the very thing that was going to save her life. To think that all of what's good within her had to get destroyed along with the bad—essentially, a casualty of war. Hanging those bags and tapping them into the PICC line was a point of no return. Another opportunity to pray and commit all of our trust to Him who is able to restore these bones.*

> "So we do not lose heart. Though our outer self is wasting away, our inner self is being renewed day by day. For this light momentary affliction is preparing for us an eternal weight of glory beyond all comparison, as we look not to the things that are seen but to the things that are unseen. For the things that are seen are transient, but the things that are unseen are eternal"
>
> *(2 Cor. 4.16–18 ESV)*

It wasn't until 9:30 p.m. when they came in with the platelets—*seven and a half hours* later! A different doctor visited us at 10:30 p.m. to discuss whether or not we were going to proceed with the lung draining procedure. Brian and I had been praying about it (we had plenty of time for that), and while a relief sounded nice (several hours ago), it was also late (the platelets still had to be infused, which would take some time). When the doctor returned to the room at 11:40 p.m., I decided at this point I'd rather just get to bed. (Well, I guess I was already "in bed"—but I wanted to sleep!) They left and the nurse (a different one, I believe) gave me some pain meds through my PICC line. Within *minutes*, I was asleep.

Peace at last.

CHAPTER 3

UNEVENTFUL

It genuinely made me chuckle to type out the title of this chapter. I mean, let's be honest—could a month's hospital stay possibly be considered anything other than *eventful?* Under normal circumstances, I would answer with the obvious, *"No way!"* However, we had *not* been operating under "normal circumstances" up to this point. In comparison with the story's beginning, I would certainly consider what remained of our time in Room C22 of Simon Cancer Center rather *uneventful.* Still, I don't anticipate you dozing off during this part of the story.

Hebrews 12:2

June 27, 2017

Darla here.

I feel like I should begin this post the way Paul started his letters.

To the saints in (fill in the blank, since you represent various demographics), the faithful in Christ Jesus: Grace and peace to you from God our Father and the Lord Jesus Christ.

"Overwhelming" is the word that keeps coming to mind—and I mean that in the best possible sense. Overwhelmed by your words of encouragement, gifts, prayers, texts, phone calls, and general load bearing of responsibility with our house and girls. Your role in this journey is crucial, and I attribute much of the supernatural peace we've experienced to you. "Thank you" isn't sufficient in expressing our gratitude.

And then there's my husband. Brian's doing a phenomenal job keeping all of you updated, isn't he? I appreciate how he's able to articulate our hospital happenings in a concise yet informative manner. I can't even begin to express how grateful I am for him. If you could only see him "in action" day to day...he is following Jesus' example in John 13, and because of that, I know with certainty he will be blessed (Jn. 13:17). Our wedding vows are being tested—"in sickness..." "for worse"—and will come out of the Refiner's fire as gold.

So, the post title...why Hebrews 12:2? Well, back last fall, God brought this verse/passage to mind and really hasn't let up on it since. Seems like not a day—certainly not a week—has gone by since October of last year that God hasn't reminded me in one way or another, "Fix your eyes on Jesus." And while it was helpful to be reminded of this command/challenge as we faced just the "usual" responsibilities of life prior to my leukemia diagnosis, I truly believe God was using it to "train my hands for war" (Ps. 144:1 NLT) in such a time as this.

It's not the first time I've realized this about myself, but this stretch in the hospital has only magnified my bent toward believing in the false hope that "ignorance is bliss." If you don't know, you can't worry, right? Sometimes I wish it were socially acceptable for a thirty-four-year-old grown woman to plug her ears and close her eyes all while saying "la, la, la" as loud as possible when being told things she'd rather not know. But in all seriousness, I cringe when nurses go into unnecessary detail and discussion about my veins being small and hard to "thread." (I'm sorry, but *thread*? Could there be a better word choice?) I avoid at all costs to look at my PICC line or even think about it being there. And if my mind starts pondering "next steps" in this whole process toward complete healing and remission, I stop myself...and pray. "Please Jesus, help me to just fix my eyes on you." Otherwise, the sound of the wind and the sight of the waves will cause me to sink.

But remaining ignorant shouldn't be the goal; in fact, that sounds downright foolish. I sense through all this that God is doing a work to refine my faulty thought process, gently encouraging me out of fear-driven surviving into faith-based thriving. While it's "easier" to "not know," it's not realistic and paints a false picture of faith.

Enter our case worker.

Not only is she a case worker in the unit, but an RN as well who's been here twenty-eight years. Needless to say, she knows a thing or two about this stuff. She also has firsthand experience with breast cancer, so her perspective stretches beyond textbook expert to a fellow patient who can relate with the questions, concerns, and "what-ifs" that come with the territory of any serious illness. She's a great resource, and we've appreciated the times she's been in our room mapping things out for us. But today, when she walked into Room C22, it's as if Satan simultaneously seeped his way in underneath the door. As she spoke candidly about next steps...potential setbacks...extended time... remission...and the like, the devil began feeding me fear, anxiety, hopelessness, and defeat. He even guilted me for the few silent tears that began to stream down my face. *Why is she telling us this?* I don't want to be reminded that this might not work, that we may need more chemo (even several more rounds depending on if there are any lingering cancer cells), or be forced to consider implications of one of my siblings not being a donor match. I wanted to yell, *Please stop!* but also knew that her information was important and that her honesty was better than being strung along with a false hope that everything is going to "work out" in our timing and best case scenario.

After she left, I needed to go to God...ask that He forgive me for giving the devil a foothold. Ask that He guard my heart and mind with supernatural peace; once again, that He help me fix my eyes on Jesus. I spent the afternoon with my Bible recalling times in Scripture when specific hardship "was" known ahead of time. Moses was told candidly from the Lord that "Pharaoh will refuse to listen to you" (Ex. 11:9 NIV), but that didn't stop him from faithfully approaching Pharaoh time and time again and asking for his favor. Joseph and Caleb remained confident that the Lord would help them enter the Promised Land despite the scary giants that had others fearing and doubting. Jesus informed His disciples on more than one occasion that "the Son of Man must suffer many things" (Mk. 8:31 NIV), but that didn't stop Jesus from trusting His Father's plan and allowing it to play out. In Paul's farewell to the Ephesian elders, he admitted "I am going to Jerusalem, not knowing what will happen to me there. I only know that in every city the Holy Spirit warns me that prison and hardships are facing me" (Acts 20:22–23 NIV). And did that stop Paul? No! He goes on, "I consider my life worth nothing to me; my only aim is to finish the race and complete the task the Lord Jesus has given me—the task of testifying to the good news of God's grace" (Acts 20:24 NIV).

The Word of God is a wonderful gift, isn't it? I'm so thankful for Truth, especially in the midst of uncertainties. Jesus promised in John 16:33 that we WILL have trouble in this world. But we can rest assured knowing that the One who has overcome the world is on our side. So whether what's ahead is kept hidden or mapped out, need not shake the fact that I am in the palm of my Creator's hand.

Contrary to what you may expect, the longer I was on chemo, the *better* I felt! The rib cage pain grew less and less pronounced with time, which—according to another doctor we met—made sense. Apparently, the cancer increases the size of the blood cells, so as these bigger-than-usual cells were attempting to pass through *tiny* blood vessels (bones contain the smallest vessels), they hit a roadblock. Translation: *Oww!* But as the chemo began to attack the cancer, the blood cells became smaller and able to flow freely once again. I also wonder how much could have been contributed by the pneumonia I was fighting upon arrival, which we didn't even know I had! A couple weeks into our stay, our nurse mentioned it as a *past tense* thing, giving further evidence to her statement that, "Because you were so sick when you first came..."

Plus, when one of the nurses introduced me to these little square hot packs (which activated upon squeezing), they soon became to me what the *My Buddy* doll was to kids of the '80s—*Wherever I go, heeeee goes!* They helped ease the remaining side discomfort *and* kept my chilly fingers warm. Bonus! Their heat lasted a half hour tops, but that only gave me (or Brian) an excuse to *POP* another one. They were fun to activate—right up there with those packaging bubbles.

So now that the rib cage drama was mostly behind us, let me introduce you to life on "3rd East," as it was known.

One of the questions I was frequently asked took on a couple different forms. Either, *What do you do all day?* or, *Aren't you bored?* To start with the latter, I can answer with full sincerity that I was *not* bored in the hospital. For one thing, Brian was with me. That's *right!* He spent all those days (Yes, *and* nights!) at the hospital, fully embracing the "bed" (aka couch)—just one of *many* inconveniences he never *once* complained about. What...a...husband. Moving on to what in the world could have possibly filled the minutes, hours, and days. Between time in the Word and various devotions, praying, reading, listening to online sermons, singing along with a variety of praise and worship tunes (Brian, I'm sure you have a playlist running through your head from that season too), coloring, journaling, going for a walk in the hallways, working on a puzzle in the lounge, playing *scrabble* or *cribbage* (I couldn't decide if it felt like we were newly married or empty nesters), and engaging in conversation with whomever I had contact (visitors, nurses, techs, cleaning crew, food service, other patients, and caretakers)...I actually kept myself quite active. Not to mention various medical procedures, "challenges" set by the physical therapist (timed walks or even obstacle-like courses to weave in and out of with my IV pole), and visits from the art therapist (we even got to do a project as a family when the girls were in town).

My room was spacious and well-lit. The blue summer sky and steady stream of sunlight was a glimpse of heaven flooding my view and space on a daily basis. This alone served as a consistent reminder that the Lord's mercies are indeed new every morning. Besides the outdoor beauty, friends and family transformed my otherwise sterile room into a colorful oasis. There were pictures of loved ones gracing countertops, posters plastering the walls with bold reminders of Truth, décor dangling from the ceiling in various hues of oranges and teals (personal favorites), a window prism splattering the room with rainbows, and cozy blankets in the most vibrant coral shade keeping me warm (morning, noon, and night). If there were any place we had to stay for thirty days that *wasn't* our home, I must say this was a pretty great alternative.

In our initial flurry to get to the hospital—not to mention our cluelessness as to the length of our stay—I didn't have extra clothes on hand (besides the ones I wore when I shuffled into the ER). My mom ever so kindly offered to shop for me at a near-ish-by Walmart, picking up several pairs of pants and underwear. As far as a top goes, we kept it simple and went with the hospital gown. I would have happily swapped it out for something less "flowy" and more "me," but didn't for one main reason: *I didn't know I could!* It wasn't until much later that it dawned on me: *Wait a minute. Some patients here are actually wearing shirts...normal shirts! How is that even possible?* My non-engineering brain was baffled. Between the PICC line and multiple tubes connecting it to the IV pole, I couldn't figure out how it was feasible to slip a shirt over your head. It wasn't until another whole stay at the hospital when the nurse asked, "Would you like me to unhook you from the pole while you change?" that their secret was revealed!

Being considered *neutropenic* (meaning, my body was helpless to fight infection) had several implications. I couldn't be around any sort of flower or plant because of their fungal spores. Since these are often "go-to's" when it comes to get-well gifts for patients, we had several beautiful floral arrangements from thoughtful friends and family which (sadly) never made it to our room. It also meant I couldn't eat already prepared or "fresh" foods from the "outside"—no carry-out or raw fruits and veggies...things like that. Thankfully, I'm not terribly picky, so I was able to find *something* I enjoyed from the hospital menu at every meal (when I had an appetite, that is). Plus, we always looked forward to the food service woman swinging by our room. She was full of spunk and charisma, and we often raised shouts of praise (as well as petitions) up to the Lord together.

Brushing my teeth with toothpaste was *also* forbidden because of the bacterial risk. And since the potential for bleeding posed too much of a threat (due to low platelets), flossing was out of the question as well. Thankfully, I could at least use the extra soft bristled toothbrush marinating in Paroex (a pink medicated oral rinse) to scrub my teeth. It was also part of the "regiment" to gargle and swish a packet of the Paroex after each meal and before bed. Not being able to do more than this for my teeth took some getting used to, I must say. When your dad is a dentist and your mom a dental hygienist, caring for your teeth is just a normal part of everyday life. This was just one of many preferences I needed to "surrender" during my hospital stay. It ended up serving as a helpful reminder that no care is too "little" for God to hear or answer. I prayed, *Well, Lord, I know this may seem like a silly prayer request in the midst of everything else going on, but you also know it's important to me. Would you do more to protect my teeth and gums than toothpaste and floss could ever do? I know you are able.* And you know what's astounding? HE DID! The next time I had my teeth checked at the dental office, everything looked good. No cavities or anything.

The rounding physician was usually our wake-up call, along with his large entourage of med students at various points of education and experience (interns, fellows, etc.). I always found it a little awkward to have so many people at once surrounding my bed first thing in the morning, watching me like some sort of specimen. At times, I felt more like a "thing" to be researched than a living being with a soul. Then again, I often wondered if some of them even spoke or had a name. One of the first questions I was asked each morning was whether or not I'd had a bowel movement that day. *Top of the morning to you too!* As early as they swung by my room, I would have been concerned if I already *had!* Sheesh.

A brief pause for background: With rare exception, I am *not* a "chipper chicken" in that initial groggy, waking-up phase. (All of you who have been around me in that state are chuckling right about now.) Keep this in mind as you continue to read.

Well into our stay—having once again been woken by the doctor and crew from my abbreviated slumber—I was feeling particularly snarky. Still in that initial not-so-good morning haze, the "flesh" part of me was tempted to answer their predictable question—"Have you had a bowel movement today?"—with, *No, have you?* Thankfully, the Holy Spirit kept a tight enough reign on my tongue to successfully prevent those words from actually leaking out.

But what the physicians became *mostly* fascinated with over time was my "output" of another kind (the clear-ish liquid counterpart, if you know what I mean), to the point where it became an actual "thing" with me—collecting and testing urine samples and keeping an accurate log of how much liquid I was taking in (between IV fluid, water, and other liquids) were in order. They basically couldn't get over how much I urinated in a day—especially someone my size—and had genuine concerns. In the end, nothing proved to be "wrong," which seemed only to *add* to their intrigue.

Ah, the things that put you on the map.

Darla J. Peters, MLL-AML: *The Urinator Dominator.*

My resumé was growing more enticing by the minute.

Like other hospitals, there were day shift nurses and techs (7:00 a.m. to 7:00 p.m.), followed by night shift nurses and techs (7:00 p.m. to 7:00 a.m.). My care, you could say, was literally *around the clock.* While some we preferred to others, I can't say that any of our healthcare providers left a bad taste in our mouths. (That was the chemo's job...wink!) My nurse would administer my oral meds, change bags on my IV pole (whether it be fluids, chemo, or antibiotics), listen to my heart and lungs, draw blood from my PICC line, and update my calendar (more on that later). The tech took care of daily weigh-ins (the wheeled-in scale each morning was *never* a favored sight of mine), checked vitals every few hours, filled my water pitcher, removed meal trays, restocked towels and hospital gowns, and emptied my hat (the kind in the toilet, not on the head).

The calendar that I mentioned in the previous paragraph was on the wall across from me. First thing in the morning, the nurse would write my new blood work numbers from the middle-of-the-night draw, which included white blood counts, platelets, and hemoglobin. The assumption (and reality) was that after chemo, all the numbers would bottom out, which gives reason for the extended hospital stay—it takes time for those numbers to work their way back up to a "safe" enough place to return home to the "real world." When platelets and/or hemoglobin dipped below a certain number, it was time for another transfusion. I was *shocked* by how many bags of each (platelets and blood) I was given during my stay. It certainly gave me a new appreciation for those who so selflessly donate.

Because we entered the scene on a weekend, we were unaware how vastly weekends differed from weekdays...but we'd soon find out. Once we recognized the ebb and flow of the hospital, we came to understand that weekends were the best times for visitors; our time was less divided than on most days of the week. We were truly blessed (and humbled) to have so many people make an intentional effort just to spend time with us, not just weekends but throughout the week: family members and friends from near and far, even some people we had never met! Who needs fresh flowers when you can have loved ones surround your room with joy, love, and life? It was always a welcome sight to see a familiar (Even *unfamiliar!*) face walk through the door.

But while we're on the topic of visitors, even though we knew Room C22 wasn't our actual home and that no one coming to visit was expecting anything from us, we felt a strange sense of responsibility for their well-being. Similar to my thought processing when guests come to the house, I would sometimes internalize things like: *Are there enough seats for everyone? Is he tired of standing? Are they comfortable? Should I offer her something?* And if I weren't quick to silence the inaudible (yet loud) commentary going on in my head, the result would be a feeling of *guilt.* When visitors left the room, I would begin to question if all their hassle (travel time, paying for parking, figuring out how to get through the maze of this place) was worth it to them.

Man, the enemy is sneaky. If he can't take you down with the word *leukemia,* he will gain access using a more innocent looking entry.

Mondays, by contrast, were by far our *busiest* day. After the weekend lull, it was as if every hospital worker in the entire facility came out of the woodwork...*especially* that first Monday. A physical therapist, social worker, case worker, two chaplains, and a slew of IU med students (interns and fellows as well) with the new (to us) doctor on call all swung by. A student making rounds with him quickly became a favorite of ours. The poor kid was a bit scatterbrained—a couple times leaving his journal of patient notes in our room—but truly seemed to have a unique bond with Brian and me. He was most often the first out of anyone in the room and referred to me as *Champ.*

The entire unit consisted of twenty-eight beds, made up of three different pods. Patients were restricted to the floor, but there was a really nice hallway loop to walk. Along one of these walls were large windows facing the outside world. When we needed a change of scenery, it was nice to sit out there and let the rays of the warm sun touch my skin. Sometimes I went there just to read, journal, or color. The only "catch" was I needed to wear a surgical mask anytime I was outside of my room, not to mention bringing along my awkward six-foot tall companion. (I'm speaking of my IV pole.) Whenever an infusion was complete (whether for fluids, chemo, blood, or platelets), or when there was "air in line" (which seemed to happen a lot), it would let out a slightly annoying and repetitive beep until a nurse came to stop it. So sometimes our visits to the "outside world" were shorter than others. Still, we had a welcoming "home" to walk back to.

There were two separate family lounges on the unit as well. The bigger of the two is where the laundry room was, as well as a microwave, refrigerator, and coffee maker. We often worked on puzzles there and occasionally gathered for a game or conversation when larger groups were in town. The other lounge was on the completely opposite side of the unit. Even though it was smaller and maybe less private in a sense (there was no door and it opened to the hallway), something about it appealed to me. It seemed quiet and undisturbed somehow, and as close to a taste of life beyond the walls of 3rd East as I was allowed to have.

Our days ended with me getting cleaned up. I was thankful for Brian's motivation and help with this process, because it was difficult to willingly leave my warm bed knowing a chilly sponge-like bath was ahead. It's almost hard to believe now (as I type this sporting little-to-none hair) how *long* my hair was upon entering the hospital. Since showers were out of the question (the line couldn't get wet) and because the PICC line was in my dominant arm (limiting my range of motion), I found that it was easiest to shampoo my hair in the sink, which I could mostly do on my own. Every so often I would clean my hair using one of the rinse-free shampoo caps they offered, which were so much fun! (They looked similar to a shower cap, but when you massage the head, it activated the soap.) When I was done rinsing out the shampoo in the sink, Brian would begin getting the washcloths (twelve to be exact) soaking in hot water for the Hibiclens (a pink foamy antiseptic cleanser). There was a specific order and process to it, and the tech was faithful in asking, "Did you do your Hibiclens today?" It was an important step in keeping me as germ-free as possible.

As "uneventful" as our time was, there were a few experiences that made it more exciting. Once the rib situation was mostly a thing of the past, the oddity which vied for my attention was a little pink bunny (my best effort at describing it) in my left eye. When it first showed up, I thought surely it was just a bit of lovely morning eye gunk. But after blinking a couple of times—even rubbing the eye—I realized it was there to stay. Yes, a patch in my field of vision, shaped like a little pink bunny! I wouldn't say my new pet necessarily affected my ability to see, though it did limit the viewing field. It was only a slight nuisance (mainly when I tried to journal, color, or read). After a full eye exam by an ophthalmologist who swung by the room, he confirmed that I wasn't crazy after all! He saw the same "pink bunny," and explained it (in more professional terms) as a small leak of blood that had made its way into the jelly-like substance near the retina. As long as it didn't grow bigger or start causing pain, he wasn't terribly concerned about it. He did, however, ask that I not lay flat, because sitting upright would allow gravity to take care of it with time. From then until the end of our stay, I slept at an incline. The bunny eventually went from pink to more of a grayish hue, and finally disappeared altogether.

Having a stomachache is so commonplace for me that it rarely raises much "concern" in my mind. In fact, *not* having one is almost more noteworthy. Seriously. Even as a baby, my parents said they would sometimes place a hot water bottle under my tummy to ease my fussiness and assist my sleep. Needless to say, when you have a continuous flow of antibiotics, fluids, and chemo pumping through your PICC line—not to mention you're eating atypical foods and moving less—your stomach is *probably* going to ache. Mine, you could say, was the definition of "uncomfortable" my entire stay at the hospital. And it never crossed my mind to mention it to the nurses or doctors. Even when I was having diarrhea on the daily—I was told every patient on the floor would experience it to a certain degree at one point or another—I didn't think twice about it.

Until, that is, the Fourth of July.

Legend had it that if we walked down to the main family lounge, we would have an unbeatable view of the downtown fireworks. So, strolling out into the hallway, bringing the glow bracelets we were given by a friend (some to wear and some to hand out to interested passersby), we made our way to the lounge. Unfortunately, legend had it wrong. Try as we may to see these *bombs bursting in air*, what we saw instead were the same drab buildings we'd seen oodles of times. Only this time, in the dark. But *if...juuuust* if...we were fortunate enough to actually detect color, we saw what may have been the top *sixth* of the burst. Sort of like going to the movies and much of your viewing field being overshadowed by the heads and shoulders in front of you.

We made our way down to the *other* lounge, thinking maybe this was the location the nurses were raving about (even though we were both pretty sure we heard correctly). Sadly, it was the same story over there, though this time, it was the parking garage blocking our view. But as it turned out, it was for God's providential best that there wasn't a show worth staying to watch. An intense cramping sent me into a doubled-over position, and if we didn't get to Room C22 *stat,* the most colorful bomb bursting was going to be in my pants. Thankfully, we made it back unharmed.

Okay, I *think* it's safe to say I'd officially moved past the *"normal"* stomach ache. The nurse collected a stool sample and determined (several days later) that it was C. diff. Looking back, I wonder how long I had been "putting up" with this nasty colon bacteria. Its lengthy list of symptoms were on par with what I had been experiencing for quite some time. Oh well, it mattered not at this point. Antibiotics were started, and within a few days, I was feeling some relief. This *did,* however, make things more interesting for visitors. Because Clostridioides difficile is a spore-forming bacteria, anyone who entered my room was required to take extra precautions; no one wants to go home carrying a little spore with them! So they "robed up" in these yellow robes and wore surgical gloves. I still can remember the look on our daughter Wendy's face when she came to visit. She was *not* pleased with the glove situation, and her exaggerated furrowed brow didn't hide it. They were preventing her from sucking her thumb. *Not* okay.

Perhaps the *biggest* news came shortly before my C. diff diagnosis. At the tail end (no pun intended) of June, I had my second bone marrow biopsy, but the *first* which I'd experienced in "full force," so to speak. They didn't treat it as Ball Hospital had (where they put me fully "under"), and my nurse (who seemed to find some sort of strange thrill in going on about how unpleasant a procedure it is) said they didn't even offer sedation. Here's what I wrote about it at the time:

Trust Me

June 30, 2017

Shortly after waking up this morning, our nurse and faithful student doctor were in the room, discussing today's bone marrow biopsy. To give them the benefit of the doubt, I'm going to assume that certain health professionals believe they would be doing a disservice to their patients if they failed to warn them of the upcoming procedure's potential unpleasantries. Thankfully, God was already working to answer prayers for courage and strength, because after their exit, I looked at Brian and said, "This is just silly." He agreed, and quickly made the comparison to Goliath's roaring threats. So, I had one of two choices: I could melt in fear like the crowd of Israelites, or I could stand like David in the confidence and full assurance that my God was bigger than this giant. I chose the latter.

I sat down on the couch and opened my Bible to what I thought was 2 Kings 17, which is where I had left off from yesterday in my Bible reading plan. I paused for a moment to pray that God would open my ears to hear Him through His living Word; then, I began reading. Wait a minute! Elijah being fed by ravens? I knew I had recently read this story, and then quickly realized my mistake: I had flipped to FIRST Kings, instead of Second. But as I reread this short, but powerful story of how the Lord sustained Elijah during a drought by providing water from a brook and food from the mouths of ravens, I knew my "mistake" was actually God's very gracious plan all along. *Darla*, I heard Him say. *Trust me. I will supply you with what you need during the biopsy today.*

Next, I flipped over to 2 Kings 17—for real this time—and read about how

God's chosen people were choosing to imitate the nations around them by bowing to false gods. The Lord had made it clear to them: "worship the Lord your God; it is he who will deliver you from the hand of all your enemies" (2 Kin. 17:39 NIV). But..."They would not listen, however, but persisted in their former practices. Even while these people were worshiping the Lord, they were serving their idols" (2 Kin. 17:40–41 NIV). It's easy to read these kinds of disappointing accounts and be overly critical and condemning of the Israelites. "How could you?" is perhaps a question that comes to mind. And yet, as I was reading and asking God to reveal if there was anything in my own life competing for his rightful place, I realized perhaps there was. See, when I had my first bone marrow biopsy at Ball Hospital, they treated it as a surgery and put me out for the procedure. Well, here at University Hospital, they don't do that. And in talking with the nurse this morning, sedation wasn't an option either. The news wasn't thrilling to me, but what else could I do? What else, but trust that God would supply all of my needs...trust that His grace would be sufficient for me during the procedure...trust that He is my rock, my shield, my refuge, my strong tower, My ever-present help in time of need. While there's nothing wrong with pain relief, I realized that—similar to the Israelites—I was wanting God PLUS the idol of comfort/ease. As I read on in 2 Kings 18, I read about King Hezekiah, how "[He] trusted in the Lord.... He held fast to the Lord and did not stop following him.... And the Lord was with him" (2 Kin. 18:5–7 NIV). What a contrast to the previous chapter. *Yes, God! Make me as Hezekiah. May I put my trust completely in you!*

No sooner had I reached this point of absolute trust that the Lord Himself would provide for the next phase of the journey, then in walks the nurse to tell me he could give me pain meds before the procedure began. It felt a bit like the moment when Abraham looked over and saw the ram caught in the thicket. Thankful for that unexpected blessing in the midst of this testing of faith. When the doctor walked in at noon to do the procedure, I had not a hint of nervousness. That, my friends, is the Lord's supernatural doing. And while there was the uncomfortable pinching and tugging of which I was warned, I was able to hum and sing through the entire procedure...mostly simple songs like "Jesus Loves Me." Before I knew it, the biopsy was complete, and God proved once again that He is more than able.

It wasn't until a couple of weeks later that we found out the results of the biopsy—*NO detectable cancer!* We were thrilled and relieved. Not having to endure another round of chemo (which would have extended our stay by another month) was such welcomed news. While we never doubted God's ability to accomplish such a miracle, we also knew He had every right to lead us down a less straightforward path. Whether or not things went the way we preferred, He could be trusted. Reality and faith hung in a constant balancing act.

While a hospital would have certainly been at the top of my list of *Places I'd Least Like to Visit,* it became a place I actually *enjoyed* being. (*Ha!* Isn't that just like God?) It was a consistent prayer of ours that God would fill us with His love and joy, and then enable us—through the power of the Holy Spirit—to live out Christ well. To make HIM look good, because HE IS good! To be an *accurate* representation of who Jesus is. Not that we were expected to live it out perfectly—it wasn't about us and what we could "do"—but that even when we stepped out of the light, we could recognize it, confess it, and ask God to help us keep in step with the Spirit. While circumstances were completely outside of our control, we *did* have a choice as to whether or not we were going to "let [our] light shine before others, that they may see [our] good deeds and glorify [our] Father in heaven" (Matt. 5:16 NIV, paraphrase mine).

From the very beginning, we recognized that 3rd East was our "mission field" and that God was providing "on-the-job" training for us there. By eliminating all other responsibilities and concerns in life, it was more noticeable when the enemy was making an appearance. If the *light* grew dark around us and fear replaced His *peace*, we knew we had given Satan an entrance into our minds. We had shifted our gaze from the Savior to the storm...and the storm *never* looked favorable. *O, Father, fix our eyes back on you. May your perfect love drive out all fear. Fill us anew with your incomprehensible peace. Shine your light to pierce through this darkness.* Over time, we came to recognize the things that most likely would trigger fear—doing too much research on *AML* or *Stem Cell Transplants* (more on that in the next chapter), others starting conversations with us about next steps and what-ifs, and thinking about the girls and their future. And while we weren't sure of the "effect" TV would have on our minds, we chose to not turn it on. It just seemed like another potential outlet for a whole lot of noise and junk to fill our minds and room.

We have many fond memories of that first hospital stay. To this day, I think of (even *miss)* many of the people we met. We formed unique connections with various health professionals and bonded with fellow patients (and caretakers) through our similar battles. And even some we didn't particularly enjoy at first, God used as opportunities for us to pray and witness miraculous changes in our perspective and even in their demeanor. Here's one example that stood out which I wrote about in my journal:

June 22, 2017

When we saw which night nurse walked in, my heart sank a little. She was one of the first nurses we met when we arrived at the hospital, and she didn't leave us with a good impression. She...just seemed like maybe she was spent and needed to move on from the job. So when she left our room to get something, we just started praying for her. "God, lift the load of whatever our nurse is burdened with; renew her spirit, give her joy, etc.," and when she walked back into the room, she was an entirely different person! Smiling, warm, interested, engaging. We even got to talking about our faith. She spoke about how some people believe in a false gospel that with Jesus, you'll never face problems...but contrary to that, it's hardship that grows our faith. It was so amazing and a testament to the power of prayer. Truly a miracle. Thank you, God, for this.

The rounding doctor for our first couple of weeks was a pleasant man, well past the age of retirement. The warm smile he wore and the gentle voice with which he spoke left me with an assurance that everything was going to be all right—what a wonderful gift! Especially for a doctor treating patients with life-threatening diseases. It was hard not to think of my late grandfather every time he walked through the door. In fact, I half expected him to offer me a bowl of popcorn, a glass of strawberry pop, and a round of dominoes or *Skip Bo*...maybe both. I appreciated how he never concerned himself with numbers—fluctuations didn't rattle him and statistics didn't faze him, nor did he allow them to define me. With as much experience as this man had in the world of blood cancer, he'd seen it all. Sure, there were patterns, but there were always exceptions as well. A phrase he used at each visit soon became a favorite of mine: *Just another day in the journey.* It was his graceful way of consistently reminding us to appreciate this day for what it is and what it brings. It's all we are guaranteed, especially in the finicky world of *AML*. Today is going well, so let's not worry ourselves with the *what-ifs* of tomorrow.

It's not often that science and Christianity so naturally intertwine. This was one of the rare times the correlation was clear. "So don't worry about tomorrow, for tomorrow will bring its own worries. Today's trouble is enough for today" (Matt. 6:34 NLT).

(Un)Becoming

Through the Storm

July 11, 2017

February 23rd. I was sitting on the couch with my guitar in an unusually quiet family room (Clara was at school and Wendy was napping). No sooner had I started strumming "How Great Thou Art," I peered out the window and saw a bird fly and rest on the flimsiest-looking twig in the front yard. The landing wasn't exactly "smooth," judging by the winged creature's exaggerated teetering and tottering—up and down, up and down. Was the bird scared? No. Utterly confident. Did the bird fly away? No. He remained. Did the seesaw-like motion cease? Eventually. Why? Because the bird stayed put; his feet did not move or falter until all was at rest. As this beautiful scene unfolded, God made it clear: He can be trusted even in the most uncertain circumstances. The bird didn't question the integrity of the branch, nor should I doubt the One who created everything out of nothing and raised the dead to life.

God was preparing me. In His kindness, He was speaking truth to me long before this storm blew in.

A story that God continues to bring to the forefront of my mind is found in the Gospels. It goes: "Then he got into the boat and his disciples followed him. Suddenly a furious storm came up on the lake, so that the waves swept over the boat. But Jesus was sleeping. The disciples went and woke him, saying, 'Lord, save us! We're going to drown!' He replied, 'You of little faith, why are you so afraid?' Then he got up and rebuked the winds and the waves, and it was completely calm. The men were amazed and asked, 'What kind of man is this? Even the winds and the waves obey him!'" (Matt. 8:23–27 NIV).

The Lord has reminded me on several occasions throughout this stretch of time that He is in this boat with me. And He isn't biting His nails looking at the size of the waves, nor complaining about the seasickness they induce. Nope. He is sleeping. Not because He is checked out. Not because He is disengaged. Not because He is unable. But because He knows that the wind and the waves are no match for the very One who made them.

CHAPTER 4

UNMATCHED

B ack in 2013, we were living in Minnesota (where Brian is from), but sensed a strong call to move to Indiana (my native land and where *both* sets of parents now lived). There was no job lined up, no house to call home, and no city—that we knew of yet—to welcome us. I guess you could say a certain amount of "risk" (we call it *faith*) was involved. While we couldn't *begin* to foresee all the reasons God had for this uprooting and relocating, two things were sure:

One, we were following the Lord no matter how scary and uncertain this felt.

Two, moving near family carried with it more significance than we could see or know at first.

Thinking things through logically, we wondered if one of our parent's health would be compromised in the near future. This seemed to "make sense" since living in closer proximity would mean being available to help. *Ha!* Try the other way around! We seriously never *dreamed* that *we* would be the ones needing *them* in such a profound way.

The cancer experience really made us aware on a whole other level of what an *incredible* support system God has blessed us with: Both sets of parents, immediate family *and* extended, church, small group, friends (near and far), neighbors, and—as it turned out—even complete strangers! Because cancer struck in the middle of summer break, the girls could camp out at various family members' and friends' homes *without* the hassle of preschool and school schedules to juggle. (Don't you just *love* the Lord's *perfect* timing?!) While we missed those two like *crazy*, we never "worried" about them. Not only were they being covered in prayer (by us and *many* others), but they were also staying with people we trust. We had no doubt that they were being fully embraced and enveloped in Jesus' love in our absence. What a *huge* gift this was to us as parents! The load that was lifted from our shoulders was life-giving. Plus, the girls were kept entertained and distracted by all kinds of fun summertime experiences—shopping, blueberry picking, swimming, fishing, homemade Slip 'N Slide and fireworks, and a jam-packed week of Vacation Bible School. Several months after the fact, Clara even admitted to me—seemingly out of nowhere—that, "Mommy, last summer was hard...but also really fun." I can't tell you how reassuring the words after the pause were to a mama's ears and heart.

Oh, and of course, Brian...

July 4, 2017

Last night, as Brian once again knelt on the hard, cold tile floor of the bathroom to wash my swollen feet, I broke down in tears. I could barely be understood through the sobbing, but was able—in so many words—to reiterate how much I love him and how he has been nothing short of a representation of Christ to me on an ongoing basis these past two-and-a-half weeks. He is a true disciple of Jesus, denying himself—his job, his sleep, his own wants and time table—and daily taking up his cross to follow the Lord's example (Lk. 9:23). Never once has he complained about serving my needs. Never once has he appeared even slightly annoyed. Never once has he sighed or given an air that he is "so above this." On the contrary, every day, he vocalizes his love for me. Every day, he sees me in a hospital gown with not a lick of makeup, water retention, and now thinning hair and says with sincerity, "You are so beautiful." Makes a girl mist up just writing about it...with no fear of makeup smearing. Bonus! And perhaps what's most astounding about it is that Brian has zilch concern with ever being noticed or receiving applause for all that he is doing and all that he is forsaking. In fact, he would prefer it that way. (Hope he doesn't mind me posting this...too late now.) His humility, patience, joy, and laughter bring so much life and healing to a potentially dark season. I can't imagine walking this road without him.

Anytime we got to see the girls walk through the door of Room C22 was a welcomed sight. And as it usually goes when you haven't seen your kids on the daily, they suddenly looked older, spoke more maturely, and (being as it was summer) had that unmistakable sun-kissed glow written all over their cheeks. We enjoyed listening to tales of their various adventures while we snuggled, colored, worked on puzzles, and took strolls together in the hallway. Modern technology is *wonderful* (*FaceTime* and the like), but there's nothing like sharing time *and* space with those you love. We weren't exactly sure what to expect as far as their demeanor in the hospital goes. *Would they be sad? Scared? Angry?* Oh, what a blessing that they were themselves...for the most part.

After a couple of their visits, we discovered that Clara's way of coping with life's current trauma was to play the role of "tough girl." Graffitied with the letters *I--A-M--F-I-N-E* were walls she had built to hide behind—a safe place where she could "escape" from reality's wildly unpredictable threats. It broke my heart knowing that, at six years old, Clara even had a reason for creating a self-protecting strategy in the first place! And while it probably isn't the healthiest way (long term) for any of us to handle menacing circumstances, I can't say I haven't adopted the same instinctual method for survival (even as an adult). We noticed too that with the walls Clara had formed came a feeling of detachment (almost coldness) as well as a determination to keep talking, keep doing, and keep moving so as to avoid having to face the "cancer" that was right in front of her.

Then there's Wendy, who had just turned four a little over a month before my hospital stay. While she has always been—or had a *longing* to be—highly independent ("I do self!" is a phrase she often used once she could express herself with words), there are two comforts upon which she had *no* shame parading her dependence: her thumb and Mommy's hair. In fact, where there was one, you were most likely to find the other. She wanted to be near me for the sole purpose of feeling my hair, and especially for taking a strand of it and using it to "paint" all over her face, ears, and neck. As hair loss became more of a noticeable reality, I mourned more for Wendy's loss than for mine. Her security blanket was unraveling before her very eyes. But with each visit, she reached over to give a tug and twirl just as she had done every time before. Only I think it meant even more to the both of us now. To her, because it wasn't part of her daily life like it had been when I was home. To me, because I knew by the thinning conditions of my hair that these days were numbered.

Since we're on the topic of my locks, this is what I wrote on the same day the beautician came to my room and trimmed my thinning hair to shoulder length:

Beauty

July 6, 2017

While our world is constantly redefining "beauty," God has remained firm on the issue from the beginning of time. (Quick side note: Can I just say one of my favorite attributes of God is that He is unchanging? It's incredibly reassuring to know we don't have to guess if His character or His viewpoints will be the same tomorrow as they were today.) And because He is the Creator of all things, it seems only natural that God would know best. So...what does He have to say about the topic? Quite a bit actually:

"The Lord does not look at the things people look at. People look at the outward appearance, but the Lord looks at the heart."

(1 SAM. 16:7 NIV)

"Charm is deceptive, and beauty is fleeting; but a woman who fears the Lord is to be praised."

(PROV. 31:30 NIV)

"Though outwardly we are wasting away, yet inwardly we are being renewed day by day."

(2 COR. 4:16 NIV)

"Clothe yourselves with compassion, kindness, humility, gentleness and patience."

(COL. 3:12 NIV)

"Don't be concerned about the outward beauty of fancy hairstyles, expensive jewelry, or beautiful clothes. You should clothe yourselves instead with the beauty that comes from within, the unfading beauty of a gentle and quiet spirit, which is so precious to God."

(1 PET. 3:3-4 NLT)

"Women who claim to be devoted to God should make themselves attractive by the good things they do."

(1 TIM. 2:10 NLT)

"For physical training is of some value, but godliness has value for all things, holding promises for both the present life and the life to come."

(1 Tim. 4:8 NIV)

Even though we all know beauty comes from within, it doesn't necessarily make it "easy" to ignore the externals. I'll admit that vanity is a sin I've confessed daily during this battle with leukemia. It's humiliating to even admit—you have "cancer" and you're concerned with how you "look"! But once again, Satan will use whatever tactic he can to focus our attention on what doesn't matter. Also, it's often not until you're faced with the reality of something being taken away that you realize how much of an attachment you'd formed.

The good news is that through this daily recognition of sin, I sense that God is bringing about true repentance...working out a much-needed reshaping of my heart. I still don't "prefer" what I see, but in light of my body being healed of a death-threatening disease?! There is no comparison.

"Turn your eyes upon Jesus, Look full in His wonderful face; And the things of earth with grow strangely dim In the light of His glory and grace."

("The Heavenly Vision," hymn by Helen Howarth Lemmel) [1]

I woke up on July 13th feeling the worst I'd felt in a while. That all-too-familiar pervasive rib cage pain was plaguing me again, and my sleep was so restless that my upper back seemed to be in a bind as well. I could tell before the day even began I was going to be moving at a slower pace. So you can imagine my utter dismay when the doctors walked in the

---

[1] Helen Howarth Lemmel, "The Heavenly Vision," 1918, Public Domain.

room later that morning to tell me I WAS *GOING HOME!* My absolute neutrophil count (the component of white blood cells which fights against infection, also known as ANC), had finally done what it needed to do in order for us to leave. Of course, I was happy at the prospect of being reunited permanently with the girls. But I wouldn't be honest if I didn't also share my apprehension about reentering "normal life." *What about this rib pain? Is it possible that the cancer was back after all? And if it hadn't returned, what if it made a soon reappearance?* Yes, you could say I was a bit "uneasy" at the thought of being back in the real world, but I also didn't want it to take away from the victory that this moment represented. I hadn't even gotten home yet, and it was already obvious that the concept of *fixing my eyes on Jesus* was going to be just as important there as it had been in the hospital.

For those of you who have endured the hospital discharge process, you know that it can be a fierce test of patience; no one on their end seems to be in much of a hurry to get things started. But we found that the extra time was actually an asset in our case; apparently, there's a lot you can accumulate in twenty-eight days. After packing, listening to discharge instructions and receiving the medications I'd be taking home with me, it was time for the PICC line to be removed. *Not* something I was looking forward to *at all.* With as much of a procedure as it had been to have the line placed, I wasn't sure what to expect for its removal...and I wasn't sure I wanted to find out. Needless to say, I was surprised that when the nurse came in the room to take it out, it required nothing more than one big yank. *Hold your breath on the count of three. One...two...three!*

And just like that, I was free to go.

It all felt so strange, maybe even surreal. I slipped my newly untethered arms back into a T-shirt for the first time in a month and walked out of Room C22 for the last time. (Don't worry, I already had pants on.) It was no longer "home," and this hallway where I had walked countless laps with Brian, the PT, a friend I met on the floor, and even solo was no longer a destination in and of itself. Now, it was but a stepping stone, getting me from where I had been to where I was going. And where I was going was *beyond.* Beyond the set of double doors that had always served as my boundary. Beyond the third floor. Beyond Simon Cancer Center.

When we pulled up to the house, it was a little after 1:00 p.m. Brian's parents were there with the girls, and they were *just* putting the final touches on the beautiful *Welcome Home* sign they'd made for us. Of course, hugs and kisses were in order, as well as posing for a picture sitting underneath the banner. This was a milestone worth remembering. Once Bapa and Nana left, we had time with just the girls. It's funny how immediate "life as usual" took over. We talked, cuddled, read, and played *Go Fish.* Brian headed upstairs to give his burly beard and puffy hair (imagine a Chia Pet, if you will) a long overdue buzz. Then it was dinner (Brian's mom had already prepared for us delicious meatloaf and sides), time outside, baths, pj's, Bible, and prayer.

At this point in the evening, we'd usually kiss the girls one last time and bid them a good night's sleep. But this night was special and carried with it more weight; it was, after all, our *first* night under the same roof in a month. Brian and I stayed at least another half hour in the girls' room, holding them and releasing the tears that had finally caught up with us all. The most noteworthy event was being able to witness Clara's protective walls come crashing down through the expression of all her pent-up emotion. She no longer cared to masquerade behind this facade that she was "tough" and "fine," but willingly shared—through sobs—how much she had missed us, how she looked at the card I gave her every day, how she missed Mommy being able to play basketball with her, how difficult it was to be in different places from one another, and that every morning we were gone, she still walked into our bedroom to see if we were there. "It was so hard…it was so hard…it was so hard," is the phrase she continuously repeated. All I could say as I cried and held her was, "I know, Clara, I know. I'm sorry."

July 25, 2017

People have been asking, "How does it feel to be home?" and assuming, "I bet it's nice to sleep in your own bed!" The best way I can describe our initial reentry is surreal. Things pretty much looked and smelled as my memory serves me (minus the color of the kitchen counter tops—they appeared darker than I had remembered), but it didn't necessarily have the "it's good to be home" feel for which I longed. Don't get me wrong, it was absolutely fantastic to be reunited with Clara and Wendy for good. But even the joy of holding them and reading to them couldn't drown out the myriad of questions playing and replaying in my mind—all of which boiled down to, "Now what?"

As far as my bed goes, "nice" is not the word I would choose to describe our first evening back. Staring at the bumpy ceiling with a heating pad wrapped around my sore ribs, I began counting the beats of my racing pulse against the ticktock coming from our bathroom clock. Aware of my elevated temp, I wondered what would happen if I slept through a fever of 100.8 (the number at which I would need to seek immediate medical attention). There were no longer nurses to monitor me while I slept, which brought with it a sense of insecurity. Enough! With Brian by my side, I began audibly confessing my fears to God. I had taken my eyes off Jesus and needed Him to fix my gaze aright once again. After asking for peace and courage, God gently reminded me that He neither sleeps nor slumbers (Ps. 121:4). His watch-care over me during the night was more constant and attentive than anyone's wearing a red scrub top ever had been.

That was the last day/night since being home that I've experienced those overwhelming reservations. The same supernatural peace that enveloped us in the hospital met me here as well. In fact, so much so that this past weekend I was almost bothered by my foreign state of unthinking and unfeeling. I began questioning whether the enemy had crept in and stolen these human abilities from me. I'm not accustomed to being so removed from thought and void of emotion. But in the past couple days, I've sensed it's not Satan's scheme creating this detachment, but rather the Lord's mercy. Those prayers I've prayed (and that I know you have as well) for God to be my refuge, my shield, my strong tower, and my fortress...He is answering! To quote David from the thirty-second Psalm, "You are my hiding place; you will protect me from trouble and surround me with songs of deliverance" (Ps. 32:7 NIV). To the girl who naturally over thinks and feels BIG, God is teaching rest. *Simply abide with me,* I sense Him saying. Oh, how easy it is to assume great things come out of our analytical thinking and emotional gauges! Yet no fruit is born apart from remaining in Him (Jn. 15). So while it's foreign (Shall I say, *uncomfortable?*) to be in this removed state, I know, "He can do more in my waiting than in my doing I can do," as songwriter Bethany Dillon penned it so perfectly.

Even though life at home was becoming normalized again, I knew Brian transitioning back to work (the physical building, that is) was definitely going to give a different "feel" to things. Here was what he wrote the night before heading back:

Back to work
July 16, 2017

Sunday night.

Monday eve.

Not sure if 'weird' is the right word to describe the feeling of returning to work tomorrow (the physical building) for the first time in a month, but it will be strange going through the normal routine: Setting an alarm; waking up to said alarm (hopefully); donning a shirt and tie; lacing up shoes (flip-flops have been the footwear of choice since June 15th); commuting; walking in; sitting down; working. All while being apart from Darla for the most significant chunk of time in a long while. I can tell you my body will be at work, but it will be a struggle to keep my mind there too.

But I'd be remiss to not take a minute to brag about how great work has been throughout this past month. They have been so supportive and so accommodating to our situation. In numerous phone calls and texts with my boss, he repeatedly stressed that family was the top priority and they would be willing to do whatever worked best for me during this time. That ended up being working remotely from the hospital roughly twenty hours a week in an effort to preserve some PTO and FMLA hours for the future unknown leg(s) of this journey. Their flexibility and understanding lifted such a huge burden and really allowed me to focus on Darla and her needs, and I will be forever grateful.

That Monday is also when we started our twice a week blood draws. Thankfully, those could be done at our local hospital, which was *so* much more convenient than driving all the way to Indy. Plus, there was hardly ever a wait at the lab; with the exception of finding a workable vein, the process was quick and easy. It was fun forming new relationships at a local clinic as well—the gal who always checked me in and the phlebotomist who usually called me back became people I looked forward to connecting with.

A significant piece of information I haven't shared about our time in the hospital began with a visit from an acute leukemia specialist less than a week into our stay. Of all the doctors, medical professionals, and other staff who graced our room, no one's presence was nearly as compelling. Wearing his long white lab coat and extending a hand for a shake, his introduction was difficult to decipher amidst a thick German accent. The man almost resembled a wax figure with his unwrinkled olive complexion and immaculately placed hair follicles. Adding to the intrigue was the fact that something about his appearance resembled a comic book character, though I really couldn't pinpoint why. Initial conversation disarmed any previous misconception that he was intimidating; on the contrary, he was extremely down-to-earth and likeable. In fact, I found it fascinating... almost *moving*...that someone would dedicate his life to researching this one very specific facet of leukemia in the hopes of improving treatment for those on the "acute" side of the disease like myself. Out of curiosity, I asked him why he was drawn to this particular field in the first place. His answer surprised me because it wasn't something I'd ever thought of before: There's an ease of accessing testable material when it comes to a blood cancer like leukemia. With cancer in tumor form, you have to wait on the doctor to get physical samples, whereas with leukemia, you just need blood. And since 70% of what he did was research, this definitely made sense.

The whole reason for this acute leukemia specialist's visit was to explain to us about something we never even knew existed up until this point—a bone marrow transplant. He said I was a good candidate for the procedure and that it would offer the best chance for a sustained remission. At the time he was explaining it, I felt far removed from the thought or idea of this. And quite honestly, I considered it much more of a "nice option" than a necessity; I was still quite naïve as to how severe my particular case was. The process would start by testing my siblings to see if they were a "match." This whole thing is way more complicated than I understand (let alone can summarize for your reading pleasure), but basically, there are ten "markers" (or "identifiers") in these specific proteins (HLA or human leukocyte antigens) that needed to line up with one of my siblings to proceed. Just one or two unmatched identifiers out of the ten could be risky and present significant problems. So if none of my siblings were a perfect match, they would move on to a national registry (through *Be The Match*) to see if a stranger and I happened to be a ten out of ten. Still, a brother or sister offered the best chance. I have three older siblings, and each one of them provided a 25% chance of matching.

I knew having my brother tested would be "easier" given the fact that he also lives in Indiana. Both my sisters live out of state—one in Ohio and the other in Kansas—but how *perfect* that they each happened to be in town for a visit! (God is so good, isn't He?) We were able to start the bone marrow matching process the same day as the doctor came and spoke with us. Two days later, my brother swung by and had his blood drawn for testing as well. I was so thankful for each of their unflinching willingness to participate.

And then it was time to do what you do with these sorts of things: We waited for results.

Two weeks after my sisters' blood draws, our quirky (but loveable) medical student swung by our hospital room to break the news that neither of my sisters was a match. While it was disappointing to hear, I had a strong conviction that Daniel, my brother, was "it." He and I share some physical resemblances, which probably has *nothing* to do with anything blood-related, but still...here's hoping, right? It was a full week later (we were home at this point) when I received a call from our transplant coordinator nurse. My brother's results were in, and unfortunately, his type-match wasn't compatible with mine either. Sure, it was not the news we were wanting to hear, but we also continued to trust God's plan as well as His timing. The nurse indicated that she would begin utilizing the national registry (via *Be The Match*) right away to see if "someone out there" would be that perfect ten out of ten match.

CHAPTER 5

UNFATHOMABLE

It was just four days after the phone call regarding my brother's mismatch that we were back in Indianapolis, this time to meet with the director of the Bone Marrow Transplant Department. Our transplant coordinator kicked things off with an *incredible*—not to mention, fascinating—update regarding the national registry hunt. Over 200 matches (that's right... TWO *HUNDRED*) were found! She whittled it down to *four* candidates who would be the most ideal—three males and one female, all in their twenties—and was currently in direct contact with each of them. I really can't say if this is par for the course (since I have no one else's story with which to compare it), but I had a hard time thinking such a broad range of matches was "normal." Kind of made me think of the time Jesus told His disciples to cast their fishing nets on the *other* side of the boat (Jn. 21:6). Here, they'd spent the whole night fishing with no fish to show for it, and then in one fell swoop, the "other side" brought in such a large catch their nets were breaking! Miraculous...simply miraculous.

Even though we were praying for the Lord's clarity and guidance going into this meeting with the BMT doctor, I was nearly settled in my own mind that this whole bone marrow transplant thing wasn't for me. If my latest biopsy didn't reveal any detectable leukemia, I really didn't see the need to pursue further treatments and procedures. Why not leave "well enough" alone? But shortly after introductions, the doctor was direct and candid with us; there was no sugarcoating what he was about to share. The deleted half gene of my seventh chromosome (discovered in that first biopsy) put me in a "high risk" category. With chemo alone, I had twelve to eighteen months to live. Even though there were potential risks, the transplant would give me the greatest chance of long-term survival.

My mind was reeling a bit from the news. How did I not know it was *that* bad? Only the Lord's protection, I guessed.

As startling as the news was, I still wasn't convinced. Sure, the transplant may boost my chances a little (there was a 30%–40% chance it would "cure" my leukemia), but at what cost? More time away from the girls? Elongated existence, but with a significant decline in quality of life? Also, "thirty to forty percent" had *anything* but a nice ring to it; I mean, that isn't even a passing grade! There were many risks that came with it, and any research I did led me to the same conclusion: The "trade-off" wasn't worth it.

Truth be told, I didn't know if we could even trust this director of the BMT Department, anyway. After all, we'd just met him, so it was hard to know if he was really on our side or motivated more by his prestige. As we listened, a question that was swirling around in my brain but never uttered (for fear of an overly emotional tone) was whether or not he would go through with this risky procedure if he were a mom with two young girls.

So God (in His kindness) did the work for me.

The doctor interrupted my stream of thoughts with these words: "If you were my sister, I would encourage you to do it." It felt genuine and as close to compassionate as he could get (especially for having just met us).

He shook our hands one last time before exiting the exam room. And then there were two...Brian and me.

Or were there *three*?

Clearly, the Holy Spirit was there with us as well, for in that moment, I heard an undeniable message spoken in His voice: *Submit to authority*. It seemed a bit strange at first, maybe even out of place; I mean, it's not like the doctor was my dad, teacher, coach, police officer, or pastor. And yet who gifted this man with an incredible mind for learning, understanding, and retaining this kind of complex matter? God did! It's like the Lord was telling me, *Darla, trust this man. I taught him everything he knows. You're in good hands.* He's right (of course). Who was I—someone who had spent all but a week researching (on *Google,* no doubt)—to think I knew more than this man who'd dedicated the majority of his *life* to this stuff? There was no comparison, and it's *laughable* I ever contemplated there being one.

It was nearly two weeks after this discussion that we were back at the hospital for a third bone marrow biopsy and meeting with the acute leukemia specialist. (Remember the "comic book character" guy?) We didn't realize until we were already checked in and waiting in the exam room that we were on the wrong side of the second floor. *Oops!* Thankfully, the doctor was super understanding and nice enough to find us (instead of us finding him). From the improving numbers shown in my blood work, he was not only pleased with the progress but expressed confidence that the bone marrow would come back clean as well. "Oh good! So does that mean we don't need the biopsy?" I teased.

It was worth a try.

After two blown veins from their last attempt at starting an IV, we were proactive about asking if the vein specialists could be brought in. Using their ultrasound machine, they detected a vessel and got it in one stick. It was a "stinger" (never did let up until it was out), but at least it was in. Sedation was administered, and the RN (who we'd soon discover was our *favorite* for performing these biopsies) got the job done quickly and smoothly.

Which reminds me of an absolutely mind-blowing fact the doctor shared with us that day. Brian was able to explain it best. In his words...

Prior to treatment, Darla would have had 10^{12} (or 1 trillion [1,000,000,000,000]) cancer cells in her body. After treatment, that was reduced by 99.9% down to 10^{9} (or 1 billion [1,000,000,000]) cancer cells. Those are huge numbers, but at the cellular level, I suppose they aren't "that" big. He gave some context to that by providing another analogy. Within her six liters of blood, suppose one liter is cancer, chemo knocks that down to one milliliter. All that to say there is still some residual cancer left after the first round of chemo, but it's virtually undetectable from biopsies. The biopsy we had done today is to prove that the cancer isn't back at a measurable level.

The other piece of information the doctor discussed with us had to do with what he called "consolidation chemo." Given the time we had until the stem cell transplant, we needed short bursts of chemo to keep the leukemia suppressed. Even if the latest biopsy came back "clean," it was crucial no leukemic cells returned to the marrow before having the transplant. This would be an extra "blast" to kill off any potential strays. He wanted to get this consolidation chemo started sooner than later, so the plan was to be admitted to Simon Cancer on that Thursday (August 3, 2017) to start a three-day chemo treatment. This would likely mean we'd be home that following Monday, the day *before* Clara headed back for another year of school. In other words, chances were good we'd be back to commemorate her first day of first grade. God's timing amazed us once again!

With little time before my readmissions and start to school, the girls and I headed to the grocery store to make sure we had the necessary foods to start packing school lunches again. It was on our way home that I realized I had missed a call from an Indianapolis number. *Hmm.* Whoever it was left a message too. I assumed it was going to be an update about my biopsy or more information about the upcoming consolidation chemo. But it was a much better update than that...*much* better.

Here's the journal update I wrote:

Match Made in Heaven

August 2, 2017

After being diagnosed with leukemia, the concept of "planning ahead" lost much of its perceived power. There were several things I attempted to schedule this week, but those soon were canceled or altered once we found out about the consolidation chemo at the end of this week. It's not easy to live moment by moment in a forward thinking culture, but I believe it's out of this idea of "daily" that true faith is born and grown. King Solomon—the wisest man to ever live—once wrote, "We can make our plans, but the Lord determines our steps" (Prov. 16:9 NLT). I'm gaining a greater understanding these days of just how much wisdom is behind this truth.

This being said, my original plan for Wednesday morning changed once I realized my hospital stay was tomorrow (so I thought...this also got switched). There were overnight bags to pack for the weekend and groceries to buy for the start of school next Tuesday. When the girls and I arrived home after our trip to ALDI, I saw I'd missed a call from an Indianapolis number. We were anticipating a call to give us biopsy results and more details about the upcoming chemo, so I listened to the voicemail (recorded at 11:40 a.m.) expecting something other than what I heard:

"Hi, Darla. This is your bone marrow transplant coordinator. I'm calling because I have been in communication with the doctors about your case. I do have an unrelated donor that is a perfect match for you. I have confirmation of that, so we can move ahead as soon as you're ready to move ahead."

The message brought me to instant tears and immediate praise unto the Creator God who orchestrated all of this. I called Brian right away, and he drove home since it also happened to be the lunch hour. I waited until he arrived to call the nurse back and tell her YES! We are ready to move ahead with the transplant.

There isn't much that can be disclosed (yet) about my donor, but my coordinator was able to tell us that he is a male in his twenties. She also mentioned how he was really on top of things; as soon as he was contacted, he got his blood work sent in right away. One of my specific prayers was that those who matched would be diligent on their end of things, so as not to unnecessarily delay the process—*thank you, God, for hearing and answering!* I can't say that I've met many men in their twenties who give much thought beyond themselves and their hobbies, so this is truly a supernatural working of the Father. Perhaps, too, it's a reassuring reminder that there are still exceptional people in the world who are willing to make significant sacrifices for a complete stranger. The coordinator also said that the transplant would be approximately four weeks after our consolidation chemo is complete, putting us at the beginning of September for the procedure.

What else can I say? His praise will ever be on our lips.

As I was reading Romans 15 yesterday, verse 13 jumped off the page at me. It's a beautiful prayer for this season, as well as a great thought to end the post:

"May the God of hope fill you with all joy and peace as you trust in him, so that you may overflow with hope by the power of the Holy Spirit."

(Rom. 15:13 NIV)

The story just kept getting better. On his way back to work, Brian got a call about my latest biopsy—it was clean! And that evening, it was "Meet the Teacher" night for Clara. Here is what I wrote:

Another Perfect Match

I've been itching to share with you yet another story of the Lord's unfathomable provision, but other updates have put it on hold—until now! Rewind with me for a moment to this past Wednesday, the very same day I received the call about my perfectly matched donor.

It was "Meet the Teacher" night for first graders. We arrived at Clara's school around 5:30 where lots of other six-going-on-seven-year-olds were abuzz with that unmistakable back-to-school anticipation. Our goals were as follows: Find her classroom, drop off supplies, and, of course, officially meet her teacher. Seemed easy enough.

Dot, dot, dot.

Before parting ways, I let the teacher know about our further cancer treatments and the implications this will have on Clara. I anticipated doing a whole lot more explaining, but she saved me the words. "I know exactly what she's going through," she explained. "When I was in third grade, my dad was diagnosed with Hodgkin's disease, so I was bounced around from cousins' house to cousins' house to grandparents', etc."

In the very moments following the teacher's testimony, I experienced such reassurance. God, in His grace and sovereignty, had pieced together a perfect match once again; this time, with a daughter who needs someone like this—a role model who can empathize with Clara's displaced feelings and offer her compassion when the weight of it all feels heavier than usual. *God, thank you, thank you, THANK YOU for yet another match made in heaven!*

I also would like to encourage anyone reading right now who may be in the midst of sorrowful battle not only to hang in there, but know that God can use your story to one day breathe life into another soul. Just this past week, I found out about a loss some friends are experiencing, and as I was praying for them, God whispered these words to me: *Someday you'll understand.* Does that erase the current sting? No. But it certainly helps knowing the pain is not for naught—it's accomplishing a future glory that far outweighs any momentary struggle.

I'm not sure if Clara's teacher has had a student before Clara to whom she could say with such sincerity, "I understand." She may, for all I know, have waited forty years for this unique opportunity. But I would have to think she'd count her own childhood hardship worth it to now have the privilege of caring for a little one's tender heart.

> "All praise to God, the Father of our Lord Jesus Christ. God is our merciful Father and the source of all comfort. He comforts us in all our troubles so that we can comfort others. When they are troubled, we will be able to give them the same comfort God has given us. For the more we suffer for Christ, the more God will shower us with his comfort through Christ. Even when we are weighed down with troubles, it is for your comfort and salvation! For when we ourselves are comforted, we will certainly comfort you. Then you can patiently endure the same things we suffer. We are confident that as you share in our sufferings, you will also share in the comfort God gives us."
>
> (2 Cor. 1:3-7 NLT)

There is NO ONE like our God!

One last entry on the topic:

POWER in the Blood

August 5, 2017

I'm still reeling with wonder over the reality of a "perfect match." It leaves me questioning, "How did God do that?!" Followed by, "God, you are so much BIGGER than my mind can even begin to comprehend!" A few passages of Scripture entered my thoughts as I pondered the magnitude of this.

"O Lord, God of Israel, there is no God like you in all of heaven above or on the earth below...even the highest heavens cannot contain you."

(1 KIN. 8:23, 27 NLT)

"Lord, our Lord, how majestic is your name in all the earth! You have set your glory in the heavens....When I consider your heavens, the work of your fingers, the moon and the stars, which you have set in place, what is mankind that you are mindful of them, human beings that you care for them?"

(PS. 8:1, 3-4 NIV)

"Who am I, Sovereign Lord, and what is my family, that you have brought me this far?... How great you are, Sovereign Lord! There is no one like you, and there is no God but you..."

(2 SAM. 7:18, 22 NIV)

"You are worthy, our Lord and God, to receive glory and honor and power, for you created all things, and by your will they were created and have their being."

(REV. 4:11 NIV)

"I will praise the Lord at all times. I will constantly speak his praises. I will boast only in the Lord; let all who are helpless take heart. Come, let us tell of the Lord's greatness; let us exalt his name together."

(Ps. 34:1-3 NLT)

"You have searched me, Lord, and you know me. You know when I sit and when I rise; you perceive my thoughts from afar. You discern my going out and my lying down; you are familiar with all my ways. Before a word is on my tongue you, Lord, know it completely. You hem me in behind and before, and you lay your hand upon me. Such knowledge is too wonderful for me, too lofty for me to attain.... For you created my inmost being; you knit me together in my mother's womb. I praise you because I am fearfully and wonderfully made; your works are wonderful, I know that full well."

(Ps. 139:1-6, 13-14 NIV)

A few days ago, Wendy was in the room next to me, working on a puzzle at the dining room table. Seemingly out of nowhere, she began singing, "There is POWER, POWER, wonder-working POWER in the precious blood of the Lamb," by Lewis E. Jones.[2] First to be noted—I didn't even know she knew this hymn. I'm sure it's come up at some point, but I can't recall context or specifics at all. So that had me contemplating for a while with no concrete conclusion. Secondly, she sang just that line on repeat for probably half an hour. Now, normally, when kids take something and run it into the ground, it's a test of my patience and endurance. Broken records are not pleasant, folks, are you with me? But to be proclaiming TRUTH on repeat...wow... there is POWER in that! Quite honestly, I began wondering if in some mysterious, supernatural way, God gave voice to words He'd earlier planted in Wendy's mind for such

---

[2] Lewis E. Jones (1899), "Power in the Blood," Public Domain.

a time as this. For as she pieced together that puzzle giving declaration to God's omniscience, my Maker was matching pieces between my donor and me. It was, in fact, just a day (Maybe two?) before receiving the call about the "perfect match" when this scene unfolded. I will never know this side heaven, but there was something that seemed significant...something much more than a preschooler singing a song.

There is indeed power in the blood. Peter once wrote, "For you know that it was not with perishable things such as silver or gold that you were redeemed from the empty way of life handed down to you from your ancestors, but with the precious blood of Christ, a lamb without blemish or defect" (1 Pet. 1:18–19 NIV). Nothing but Jesus' blood is capable of washing away our sin. Nothing. No amount of trying, good work, commendable service, money given to the poor can eliminate the sin stain that comes between us and the Father.

Very early on, I recognized the parallels with leukemia and the Gospel. My blood is sick, and there is nothing my own body can do on its own to fix it. I've already relied on countless individuals for their healthy blood and plate-lets, not to mention chemotherapy to kill off the disease. The deleted seventh gene they discovered after my first biopsy put me in the category of "high risk" leukemia patient, which gives me a twelve- to eighteen-month survival rate with chemo alone. My greatest fighting chance at longer term life (from a medical standpoint) is through this transplant. I need healthy bone marrow to replace my diseased bone marrow in order that it may work to kill remaining and future leukemic cells. Do you see the connection? While I am eternally indebted to Jesus for His atoning sacrifice to save me from everlasting dam-nation, so I am exceedingly grateful for the man in his twenties whose healthy stem cells will replace mine to save me from cancer.

I sincerely hope that someday, I can meet—or at the very least, be in cor-respondence with—the young man who is donating his stem cells. Certainly, he has to know it means "a lot" to the person on the receiving end (me), but does he know just how much? I pray that if he doesn't already, he may begin to grasp also this Gospel connection and form a deep, intimate relationship with his (our) awesome Creator.

The consolidation chemo ended up starting Friday (August 4) instead of Thursday. It was nice to have an extra day at home *and* discover we'd still be back in time for the start of Clara's first grade year. After a rough blood draw (those were becoming commonplace), it was time to meet with the acute leukemia specialist again. As he went over various consent forms with us and made sure we were "done having kids" before signing my name (the procedure would lead to infertility), he asked if my diagnosis followed a similar pattern: "Let me guess, you had flu-like symptoms, no energy, you got in and were treated with an antibiotic but it didn't treat your infection; you got admitted to the hospital, had blood work done, and discovered you had leukemia." As a matter of fact, yes! He sure knows his stuff! Apparently, this is "classic" in terms of patients discovering they have AML.

We left his office with a handshake, smile, and warm send-off: "We'll see you after transplant!" Ironically, we've never seen the man since that day. What we didn't realize at the time was that once I entered the transplant world, there was a "baton toss" that occurred between him and the bone marrow transplant director we'd met earlier that week. From then on, I was under other care.

Waiting for my PICC line insertion (yes, I needed another one) was quite the test of patience; it was a full hour before they called my name. But whatever the holdup was worked to my advantage; it allowed me more time to pray, for which I was grateful. I'm honestly not sure which is more difficult: Entering the unknown? Or *knowing* what to expect? To keep my fears at bay, I quietly sang the song "You Are My All in All" a good fifteen or twenty times (and that's more likely an underestimate than an exaggeration). It was helpful to focus my mind on who God is (strong and capable) instead of on myself (scared and weak).

There were other songs too that God put in my head to sing. One called "Ever Be" *(by Kalley Heiligenthal)* was a good reminder for me to offer a continual sacrifice of praise to the Lord, and there were a variety of other tunes He gave me set to the words of Psalm 23. At the beginning of that week, I had sensed that this familiar psalm was a new "theme" God was setting my heart and mind to as we prepared for this chemo stent. There is such power in praise...more than we can really see or know.

When I was finally called back to have my PICC line put in, I gave a forewarning to those who were doing the procedure about my small veins. Getting out the ultrasound machine, they first scanned all the veins in my right arm; nothing was even remotely workable, except in the armpit. *Noooo,* thank you! Unfortunately, the left arm was no better. All my veins were too tiny and wouldn't compress. The biggest of them was 0.2 millimeters, and the smallest catheter they had available was 0.4 millimeters. The risk for a blood clot was too high if they tried to force it, so they came up with an alternative. It wasn't necessarily ideal (because of the risk of "blowing" at some point and the fact that blood draws in the night would require extra pokes), but a regular IV was the route they went. He placed the biggest gauge he could in my right bicep, and I've got to say that thing pinched and ached the whole time it was in. I prayed continually that it could "handle" the chemo pumping through it for the next few days.

Same But Different

August 6, 2017

We knew going into consolidation chemo things were going to look quite different than before. Shorter stay, shorter rounds of chemo, and shorter hair. (Ha! Truth.) Turns out they also had to go with an IV versus a PICC line because my veins were too small and wouldn't compress this time around. The only thing I haven't preferred about the IV is they actually have to poke me in the middle of the night for blood draws.

I just recently completed my fourth dose of chemo; I will have six total. The regiment this time is two hours of chemo every twelve hours for six rounds. So 6:00-8:00 both a.m. and p.m. have been when I'm receiving treatments, my final one being tomorrow morning. Then we should be free to go.

Thankfully, I haven't experienced any unpleasant side effects. The dosage is more concentrated this time around, so they gave me a complete sobriety test of sorts every few hours to see if my brain is functioning as it should. I also have to write a sentence for them—the same one every time. Medicated eye drops are administered twice a day, as that also is an area often targeted with this chemo. Some aspects are the same as last time—morning and night meds as well as the mouthwash to prevent mouth sores (as much as possible).

When the doctors met with me this morning, they reminded me that it will be about a week after I return home that my body will feel the effects of the chemo—fatigue, more hair loss (I still have a little left, but most of my scalp shows now), possible mouth sores and other complications. I need to closely monitor my temperature in case I spike a fever and will most likely need blood transfusions in Muncie as well.

Another difference has been the time without Brian. We had agreed upfront it wasn't as crucial that he stay with me this entire stretch. He was sensing a need to save up work days for the upcoming transplant, and I was sensing the need for the girls to spend as little time away from him and home as feasible. Our oldest daughter, Clara, is really worried about us leaving her again. She gets pretty emotional about it (especially in the evenings) and asks every time we have even an afternoon appointment, "Are you going to be gone for thirty days?" Breaks a mother's heart. But I know God is using this time to grow the girls' faith as much as He is growing ours. This time is not being wasted. "We can rejoice, too, when we run into problems and trials, for we know that they help us develop endurance. And endurance develops strength of character, and character strengthens our confident hope of salvation. And this hope will not lead to disappointment. For we know how dearly God loves us, because he has given us the Holy Spirit to fill our hearts with his love" (Rom. 5:3–5 NLT).

After getting me settled in here Friday, Brian headed back to Muncie to work for a few more hours before returning for the night. Yesterday, he drove to Richmond late morning to pick the girls up from Grandma and Grandpa's. They got here around 2:30 and visited until dinner time. He spent the night with them at home in Muncie and will have the normal church, lunch, nap routine today. This afternoon, the girls head to a dear friend's house to stay until we return home tomorrow.

Neither of the nurses I've had this weekend attended to me during my entire stay last time. Seems kind of crazy considering how long I was here! But they've both been as great as the others. And speaking of the others, it's been fun running into several of them and catching up as I walk laps around the unit.

There was one nurse we were especially excited to see again and catch up with. She said she was thinking of us when she walked into Room C22. And then she said the new patient in there is equally sweet. The tech in the room agreed and said, "You left a presence in there." That, my friends, is the Lord's presence. Praying that the patient in there recognizes it as Him as well.

Just as scheduled, my last chemo treatment was early Monday morning (August 7, 2017). After the doctor made his round, the nurse came back in our room and said, *"This may be the earliest discharge ever!"* Of course, God would bless us in that way! He continued to show up and provide for us in so many amazing ways. She went over discharge papers around 9:00 that morning and then pulled the IV out. Man, did it feel good to be free of that thing! And praise God it lasted for all the treatments! We picked up our prescriptions from the hospital pharmacy, and by 9:45, were out of there and on our way to pick up the girls! When we got back to Muncie, Brian headed to work and I got to spend the rest of the day with Clara—the last day before starting first grade.

CHAPTER 6

UNWAVERING

Now that a "perfect match" had been discovered, it was time to prepare for the transplant. Back when the BMT (bone marrow transplant) was first being discussed, I had no idea how soon around the corner they meant. But it only made sense to get the process started since the cancer was at bay *and* a willing donor was solidified.

You may have picked up by now that this "transplant" has interchangeable names. Sometimes I refer to it as a "bone marrow transplant" and other times as a "stem cell transplant." Really, the latter is more accurate in my case. While such a thing still exists—where they surgically remove part of the actual bone marrow of the donor and surgically insert it into the recipient—the more common method is what I had. In fact, a stem sell *infusion* may be the most precise title of all. My knowledge of the technical side of things is minimal, but from what I've read about it, the donor gives himself/herself Neupogen injections for the five days leading up to the donation. The medication works to stimulate the stem cells in the bloodstream, therefore increasing their production. After those five days, the donor's stem cells are ready to be collected. With an IV in each arm—one busily removing blood and the other working to return the blood that has had the stem cells spun out of them (thanks to the machine that's doing all the work)—the cells are collected in a bag, which is soon thereafter infused into the cancer patient. Quite fascinating, eh?

This process can't be jumped into blindly but requires a lot of background work leading up to it. Not just anyone can donate, and tragically, not everyone is healthy enough to receive new stem cells. As you may imagine, it takes a toll on a person's body to be, in essence, reset. There's a reason the medical world refers to it as a "rebirth." Out with the old (cells) and in with the new (cells). There are a variety of tests that need to be cleared before being considered eligible.

Leaving our home a little after 6:00 the morning of August 16, 2017, we made our way to the hospital for my transplant "workup." From the looks of the itinerary, we had a *full* day ahead of us. "Full" was also an appropriate adjective for the two collection jugs containing my twenty-four-hour urine sample. Until we arrived at the drop-off location, poor Brian lugged those puppies around on his back in an iced and insulated backpack. Thankfully, there were no leaks despite all the movement we did that day. Have I mentioned before what a trooper he is? Beginning at 7:30, we moved from one test to the next: pulmonary function, chest x-ray, echocardiogram, CT scan, labs, meeting with social worker, and EKG.

The most difficult part about yesterday was, of course, the good ole lab work. When I counted seventeen vials to fill, I immediately started praying. I told the technician that my hands were the best bet for finding a good vein, but she decided to attempt one she thought would work on my right elbow. Poke, dig, talk about how it's "getting away" from her, aaaaaand out the needle comes. Into the hand she went. By the time we had probably seven vials left, my blood flow was not really "flowing" anymore. We slowed down to literally a drip by drip filling. Talk about slooooooow and a mind over matter game. Praying. Praying. Still praying. Now in the past, I would have been unconscious on the floor by this point with smelling salts in my face to revive me. Not so this time. God is building up my endurance...His provision still astounds me.

It was an exhausting day, but it was done! The ball was now in their court, which brought with it a certain amount of freedom and relief. While they were busy determining when the next move would be played, we had a chance to catch our breath in the waiting.

The following day was "business as usual." Preschool would be starting up again soon, and we needed a signed copy of Wendy's most recent physical for her upcoming registration. Before hopping into the car to retrieve the needed paperwork from the pediatrician's office, I received a call from the IU Health radiology department to inform me that my echocardiogram from the previous day's workup was missing. *What? Missing? There's no way! I remember being in the yellow waiting room, and I can still recall the woman's name who called me back for the test.* The receptionist on the other end said she would double check with my transplant coordinator.

By the time the girls and I reached the parking lot of the pediatric clinic, my phone alerted me to a missed call and a new voicemail. It was my transplant coordinator who reiterated the fact that no echocardiogram was to be found.

(Pause)

Have you ever experienced such a strong conviction about something that you couldn't figure out how in the world it wasn't matching up with someone else's reality?

(Unpause)

Completely dumbfounded, I dialed the number back and waited for an answer. When the transplant coordinator picked up, I again expressed my absolute assuredness that we had completed every single one of those tests. Yes, even the echocardiogram. At this point, I was starting to feel a little defensive and borderline emotional. I could *not* fathom how what I was trying to convey was anything other than truth. *Until* (now *there's* a game-changer word) she asked, "Do you recall having a test done where they put jelly on your chest?"

Sigh. No...I didn't. And it sounded too memorable to forget.

Unbelievable. How is it even possible that this got skipped? And why couldn't the department have alerted someone *yesterday* (While we were still *there!*) to the fact that, *Darla Peters never showed up for her echocardiogram. Should we be concerned?* Now we needed to reschedule the test, which would most likely push back the date of the transplant. In my flesh, I was feeling frustrated and defeated. Meanwhile, my spirit was trying its best to remind the rest of me that God's timing is always right and that all this would work out for "good" in the end.

Now that this mishap was mostly settled, the girls and I got out of the parked car to take care of the one thing we had driven to this office to do: get this signed printout. Easy enough, right? Walking up to the front desk, I explained to the receptionist the reason for our visit. She was happy to help us out, but as she pulled up Wendy's electronic records, she told us that the preschool may not "accept it" because it had been "over a year" since her last physical. *Over a year?* In the midst of my deep pondering and contemplation, I scrunched my face into my furrowed brow expression (the one I don't realize I do until it shows up later in pictures), and had that strange wave of twilight zone feeling wash over me once again. *There's no way it's been over a year! There must be some mistake.*

I stood there trying to pull up my own records (via my ever-failing memory) as quickly as I could from that previous May—just a few months before. When I did, it became clear: She's *right!* I had totally spaced on Wendy's fourth year physical! But how is that even possible? It all started to make more sense once I remembered how soon after Wendy's birthday, my health began its decline. Having a better understanding of the *how* and the *why* didn't make me feel any better about the whole unfortunate situation. Between this and the parking lot phone conversation I had just finished, I couldn't hold it together any longer. Before I knew it, an unavoidable lump (not the cancerous kind) had formed in my throat. And if that didn't make it difficult enough to communicate, the next emotional reflex surely would. My tear ducts finally surrendered to the pressure they'd tried for some time to resist. What followed was an eruption of tears. In fact, I was crying so hard that I could barely make sense of my own words. Thankfully, God graced me with enough poise to voice this last coherent thought between the sobs: "I'll call you later today to schedule Wendy's next appointment."

Yes, all was worked out in the end. An appointment was made, Wendy was checked, an updated form was printed and signed, and registration for preschool happened.

Just six days after the workup, I was back at Simon Cancer Center...by myself this time. Going into the solo adventure, I really thought I had this whole spiel down. I'd been the passenger *many* times before, so if memory served me correctly (which I was pretty sure it would), I was familiar enough with the route. And maybe more importantly, I (thought I) knew which of the several parking garages to use. Unlike Brian who is a "natural" when it comes to navigating, I am neither directionally inclined *nor* do I seem to have the capacity to think logically when lost or looking for a place to park. It doesn't help that the enemy *also* knows these particular weaknesses of mine.

I continued praying as I neared the stickier parts of the route and turned on GPS for that final stretch. But now it was time to find that specific lot, which my phone wasn't going to help me locate. One turn here and another turn there, I was *almost* sure I had found the right place. But by the time I had circled my way to the top level of the garage, I realized it had a different aerial view of the hospital than I was used to. That's also when I began noticing how the only people I saw coming and going were University kids. *Great!* I parked in the student lot without knowing it! And since any ability to use common sense proves nonexistent in moments such as these (as I mentioned in the above paragraph), there was no finding another garage. I was there, I was in between two white lines, I was late for my meeting, and I was staying put.

Quick sidebar: This is a good time to mention how grateful I am for Brian's willingness to drive us to and from these appointments. I've expressed to him on multiple occasions how appreciative I am of the heavy load that he shoulders. He usually won't take the compliment, dismissing it with a slight eye roll and a declaration that, *It's really nothing.* That's when I remind him that it's actually quite a significant *something* for me. In case he needs the refresher, it's also the moment I remind him of the fact that navigating is not my forte—to put it lightly. It really has been an incredible gift that the only thing I have to think about is the appointment itself. He'll probably never fully understand how much stress he alleviates.

So the whole reason I chose to go by myself this time around is because this visit required no pokes, prods, or physical examinations. I was, in essence, going to class to learn about stem cell transplants and what to expect for the hospital stay and beyond. (*Ha!* Perhaps the "student lot" was appropriate after all.) I knew that the information I would be given could easily be shared with Brian later (I was given a packet and took extra notes when needed), so it really wasn't necessary for us both to be present.

I first met with my transplant coordinator to go over the consent form, which was several pages long. While this was simply the "opening act" before the actual "educating" began, I found it to be the most enlightening part of the day. You know those commercials for various medications where by the time they get done rattling off a slew of potential side effects, you wonder who in the world would be so brave as to risk taking it? On a much grander scale, that's what this experience was like. But the beautiful thing is I can't recall feeling any sort of anxiety or negative emotion as she read off all the "potentials" surrounding the procedure, nor did I have any hesitation signing my name to every line of the document that required a signature. Clearly, God was my *shield* and my *fortress*, and the darts whizzing my direction seemed to only ricochet off of me. In fact, I actually found the information to be rather fascinating. His grace proved sufficient for the moment once again.

Remember that whole echocardiogram fiasco? My transplant coordinator was actually able to get a new one scheduled the day after my class. This put us exactly a week behind the original workup day, which wasn't bad from a timing standpoint. It made me even more thankful that Brian had skipped out on the class the day before, since it would have been difficult for him to leave work two days in a row. I love how God knows that kind of stuff ahead of time and gives us wisdom in the moment to make the best decisions. He's so good to us.

For all you mothers out there who have had ultrasounds, did you ever feel any pain when the wand glided over your pregnant tummy? There was always such a distinct stinging I experienced every time I had it done, but I figured it mostly had to do with the growing baby or the stretching skin in the area that was being tested. Well, that theory was put to rest the day I had the echocardiogram. The best word I could use to describe it was *excruciating*. This, I didn't expect. Between the to-and-fro motion and intense amount of pressure the tech was using with that silly wand, it felt like the skin on my chest and upper abdomen (and perhaps even the bones and organs directly underneath) were on fire. Even though I have fears and apprehensions related to medical procedures and all that comes with them, I am an extremely cordial and compliant patient. I never set out to make the medical professional's job more difficult than it needs to be, nor do I ever question what they are doing (as if I know any better). This, however, was one time when I was in such misery (for what seemed an endless amount of minutes) that I came *this* close (on multiple occasions) to shouting, *Let up, lady!* Instead, I remained silent with quiet tears rolling down my cheeks, clinging to the only rock I knew who could get me through this. After it was all said and done, I did say, "Man, that was really painful." to which she responded, "Yeah, it seems to be for some patients."

Needless to say, if I ever need another "echocardiogram" in my life, there will be no shadow of a doubt as to whether I'd actually had it or not.

I wish I could say the day only got easier from here, but more unforeseen hurdles marked the road ahead. Next in our schedule was an appointment with the director of bone marrow transplants, so we left the radiology department and made our way to the BMT unit. Normally, it wouldn't bother me that the doctor showed up an hour and fifteen minutes late—I know he's a busy man and patients' lives are at stake. But something didn't settle well with me that after all this waiting, the only topic he wished to discuss with us had to do with an experimental group. The research team presented what it would involve to be part of the study, which basically boiled down to a whole lot more pills (they were testing a drug to see if it would minimize acute graft versus host disease), extra blood draws, several more bone marrow biopsies post-transplant, and various other agreements I can no longer recall. There was a long pause, at which point I couldn't tell if they were waiting for me to sign on the line or what. *Was that all this was? Just some sales pitch?!* I had questions—lots of them. If they were looking for a decision, I didn't have one. There's no way I was jumping into anything without praying about it first. "We'll take the paperwork home with us."

Our day ended with a bone marrow biopsy—fourth and counting. As much as I would have preferred sedation for the procedure, I also knew what starting an IV entailed. In my case, the trade-off wasn't always worth it. A sweet nurse we had never met before got me all set up. The area where she began numbing felt incredibly tender, and things only got worse when she attempted to aspirate a sample of marrow. Like a poor fisherman struggling to get a bite, she pulled the needle out with nothing to show for her effort. So she tried *again* and *again!* Three strikes, and she was out. I'm so thankful that she chose at this point to humbly let the doctor know the situation. When he heard, he marched in the room and—like the Little Red Hen—did it himself. Unfortunately, this required that he numb a whole new area, but at least once that part was finished, he aspirated in one try. I remember at one point during all this, the doctor asking, "Are you laughing or crying?" I'm not sure which I was doing either, perhaps some sort of strange combination. I guess when you don't know if you should laugh or cry, you do both. Praise God for being my *joy* and *strength* once again.

We were both quiet on the drive home from the appointment that day. In every facet of the word—physically, mentally, and spiritually—we were tired; even too exhausted to make conversation. But God made sure the silence wasn't wasted. Watching the big, puffy clouds move in and out of shapes against a rich blue backdrop was surprisingly therapeutic. A glimpse of the Lord's glory through His magnificent creation proved life-giving and peace-inducing. Directly in front of us was a large semi-trailer. While our field of vision for the road was limited due to the magnitude of this truck, the words *Oversize Load* gracing the back were in plain view. How fitting all of this was to real life. The load we were carrying felt uncommonly big, and our vision "down the road" finite at best. Thankfully, we had a load-bearing God on our side—One who called us to come to Him for rest and who offered an exchange for what was heavy for something much lighter.

This journal entry overlaps some information I've already shared, but gives a good overview of the state I was in as I anticipated the soon bone marrow transplant.

Upcoming Transplant Schedule
August 30, 2017

It is such a blessing to have a week with no appointments at IU Health. I still have my Monday and Thursday blood draws at our local hospital, but other than that should be "set" (from a medical testing standpoint) for the transplant. Speaking of the transplant, my official "rebirth" (as it is sometimes referred) is September 12. At 7:00 a.m. six days from now, we will be walking into the hospital to register for my 8:30 a.m. catheter placement. I am a bit relieved that I will be "put under" for this procedure. The port is inserted into a vein under the collarbone and will take the place of a PICC line or IV. Again, this is where all medications and fluids will enter, and from which they will draw blood each night.

Once the port is inserted, I will begin receiving high doses of chemotherapy. This is referred to as my "conditioning regimen" or "preparative regimen"—the purpose being to destroy cancer cells, of course, and also suppress my immune system so that my body is less able to attack the transplanted donor stem cells. The day of my transplant is referred to as "Day 0," so I will begin chemo Day - 7 (September 5), continue Day - 6, rest on Days - 5 and - 4. More chemo Days - 3 and - 2. Rest day - 1. And then it's transplant day.

The transplant itself is rather anticlimactic. Except for the fact that its color is a lighter hue of red, it will look almost identical to a typical blood transfusion. The "excitement" could come a little later if signs of graft versus host disease (GVHD) show up. It's undetermined if or when these side effects could appear and to what extent, but common signs of acute graft versus host are a rash with burning and redness of skin (can pretty much show up anywhere on your body), nausea, vomiting, cramps, diarrhea, and jaundice. Within the first 100 days, GVHD can appear as mild symptoms, life-threatening complications, or anything in between. Major organs can be attacked, so doctors and nurses will be closely monitoring my heart, lungs, liver, kidneys, and colon. There's also GVHD in its chronic form. As the word implies, these are symptoms that either remain for life, or at the very least last for several years post-transplant.

No matter how things look from a GVHD standpoint, I know for certain that my immune system is going to be compromised; in fact, it will become like that of an infant. Needless to say, I will be practicing precaution in order to prevent illness as much as possible. Any sign of infection is concerning and will require an immediate trip to the hospital. Eventually, when my body has had a chance to build back up crucial blood counts, I will begin receiving (again) the immunizations I had in my earliest years. I can see why "rebirth" is an appropriate nickname for the procedure.

The decision to have this transplant seems like it would be a no-brainer considering my slim chance of survival without it. Yet I have found myself wavering on the issue. The more educated we have become, the more I have considered this a lose-lose situation—as if I'm trading one horrible disease for another potential one. Meeting the BMT director the first time put to rest some of my concerns.

Last Wednesday's appointment brought to the surface former questions and concerns. We sat through what seemed like a sales pitch for taking part in an experimental study. They are testing willing transplant patients on a diabetic medication in the hopeful attempts of reducing acute GVHD symptoms.

For those who have taken part in the study, results have proven favorable. As they continued their explanation of the study, I was still reeling with the thought of twelve more daily pills on top of the excessive amounts of prescribed drugs I am already taking. *What sorts of complications will this present down the road?* Even though they assured me that this medication proved less harmful than GVHD, I felt hesitant to "sign here" without more counsel and time to pray.

We left that day with the unsigned paperwork in hand. When speaking to my sister (who's a physician) about it, she informed me that the drug actually is safe with seemingly no ill side effects. Despite this reassuring news, my wrestling with uneasiness continued until this weekend when the Lord reminded me of our first encounter with the doctor *(Submit to authority)* as well as the story of Shadrach, Meshach, and Abednego. These three men's resolve to remain faithful to the one true God resulted in their being thrown into a fiery furnace. They wholeheartedly believed that God had the power to save them through the flames, and even if He decided for them a different fate, they refused to defy or defame His great Name. And what happened? Jesus was right there in the furnace with them, and they walked away from their death sentence without so much as a hint of that pervading campfire fragrance!

God has used this familiar story to alter my perspective. I recognize now that we are actually in a win-win situation. He can absolutely—in His omnipotence and omniscience—allow me to walk away from the transplant unscathed. I am praying to that end. But even if...EVEN IF...the Lord doesn't continue the plot in the direction we would prefer, I know He sees the whole picture and with every intentional, love-stained stroke is painting a work of art.

Even if.

CHAPTER 7

UNCONTROLLABLE

Two days before our transplant hospital stay, I asked Brian if he would shave what wispy hairs still remained intact on my balding head. It wasn't out of denial that I'd resisted so long; I just liked having a few strands sticking out from underneath my hats and scarves. Now that things were as sparse as they were, it was time. I wrote a haiku at the time to commemorate the event:

Hair

I thought letting go

Would hurt more than this. Surely

God's peace shields my heart.

I love how God prepares our hearts. Take, for instance, the birth of a child. When a woman is first pregnant, the concept of actually pushing the baby out someday is petrifying. But you ask any woman in her last few weeks of pregnancy how she's doing, and she'll tell you, *I'm SO ready for this baby to come out!* Oh, how perfectly God designed the length of pregnancies. To think that in that final stretch, a woman is actually *eager* for the delivery—something which earlier elevated her heart rate just thinking about—is nothing short of miraculous. And so it goes with hair after chemo. Given enough time dealing with loose clumps and shed strays, I think most patients are more than ready to be done with it. I know I was. What a beautiful gift this was.

With an early start the next morning, we knew bedtime with the girls the night before our hospital stay was going to be especially hard. Clara sat on my lap and cried while Brian read the Bible and prayed. After my last hospital stay, a friend had given us a kid's storybook of Psalm 23, which the Lord prompted me to reread before leaving their room. I was especially struck with a picture of the Shepherd holding the sheep close to His heart, coupled with the words, *Inside, my heart is very quiet.* It was Labor Day and we had spent the holiday at my brother's family pool. Before leaving, I was able to capture a picture of Wendy's favorite past time there—holding one of their cats. The resemblance between that picture and the one of the Shepherd in the book was striking. I wrote, *Just like that kitty felt absolute security and acceptance in the arms of Wendy, so do we (God's sheep) who are enveloped in His (the Good Shepherd's) peaceful, loving embrace—even as we walk through the valley of the shadow of death.*

Clara was sure to inform us that she didn't want to visit us in the hospital this time. She said the travel part made her car sick and that having to say "goodbye" after a short time together was difficult. It made sense; still, I would miss those "real life" moments. Since it wasn't summer break anymore and the girls had preschool (Wendy) and first grade (Clara) schedules to maintain, Brian's parents willingly volunteered to fill in as "Mom and Dad" at the house while we were gone. What a huge sacrifice on their part and blessing on ours! It seemed that between their school routines and lack of hospital visits, the girls would be well distracted from the harsh realities of life.

Day - 7

September 5, 2017

Yesterday marked ~~the first day~~ "day - 7" of our BMT (bone marrow transplant) adventure. Brian and I backed out of the garage at 5:44 a.m. and arrived at IU Health shortly before seven o'clock. One of the nurses on the BMT team was there to greet us in the waiting room. After registering for my catheter placement, we sat down with her and signed my consent for the experimental study.

Next, it was off to ~~see the wizard~~ register in Radiology/Echo where my surgery was scheduled. I had just opened my Bible in the waiting room when my name was called. They're on top of things first thing in the morning! We headed back to a small room where I changed into a hospital gown and answered a host of questions for the nurse about my medical history, etc. After we finished, he sort of jokingly said, "I trust you brought your good veins with you today." I'm glad he said something, because it gave me a chance to tell him, no, actually my veins aren't great—they're tiny and roll easily. Without hesitation, he ran off to get the ultrasound machine (while Brian and I prayed) and was able to find a healthy vein a couple inches above my left arm's elbow bend to start the IV. *(Thank you, Jesus.)*

We had a brief meeting with the doctor who would be doing the procedure—a simultaneous handshake and name introduction, rundown of the catheter placement, and heart listen. He also let us know that I was the first surgery of the day and would be in and out in no time. I liked the sound of that! Brian gave me a quick kiss goodbye as I was being wheeled off and before he made his way back toward the waiting room.

I had been told by my BMT coordinator that I would be "put under" for this port "small bore central catheter," but as it turned out, they just sedated me. I'm not sure how sedation is supposed to work exactly, but I was very cognizant of the whole thing—the doctor told me I would feel the burn of the numbing, and I did; he said there would be some tugging, and I felt that. Still, I'm thinking it maybe took some of the edge off. The doctor didn't deceive— "in and out in no time" was right! I'm pretty sure setting up for the procedure took more time than the surgery itself.

I was met by Brian, Mom, and Dad and they followed the bed and me as I was wheeled to the fifth floor, Room 5278. We had been "warned" on several occasions from nurses down on 3rd East that the BMT floor was tiny. I mean, *tiny*. Which, now looking back, I think was God's grace how much they exaggerated the difference in size. I was prepared for a shoe box of a room with no hallway to speak of. But actually, it's a decent size yet cozy (And warmer!) at the same time. I like it! And ironically, from our window, we can see Room C22 where we spent our first month here. Somehow seems fitting—a different side and level of this road to remission.

We felt immediately welcomed by the nurses and staff up here. The nurse assigned to my room that day was certainly an energetic and informative nurse to initiate our stay. She updated my charts, gave us some info about the room/floor and BMT procedure, and then took us on a little tour of the unit. Chemo started at four o'clock yesterday afternoon. These first two days, it's thirty-minute high doses of Thiotepa every twelve hours, so my last round will be 4:00 a.m. tomorrow. Then I will have two days of rest before my next strand and treatment regimen.

As yesterday progressed, the tenderness around my catheter increased—I expected that. The pain was tolerable, but I wondered how things would feel around bed time. I was gratefully surprised that by the time I was crawling into bed, things were actually less sore! And I'm pretty sure I slept like a baby. *God's grace is sufficient for me.*

One thing that would make this stay similar to my first one on 3rd East was the predicted length of time—approximately thirty days (maybe more, depending on complications). We had been told that the chemo I would be receiving before the transplant was much more potent than what I had been given in June. Boy, were they right! My body could certainly tell the difference, as those first days of treatment left me feeling nauseous and puny. I remember lying on my side and gripping the side of the bed to try to alleviate some of my discomfort while my parents were there for a visit. Through the fog, I expressed, "I didn't know it was going to be this hard." Oh, but more "hard" is on the horizon.

As Brian wrote:

Day - 2

September 10, 2017

These last two days of chemo have really wiped Darla out. She has been super sleepy and today hasn't had much of an appetite. This chemo has made her feel nauseous as well. In fact, we had a little scare earlier this afternoon. Darla was coming out of the bathroom but then got light-headed and passed out. She crumbled to her knees and thankfully didn't hit her head on anything. As I was hoisting her up, a nurse was coming in to address a beeping IV pump, so she was able to call for reinforcements right away. Nurses grabbed her torso and I grabbed her legs, and by the time we had her back in bed, there were six total nurses and a doctor swarming around checking vitals, drawing blood, running tests, etc. Darla was only out for maybe five to ten seconds, and since she didn't hit her head (and her platelets were high), there was no concern for running a CT scan. Within a few minutes they determined her to be stable and have her on a fall protocol where she will need assistance going to the bathroom (from nurses, not just me).

One of the medicines they have been giving her is designed to induce urination, as this chemo, if left in the bladder too long, can be harmful. So they want to force the body to get rid of it as soon as possible. Since she's been going so much, results from the blood that was drawn after her fall indicated her potassium and sodium levels are low (doesn't help that she hasn't eaten anything today either). In an effort to bring those levels up, they instituted a new restriction where she is not allowed to have more than 1200 milliliter of fluids in a day. The thought being this will help to not "wash away" the potassium and sodium levels in her body.

The nurses tied a bright yellow cloth to the end of my bed to serve as a reminder of my new bed restriction status. While my increased dependence didn't thrill me (especially the part about paging the nurse to use the bathroom), I was also aware of my need for being cautious. Fainting wasn't a new experience for me, but doing so without any forewarning was. If this incident could happen in the absence of any classic signs of passing out—muffled hearing, ear ringing, overheating, blurry vision, general weakness—it was for the best that I require an extra hand. And thankfully, the restrictions didn't last but a few days.

Day Zero had arrived, the day of my rebirth. We felt mixed emotions as we waited for the stem cells to arrive. At 1:05 that afternoon, a lab tech carrying a purple cooler plastered with a bright orange biohazard sticker entered our room (5278). He pulled out the pouch containing the stem cells, which had been donated less than twenty-four hours before.

Bones That Live

September 12, 2017

Phew. It's good to be back. The past couple days were pretty rough after the latest chemo. Thank you for all your prayers, texts, visits, encouragement and support. Couldn't have gotten through them without you. (I hope you know I don't say that flippantly. You guys have carried us and given us ammunition to keep fighting.) And Brian Peters. Your presence brings a lightheartedness and an "everything's gonna be okay" feel to this hospital room that is both priceless and palpable. Thank you for literally catching me when I fell, and for your continued updates when I've been out for the count.

The doctors and nurses told us ahead of time the actual stem cell infusion was pretty lackluster. It looked nearly identical to a bag of blood, all ready to soon be attached to an IV pole and dripping its way into my line. But man, the nurse asked me if I wanted to hold the bag of cells in my hand before she hung them up; I'm so glad she offered. That experience moved me. The bag fit perfectly inside of my hand, a meager 113 milliliter of fluid. Staring at me were lots of numbers and letters that didn't make sense to me as a patient—codes, medical stuff, etc.—but one thing that did translate was something I couldn't possibly contain inside: "Isn't God amazing?" I exclaimed. I mean, that He would create us with this blood...this marrow...these cells...and He knows exactly how to put them together to make life. And now, to create new life (in essence). Astounding. And again, of course, so very thankful for this young man whose donated stem cells were collected and mailed yesterday. That whole act is still beyond comprehension.

The nurse stayed in the room with me for fifteen minutes to make sure my body was handling the transfusion. After she checked my vitals and stepped out, I opened up my Bible and audibly read the first fourteen verses of Ezekiel 37. Around Thanksgiving of last year, I sensed very clearly that God was speaking the "valley of dry bones" over me. I have all kinds of underlines, notes, and prayers dated from November of last year written under the verses and in the margins of my Bible. At the time, I wasn't certain why the Lord was emphasizing these verses, but I felt strongly that "someday," I would understand. When mid-June came, that puzzle began to become more clear. Bones. Bone marrow. Life. Breath.

"'Son of man, can these bones live?'" I said, 'O Sovereign Lord, you alone know.' Then he said to me, 'Prophesy to these bones and say to them, 'Dry bones, hear the word of the Lord! This is what the Sovereign Lord says to these bones: I will make breath enter you, and you will come to life'"

(Ezk. 37:3-5 NIV).

Oh, Lord, this is still my prayer. That you would breathe life into my body and that these dead bones would come to life once again. Nothing is too difficult for you. May your praise continually flow from this breath you breathe.

The only notable change after my infusion of new cells was some sort of confusion between day and night. The two seemed to swap places on me! I teased that my donor must have lived in a different time zone since the first two nights were plagued with insomnia. Wide awake, I sat up in my hospital bed watching the wall clock's second hand make its way around the entirety of the circumference...again and again and again. It had to be bad if even Brian was sound asleep in his hospital recliner. I remember thinking, surely, I would crash that second night, but that proved to be a *pipe* dream instead of an *actual* one. There was also a significant (to me, at least) decrease in daytime urination and an increase at night. *Weird.* Who knows? Maybe these phenomena were triggered by a medication or were purely coincidental. Still, I preferred sticking with the time zone theory.

By far, the most grueling aspect to this hospital stay (from a physical standpoint) was the mucositis. While I had been warned of this likely side effect (due to the particular kinds of chemo I was receiving), I could not *begin* to appreciate in its description what it would feel like in reality. What started as a slight stinging in my mouth and thickening of my throat progressed into quite possibly the worst form of chronic pain I'd ever experienced up to this point...and that was saying a lot. The sides of my tongue and insides of my cheeks looked like they had been through a meat grinder. While I couldn't see what "down my throat" resembled, if its appearance matched its feeling, it wasn't pretty. Anything I consumed felt like what I would imagine eating glass to be like. If I had known it would be that horrendous, I probably wouldn't have agreed to be part of the experimental study. As if there weren't enough pills to swallow already, I had *twelve* extras to get down each day because of their research. I remembered going as fast I could to get each one consumed (I wanted to get it over with), wincing with every swallow. Needless to say, food (and even liquids) were not appealing. Neither was talking, for that matter.

In an attempt to use humor to help me cope, I wrote a letter.

Dear Ms. Mucositis

September 23, 2017

Dear Ms. Mucositis,

I am writing this letter to inform you that it's time for you to pack your bags and leave; you have overstayed your welcome.

Ms. Throat was the first to stop by my office. She was in tears recalling how on the very first day you moved in, you were carrying a box of kitchen supplies labeled FRAGILE. Crash! Glasses and dishes shattered into thousands of little pieces...and you never cleaned it up! Poor Ms. Throat said she steps on glass every time she walks across her floor.

Next in my office was Ms. Mouth. Now we all know that she likes to talk, but even she kept it brief and to the point, it actually hurt for her to speak at great length. She said you dug a couple holes in the backyard, all gung ho about starting a garden, and then abandoned the project. A direct quote from Ms. Mouth: "The very least Ms. Mucositis could do is fill the holes back in...but no."

Last, but certainly far from least, Ms. Stomach shuffled her way into my office and immediately plopped her limp self in the chair across from my desk. "Let me guess...Ms. Mucositis?" I asked. My prediction just about knocked Ms. Stomach out of her seat. She proceeded to share. "I mean, there's nothing wrong, per se, with oatmeal, cream of wheat, and mashed potatoes. It's just that...well... variety is the spice of life."

So you see, Ms. Mucositis, it seems it would please everyone if you cleaned up your mess, said your goodbyes, and boarded the next plane to Never Again Land.

Oh, but before you go, I do want to assure you that your visit was not for naught. The Bible tells us to rejoice in our sufferings "because we know that suffering produces perseverance; perseverance, character; and character, hope. And hope does not put us to shame..." (Rom. 5:3-5 NIV). Even though your stay, Ms. Mucositis, wasn't necessarily welcomed and the length of time here longer than we would like, you are teaching us in greater measures how to fix our eyes on Jesus, the One who endured the pain of the cross with joy.

Sincerely,
Every Cancer Patient Ever

The letter was stamped and delivered, but I wondered if it maybe got lost in the postal system. I never did hear back. *(Wink)*

I had forgotten that mucositis isn't only a mouth and throat issue, but it can cause ulcers along the entire digestive tract. As the nurses put it, "Anywhere from the mouth to the anus." So as time went on, you could say I was feeling the burn on both ends. *Lord, have mercy.*

Wednesday

September 20, 2017

As I was trying to get to sleep last night—but very aware of the pain coming from my mouth and bottom—I started crying. First time since being up here on BMT unit. The constant pain is just kind of wearing on me. I'm ready for those white cells to go up so that my sores can heal. In the meantime, asking God to give me patience and endurance.

While they tried to manage my misery using high-powered pain meds, I realized early on the only noticeable effect the drugs had on me was extreme grogginess. It didn't target any of the places that were screaming for relief, and the trade-off meant being super sleepy and out of it during the day. I mean, when you write things like *this* in your journal, you know some loopiness is happening: *I'm having these "spells" where I start closing my eyes, daydream, and then talk like I am interacting with the people on stage.* Once this became a more consistent occurrence, I figured out I was hallucinating. I wrote, *I'm guessing it's from the oxy that I'm on, but I've been having these hallucinations. Actually, more like daydreams that are so real I participate in them—answering questions audibly, moving my hands a certain way, throwing a pen cap over someone's leg. Bizarre stuff.*

There was a medicated mouthwash that you could swish and swallow, leaving your throat temporarily "numb." I put the word in quotes because it never fully took the pain away, but it did give me maybe a two-minute window when I could try to quick down my pills or get some food in me. Even then it was barely tolerable at best. Also, those trusty heat packs I frequented in June (when my rib cage was in so much pain) became my neck warmers. I don't know if the heat actually helped, but it was worth a try.

In one of my oxycodone episodes, I accidentally dialed my mother-in-law's number. I woke up hearing, "Darla? *Darla?*" While it wasn't my intent to call, it ended up being a really good time to catch up with her and the girls. Wendy got on the phone at one point and said she had a question: "So, since Daddy is with you in the hospital, will he get sick, too?" I explained to her that no, Daddy can't get sick from Mommy. It was difficult to suck back the tears while I talked to my sweet little four-year-old girl. Broke my heart that these were the concerns on her mind. But it also warmed my heart to think she would want Daddy to be careful.

Light

September 14, 2017

A word that God keeps impressing upon me during this particular hospital stay is LIGHT. I've sensed that there's a twofold purpose behind it: one, for inward hope; two, for outward edification.

This unit is very dark. Literally. We have one window in our room where natural light can enter, but its access is limited since our view is of the opposite side of the building. When we walk the unit hallways, there is natural light to speak of; it's completely enclosed. Now don't get me wrong, I'm very thankful for the invention of the light bulb. However, there is nothing that compares to God-made light, amen?

So while all this has the potential to mess with a person's psyche and overall mood, I must say that the Lord has protected us from the crazies, thus far. And I think it goes back to the "inward hope" thing, which I referred to at the beginning of this post. Scripture tells us that "God is light; in him there is no darkness at all" (1 Jn. 1:5 NIV). Though our eyes cannot behold Him, I'm fully convinced that the very Light of the World is here with us, shining His face upon us.

The "outward edification" can best be summed up by Jesus' words: "Let your light shine before others, that they may see your good deeds and glorify your Father in heaven" (Matt. 5:16 NIV). Which brings up a slight side topic.

See, I am convinced that we "outgrow" certain kid songs waaaaaay too prematurely. Like "This Little Light of Mine," for instance. That should totally be a song we sing to ourselves before beginning a new day. "This little light of mine, I'm gonna let it shine. Hide it under a bushel..." NO! Don't let Satan blow it out. I mean, if we all went into our days with this kind of conviction and resolve, there'd be a whole lot less gloom.

Okay, off the side topic. So right before our night nurse came in last night, we were praying again that God's presence would be evident in our room. That we would be the fragrance of Christ to whoever entered. That God's light would permeate the darkness. That we would be ambassadors who represent Him well. And as soon as our night nurse walked in the room, the Holy Spirit was already doing His work. She honed in on a beautiful poster I have hanging, made and sent by a good friend of mine. On it are printed lyrics of the Hillsong Worship song, "Cornerstone." After reading the words to her she said, "I don't get the word 'cornerstone.'" Bam! Just like that, an opportunity the Lord gave us to spread His light. I explained how in Scripture, Jesus is called our *cornerstone*, because He is the only firm foundation upon which to build our lives. That's all it took, and she said, "Hmm...makes sense."

We found out from our nurse this morning that this same night nurse wanted to take Brian and me home with her. Do you think we can take any credit for that? Nope. Straight up Jesus! That's whom she really wanted more of. HE is appealing! His light is so beautiful, especially in the midst of darkness.

Thank you, God, for being our LIGHT.

While the size of the room wasn't ever an issue (especially with fewer visits and restrictions on how many "outsiders" could be in our room at one time), the hallway could very well have become a source of frustration if I'd allowed it to. The unit itself consisted of only thirteen beds in sort of a U shape, so the length was rather compromised. Then there's the fact that when you're walking with an IV pole down a hallway with various hindrances—large medical carts, floating nurse stations, exercise bikes, communal table for puzzles and games, cleaning lady's closet on wheels, other patients mulling about (not often seen), and a group of doctors huddled in front of patient doorways—it sure could feel cramped and narrow. Hey, I was probably gaining in the way of dexterity now that I think of it! A pivot here and a sharp turn there. The ambiance wasn't helped by the fluorescent lighting or strange smells. We kept noticing this really pungent smell from time to time, and it wasn't until one of our nurses said, "Smells like someone got their cells today," that we realized the source. Somehow, that made it more gross. I guess when patients have an allogeneic stem cell transplant (where their own cells are donated, cleaned up, and put back in—*very* loose translation), the protective substance their cells were frozen in have a distinct scent. Have you ever smelled creamed corn? That's the aroma it gave off.

I hope I didn't ruin your appetite for corn. Maybe just the creamed variety.

So as you can imagine, walking down this cramped, dimly lit, and sometimes smelly hallway required its own form of patient endurance. But God had been preparing the soil of my heart with Psalm 23; in fact, it seemed that this well-known chapter in the Bible had become a new "theme" the Lord had placed on my mind and in my heart. The connection was immediate the first time I made my way through the hallway. *Wow. I am quite literally walking through the valley of the shadow of death.* Patients in the BMT unit were *sick...really* sick. The kind of sick that kept many—I'd say, most—of them captive to their hospital bed. There was a reason the nurses up there were also ICU trained. At times, the heaviness I felt passing by each room and peering in at these fellow fighters was too much to bear. I shed many tears, crying out to the Father for mercy upon them. While most of them I never met, each of their surnames was posted outside their door, so I was able to pray for them that way. Not that the Father needed names, but it somehow made a difference to me.

On these walks, I was also aware of the fact that I wasn't in the valley alone. Not just because of the other patients behind their closed doors or the medical staff buzzing around, but as Psalm 23:4 (NIV) continues, "I will fear no evil, for you are with me...." The Shepherd kept me company, and I enjoyed our conversations as I strolled my way through those hallways with Him. He brought along His rod and His staff, which provided the comfort and regrouping this prone to wandering sheep needed. I remember one specific time retreating in my mind to a safer place—my childhood. The house I grew up in. A young, energetic, carefree Darla. Not a worry in the world. I was tempted to stay in this place and—more than that—to covet this place. Without uttering a spoken word, my thoughts were starting to sound like the Israelites as they wandered in the desert, *Oh, if we could only be back in Egypt. Why did we ever have to leave it?*

Thankfully, the Shepherd did quick work in steering my mind back in a focused direction. I had outgrown my past, and wishing to go back was not only foolish but a lie. Life's résumé had overqualified me for childhood, and like any good boss knows, taking the position would only result in soon boredom, dissatisfaction, and a stunting of growth. Once this thought had been fully squelched, He replaced it with a new one. *Of course, you would give me something I have absolutely no control over.* I let out a chuckle, *You know me so well!* I was truly delighted with the Father, recognizing that I had been strapped in for the faith ride of my life. There was nothing I could "do" to "fix" what was happening (or not happening) inside of me. Changing my diet, activity level, or thoughts (*Think happy thoughts!*) wasn't going to erase the AML or keep it from returning. While we give ourselves far too much credit for the things we *think* we're controlling, this whole blood cancer thing was, without a shadow of a doubt, beyond my power. Which also meant that every ounce of glory in this story He was writing would be given to Him and Him alone.

This didn't discourage me, it *excited* me.

Adam vs. Christ

September 28, 2017

When Brian and I took a little walk last night in the hallway, it struck me again (as it had early on in our stay) that we are literally walking through the valley of death. Behind every closed door we passed is a patient fighting for his/her life. Everyone has complications—not all the same; some more severe than others—and hopes for the day all this is a thing of the past. I started to weep behind the yellow mask that protects my infant-like immune system from the germ-filled world. I'm broken for these fellow patients. Broken that sin ever entered the world. Broken that some people are fighting this battle without Christ. Broken that sickness and death are a part of life.

Oh, God, have mercy on us!

This isn't how the story was supposed to go, but there was a fruit tree; there was a serpent; there was deception and temptation; and then there was disobedience. Snap! Just like that, perfect communion with God severed. Enter sin. Enter sickness. Enter death.

Thankfully, God—in His omniscience and sovereignty—had a plan all along to remedy this devastating dilemma.

"For the sin of this one man, Adam, brought death to many. But even greater is God's wonderful grace and his gift of forgiveness to many through this other man, Jesus Christ.... Adam's sin led to condemnation, but God's free gift leads to our being made right with God, even though we are guilty of many sins. For the sin of this one man, Adam, causes death to rule over many. But even greater is God's wonderful grace and his gift of righteousness, for all who receive it will live in triumph over sin and death through this one man, Jesus Christ. Yes, Adam's one sin brings condemnation for everyone, but Christ's one act of righteousness brings a right relationship with God and new life for everyone. Because one person disobeyed God, many became sinners. But because one other person obeyed God, many will be made righteous"

(ROM. 5:15–19 NLT)

It saddens me when people shake a fist at God for the darkness in this world, as if He's the one to blame. Paul's back and forth contrasting between Adam and Christ leaves us with no question as to the origin of sin and death. One poor decision in the Garden led to the negative consequences we still deal with today. However, God—in His wonderful grace—offers us forgiveness and new life through the death and resurrection of His Son, Jesus Christ.

Yes, cancer stinks. It's an ugly, life-sapping disease. Yet as horrible as it is, it offers an opportunity for me to tighten my grasp on Jesus, as well as gain a better understanding of what it means to walk by faith, not by sight. *God, I trust you have a purpose for my leukemia; please don't let me miss it. I pray that 1 Peter 4:1-2 would be true in my life...that after suffering physically for Christ, I won't spend my days chasing my own desires, but will be anxious to do your will.*

CHAPTER 8

UNANTICIPATED

We were nearing the end of our transplant stay but not necessarily going home. Both girls were back home fighting bad colds, and with as compromised as my immune system was, the doctor wasn't comfortable sending me where known viruses abounded. Don't get me wrong, it was wonderful to find out that my ANC level had begun to rise and a soon departure was on the horizon. But what *wasn't* as thrilling was the possibility of staying two nights in a hotel if their predictions proved accurate. First of all, a hotel didn't sound exactly germ-free either; and secondly, I missed those girls! I was ready to be with them in person again. My mood wasn't helped by the fact that the mucositis was showing no signs of improvement, and the thought of bringing that back with me to the homestead was a little upsetting. Oh, how I needed the Lord's help keeping my eyes fixed on Jesus. He was in control of the wind and waves. I could trust Him.

Well, wouldn't you know, my ANC decided to do a funny thing (directed by God's hand and command). After several days of increasing at a steady rate, we found out that it *backslid* the morning they had anticipated being my last. You can imagine our surprise...and *theirs*. It was actually such a sweet gift to us. This meant no hotel stay for me, *but* two nights in a BED for Brian. Since he had already booked a room at a nearby hotel (not anticipating the ANC dip), he went ahead and stayed. I was excited for him to be able to lay horizontal for a change. While a hotel isn't a guaranteed source of a good night's sleep, *anything* had to be better than a recliner in a hotel room with beeps, buzzes, and visits from night nurses.

They decided to move forward with my catheter removal a day early, obviously feeling good with how the ANC had bounced back after its moment of retreating. Just as I had been with my PICC removal, I was curious how this one would go down. I mean, it had been a minor surgical procedure to insert, so I assumed the same would be said for its departure. I was wrong.

So Long, Catheter
September 28, 2017

Good news!

My neutrophils jumped to 600 today! White cells, hemoglobin, and plate-lets have continued to rise as well. I don't know how He does it, but God is piecing things back where they belong. Astounding. I have full confidence in the One who "made all the delicate, inner parts of my body and knit me together in my mother's womb" (Ps. 139:13 NLT). AND the One who "watched me as I was being formed in utter seclusion, as I was woven together in the dark of the womb" (Ps. 139:15 NLT).

Around 10:30 this morning, they dropped off a hospital gown—time to get my catheter pulled! (This means I'm being discharged tomorrow for sure.) After getting changed, I took a ride down to the basement where we'd had the catheter placed. It was a long wait once I got down there, but I was thankful for the time. I prayed for God to be my *hiding place*, my *shield*, and my *refuge*.

I prayed that His perfect love would drive out all fear and that He would give me the same courage David had when he faced Goliath. I also prayed against complications.

When the doctor arrived (along with a med student who was observing), he explained the procedure. After getting all the dressing unstuck and sterilizing the area, it was time to take a deep breath and blow out slowly while he pulled the catheter out. It burned, but it was over in no time. He bandaged me up, and then I was wheeled back up to my room.

It's a bit surreal to think we are actually leaving this place tomorrow and returning to our home...to our girls.

My last night spent in the hospital was the best sleep I'd gotten in my entire stay. How ironic, and what a blessing! One of the reasons for this was they chose not to interrupt my rest for my usual middle of the night blood draw. They did it later in the morning when I was already awake. And, oh, how thankful I was that they didn't try to tackle in the night! My veins were quite shot at this point. They're so small to begin with, and all the chemo and catheters left things scarred. The specialists entered the room with their ultrasound and finally found one puny thing on my left forearm. At this point, I tried to not anticipate what my *many* future blood draws would be like.

Before leaving, we were visited by the pharmacist to review medications and dosages, as well as the fellow and nurse who went over discharge papers with us. They certainly weren't shy in emphasizing the seriousness of my weakened immune system and the importance of hand washing, avoiding crowded places, wearing a mask when in public or around active coughing, faithfully checking for fevers, and even avoiding our filtered well water back home. I appreciated their candidness. Equally appreciated was their assurance that living in a bubble was neither necessary nor feasible. Good. I was beginning to wonder as they rattled off my various restrictions.

It was reassuring to hear that survival actually *was* possible outside of the contained environment I was leaving.

It wasn't until I was about to walk over to the wheelchair they had waiting for me that I started feeling nauseous. They wheeled me down to the parking garage where our car was, and again, I felt a strong wave of ick wash over me. As we made our way toward Muncie, I was especially thankful that Brian isn't a "jerky" driver and that God quieted my tummy. Pulling into the garage, it was hard to believe we were home. We had been prepared for a longer stay than twenty-five days. Oh, how gracious and kind the Lord continued to be.

Reentry

October 1, 2017

We left the parking garage at 1:08 p.m., Friday, and pulled into our garage around 2:15. Brian's dad was here to greet us—Wendy was still napping and Clara hadn't gotten home from school yet. It wasn't too long before I heard some pitter-patter of little Wendy's feet; she ran toward me and I held and hugged her for a good long while. When Clara's bus rounded the corner, I got out there in time for her to run off the bus; I lifted her off the ground with excitement. Man! It sure is great to see these girls again. Oh, how I've missed them.

As the afternoon wore on, I started to feel weak and a little nauseous. Unfortunately, that continued through the night and into Saturday as well. I ended up getting sick mid-morning and remained weak and puny most of the day. By evening, I was feeling a bit less nauseated, but still lacked energy without nourishment. I seemed to turn a corner today. I ate every meal and the food settled well. Praise the Lord! The mouth and throat are still sore when I eat, but I'm just thankful for the renewal of strength.

For the next couple of weeks I'm required to have an adult with me twenty-four seven. Brian's parents and my parents are taking turns staying here. As I was in the kitchen with my mom earlier today, I told her it's been a blessing in all of this to have them here. There's something really special about doing life together under one roof again. It carries with it that same peace and assurance I had as a kid that somehow everything's gonna be okay.

I was confused why nausea wasn't a problem in the hospital, but ever since leaving, it was. At first I thought it had to do with the low dose of oxy I was still taking (for the mucositis), but that didn't add up; after all, it wasn't an issue during my stay. That's when a light bulb finally turned on. *The patch!* See, one of the ways the nurses prevented (Or managed?) nausea was by using this medicated, circular patch (scopolamine) behind one of my ears. They would replace it after a few days, putting the new one behind the opposite ear. The thing honestly made me think of a round Band-Aid, which may have contributed to my doubt that it was actually *doing* anything. But thinking back, it was no longer than thirty minutes after they removed it before my discharge that I started to feel sick! So it was doing something, after all—keeping the high-powered pain meds from making me sick to my stomach.

After the revelation, I stopped taking oxycodone and the nausea never returned.

Being back home in time for Clara's seventh birthday was an answer to prayer and a sweet gift from the Lord. Normally, we would invite all our nearby family to celebrate, but with my immune system being what it was, we didn't think it was a good idea. So we kept things small and had both sets of parents over. Clara had a soccer game the Saturday morning of her birthday, which was ideal. Brian, Wendy, and my dad headed to the game to root Clara's team on, while my mom helped me do some minor decorating and setting up for ice cream sundaes we'd have when they returned. Oh, how thankful I was to be feeling stronger than I was just five days earlier (when we left the hospital). I had *just* put the finishing touches on the birthday banner when I received a group text from Clara's soccer coach. He was basically thanking Clara and her family for providing snacks for the game—"OH *NO!*"

My mom was in the other room, and when she heard my concerned exclamation, she became concerned herself. "Is everything okay?" It had nothing to do with my health and everything to do with the fact that I hadn't sent Clara with a snack for the team—I didn't even know it was our turn. Thank God for my mother-in-law's planning ahead! I remember her saying she had bought a big box of Pop-Tarts from Costco for soccer snacks. Grabbing the box, my mom and I headed to the soccer field to drop the snack off to Brian. Mission accomplished.

I'm not sure an ice cream sundae ever tasted so good as that day.

Two Weeks' Notice

October 15, 2017

This past Friday marked another significant milestone in our journey as my "twenty-four-hour care" officially ended. For two weeks post-discharge, I was required to have an adult around so that if anything alarming happened (I spike a fever, fall, etc.), I could be rushed to Indy for an immediate admission. Praise the Lord for being my *shield* during this time! There were no "scares" or "close calls," and this even reentering a home teeming with active colds or the potential beginnings of something. (Clara informed me on more than one occasion, "My throat hurts.") That first week, I pretty much wore a mask in the house at all times—except to eat or drink. Though I am convinced it was God who did the protecting more than the paper that separated me from them.

So now, what? Or, as some of you have asked me, "How can I be praying?" Well, of course, there's the obvious—continued healing and strengthening. But beyond that is what Psalm 85:8 touches on and what I sense God was speaking directly to me today. "I will listen to what God the Lord says; he promises peace to his people, his faithful servants—but let them not return to folly" (Ps. 85:8 NIV). Like the "Sons of Korah" who penned these words, God forbid that I come away from my captivity unchanged, falling into the same traps of sin as I fell before. But already I recognize that once life starts to settle in and become more "comfortable" again, old thought patterns and tendencies pose a threat.

This now brings me to two words I keep hearing the Lord speak: *transform* and *hidden*. Now is the time to ditch worldly customs and allow God to change my thinking, and therefore transform me (Rom. 12:2). And the way to go about this is nothing short of abiding with Christ—allowing Him to bear the fruit in me that I cannot produce on my own (Jn. 15). By remaining hidden in Him—basking in His presence and beholding His glory—the Spirit will make me more and more like Him, transformed into His glorious image (2 Cor. 3:18). A line in the opening song at church this morning (which, by the way, after a six week sabbatical, it was refreshing to be back in a corporate worship setting again) gripped me and reiterated the things the Lord is beginning to reveal. It was the Vertical Worship song, "Spirit of the Living God," and through it I sensed the Spirit saying...

Did you hear that, Darla? Lean into Me. Everything else can wait.

*"Yes, God, but what if I fall behind? What if I'm forgotten? What if old friendships move on? What if there's not a place for me to use my gifts later as there was before?"

Trust me, Darla. Waiting on me is never wasted time.

*"I do trust you, God, but I admit this 'being still' isn't always easy for me. Yet I know you can accomplish more in my waiting—my 'being'—than I ever could in my doing. Give me the discipline and strength to lean in to all you are. Satisfy me as you hide me in your presence."

*I have never left you, Darla; I won't forsake you now.

*"Oh, Lord, let me not forsake you."

The second floor of Bone Marrow Transplant Infusion Center quickly became our home away from home. With appointments every week, then every two, it didn't take long before the familiarity of the place was strangely soothing. It was a unique environment where I had an overwhelming sense of *belonging*. And this is coming from someone who once wanted to avoid the hospital (and medical facilities) at all costs. Even the hour-long drive there didn't feel burdensome; in fact, it was something I looked forward to. As I wrote:

January 13, 2018

One of the unexpected blessings through this entire leukemia journey has been quality—yes, *quality*—time with Brian. Our conversations as we drive to appointments and while we wait for the doctor to arrive are some of the most in-depth (and least interrupted) we have all week. Updates on Brian's job, how to parent each of the girls with their individual personalities, church life, and what God is currently teaching us through His Word are the topics most often covered. Even if we were completely silent through the entire experience (which is unfathomable), the shared experience alone is enough to create a closer bond. Brian's unwavering loyalty has both humbled and challenged me. He's never given so much of a hint that any of this is burdensome (even though I know it's not a light weight that he's helping to carry and certainly an inconvenience at best). It makes me think of one of my favorite lines in all of Scripture spoken by King David unto the Lord: "You stoop down to make me great" (2 Sam. 22:36 NIV84). God is using Brian to bring His quality of selfless love to life. An extreme humbling for my sake that says (without the use of words), *I make myself low for the purpose of building you up.*

One thing I would have been okay *not* growing familiar with was the good ole bone marrow biopsy. Unfortunately, it was unavoidable. Just a little over a week after being home, my first one was scheduled post-transplant...fifth one to date. My usual doctor was on vacation, so I was seen by one of the other BMT doctors. His social skills were a bit lacking, but I grew to appreciate his quirkiness and sense of humor. All of that was overshadowed by his heartfelt smile and warm interest in me as a person. When I found out by the nurse that he once asked to have a bone marrow biopsy done (without sedation) just so that he would know what the experience was like for the patients on which he performs them, my respect for him reached a whole new level.

He performed my biopsy that day.

At my next appointment two weeks later, we found out the exciting results from the biopsy. I was 100% engrafted, which meant I was all donor. Or as the biopsy report read: *From the bone marrow specimen received in the laboratory on 10/9/2017, thirteen dividing cells were analyzed plus 37 were scored, and all were donor (XY) in origin. No recipient (XX) cells were observed.* Because I wasn't graced with a scientific mind like those in the medical field, I couldn't fully grasp what all this meant. My best attempt at translating was that the healthy donor cells I received the day of transplant (September 12) began making their way through the bloodstream and into my bone marrow, via God's command and design. Once these new guys took up residence, they began to grow and form new blood cells, thus "taking over" where my old cells once lived. Simply fascinating.

100% Donor

October 22, 2017

On the ride home, I couldn't stop giving praise to God. Many tears were shed on those miles back, overwhelmed by His mercy...His grace...His favor.

This whole 100% donor thing blows my mind every time I think about it, and still I can't help but see the Gospel parallels. One of my favorite verses says, "I have been crucified with Christ and I no longer live, but Christ lives in me. The life I now live in the body, I live by faith in the Son of God, who loved me and gave himself for me" (Gal. 2:20 NIV). As a Christ follower, my life has been purchased by the blood He shed on the cross. He gave up His life in order that I might have a chance to live. Why? Because He loves me. And this isn't an exclusive offer. "For God so loved the WORLD...that WHOEVER believes in Him..." (Jn. 3:16 NIV, emphasis mine). Even greater than knowing I'm 100% donor cells is knowing I'm 100% Jesus' blood—washed clean of all my sin and shame.

I'm not sure I ever anticipated how difficult life would be after this point. For one thing, those mouth sores wouldn't let up. I ended up with two canker sores the size of dimes—one on the front tip of my tongue and the other in the back underneath. The liquid lidocaine I came home with certainly got good use; I just wished it could have completely taken away the pain. I remember the worst of it being at Thanksgiving time. Salty foods never burned so bad.

But what proved just as difficult (probably *more*) for me was this new season of "hiddenness" God had called me into. I soon discovered it was hard to be *hidden*. It was hard to be *still*. It was hard to live a life of *obscurity*. The *What now?* and *What next?* questions troubled me because there weren't definite answers. I wanted to know something more than what was right before me. *Where is all this going? Or is it going anywhere at all?* Remaining in the "this" was hard...especially with as blah as *this* was.

During my first hospital stay, I was so overwhelmed by the Lord's grace and mercy in the whole process that I *actually* had the false thought that I would walk away from it as a sin-free person. Not because this process had become my salvation or anything weird like that. I just felt as if there was *no way* I could possibly rebel against God after all that He had brought me through. Well, I'm not sure how long of being home it took before *that* was proved untrue, but I assure you not much time passed. And that bothered me. I didn't like my impatience with the girls, my retreating to food, my anger, and overall selfishness. There was obvious transformation God wanted to do during this hidden season; now I just needed to be still enough to listen.

And God certainly had some things He wanted me to hear....

Exception

November 9, 2017

Last Wednesday, we were in Indy for our usual labs and brief exam. Blood draw went well. Chemistry was fine. Levels looked good...except...hmm, *except*. Not the most reassuring word to hear, but do go on. Except my platelets dropped and were now below normal range. (That would explain the random bruises I had discovered just a day or two prior.) While my doctor didn't act terribly concerned ("Fluctuations can happen after the transplant."), he went ahead and placed an order for a follow-up blood draw one week later (that would be yesterday) here in Muncie.

Coming away from the appointment, I struggled to take my thoughts captive. *What if this is more than a fluctuation? What if my platelets are unrecoverable? Could this be the first sign of a failed transplant? Are leukemic cells starting to take over again?* It wasn't long before this over-analyzing (as well as researching...Google researching, mind you) brought worry, doubt, anxiety, and fear to the surface. Which brings me to a very important discovery—one that was uncovered long before this moment, but became all the more apparent: Being home is no different than being in the hospital. When I stop fixing my eyes on Jesus and start fixing my eyes on the storm, sinking is inevitable.

Also, setting my mind on earthly assumptions rather than on heavenly truths is a sure way to falter.

For the next few days after the appointment, I wavered between complete trust in the Lord's plan and unbridled fear. Whether or not the battle with leukemia was still being fought within my body, I didn't know for certain; but one thing I did know—war was raging spiritually. Certainly, however, it's good to be reminded that truly, "our struggle is not against flesh and blood, but against the rulers, against the authorities, against the powers of this dark world and against the spiritual forces of evil in the heavenly realms" (Eph. 6:12 NIV). And how reassuring to know that we can "be strong in the Lord and in his mighty power" (Eph. 6:10 NIV) because of the spiritual armor He supplies. The enemy does not have to win.

The Lord also provided timely, healing balm to my soul on Tuesday afternoon when He led me to Psalm 27, Isaiah 55, and Psalm 63.

"The Lord is my light and my salvation—whom shall I fear? The Lord is the stronghold of my life—of whom shall I be afraid?... Though an army besiege me, my heart will not fear; though war break out against me, even then I will be confident. One thing I ask from the Lord, this only do I seek: that I may dwell in the house of the Lord all the days of my life, to gaze on the beauty of the Lord and to seek him in his temple. For in the day of trouble he will keep me safe in his dwelling; he will hide me in the shelter of his sacred tent and set me high upon a rock."

(Ps. 27:1, 3–5 NIV)

"Come, all you who are thirsty, come to the waters; and you who have no money, come, buy and eat! Come, buy wine and milk without money and without cost. Why spend money on what is not bread, and your labor on what does not satisfy? Listen, listen to me, and eat what is good, and you will delight in the richest of fare."

(Isa. 55:1-2 NIV)

"You, God, are my God, earnestly I seek you; I thirst for you, my whole being longs for you, in a dry and parched land where there is no water. I have seen you in the sanctuary and beheld your power and your glory. Because your love is better than life, my lips will glorify you. I will praise you as long as I live, and in your name I will lift up my hands. I will be fully satisfied as with the richest of foods; with singing lips my mouth will praise you. On my bed I remember you; I think of you through the watches of the night. Because you are my help, I sing in the shadow of your wings. I cling to you; your right hand upholds me."

(Ps. 63:1-8 NIV)

Which brings me to yesterday. I headed to our local hospital on Wednesday morning to get my blood drawn—just one vial. A little after one o'clock, I received a call from my nurse with the blood results. Everything looked good—white blood counts, neutrophils, hemoglobin, and yes...even platelets were in normal range! Praise God from whom all blessings flow!

My mom has shared with me how even as a young girl I was able to easily articulate what I was feeling ("My tummy hurts."), as well as clearly define what I wanted or needed because of it. ("I want you to sit next to me on the couch and rub my tummy.") For now, my thoughts are in the forms of questions rather than answers, such as, "Now what?" While I long for God to map it all out, I realize that opposes authentic faith—"Now faith is confidence in what we hope for and assurance about what we do not see" (Heb. 11:1 NIV). And in this place He has me right now—"being" versus "doing" (which is tough for me at times)—He's not expecting or asking me to figure anything out. It's as if He's telling me, "Come to me. Seek me. Gaze upon my beauty. Find in me a quenching for your thirst and a satisfaction for your hunger." *Period*. Also, I thank God for another year to celebrate life.

Today is my thirty-fifth birthday…a day that several months ago I wasn't sure I would see. But I'm thankful for God's tender mercies and a special occasion (my "original" birth) to remember the miracle and privilege that life is. This is dedicated to my Maker and Sustainer.

December 16, 2017

This a perfect time to mention what God spoke to me two weeks ago on Sunday. A woman familiar with Muncie Alliance and still involved in the denomination on a district level came and shared with us about prayer ministry. But before she began, she asked us all to think of a burden we were bearing. The burden that instantly came to mind was my current state of uncertainty and aimlessness—the "What now?" and the "What next?" every so often come to threaten my peace and sideline my faith. She proceeded to tell us that once we had something in mind, to hand that heavy weight over to God and ask Him what He would like to give in return. It wasn't an immediate answer, but rather took a few minutes of listening, but what I heard was clear—"But I have stilled and quieted my soul; like a weaned child with its mother, like a weaned child is my soul within me" (Ps. 131:2 NIV84). In essence, the Lord was telling me, *Darla, you can rest. Cease your laborious straining to know what is ahead. Put your hope in me and trust that I will lead you where you are meant to be in my perfect timing.*

While there was nothing but ease and comfort in what the Lord spoke, it took a few days of me wrestling with this whole idea of a weaned child thing for me to finally accept it. It sounds crazy, I know, because giving someone a pass to "be still" and "rest" sounds like the best thing ever (and it is)—especially in the midst of one of the busiest times of the year! But I think, deep down, what I was hoping for was specific direction and less ambiguity. Again, it goes back to faith. Do I want it all mapped out for me? Sure, I do! Would I grow in my walk and intimacy with the Lord if I had the map and no longer needed Him to be my tour guide? Sure wouldn't.

December 23, 2017

We had an earlier appointment on Wednesday than we've had in a while, and it actually coordinated with the timing of Clara's school car drop-off (she normally rides the bus, but when we drive her, she gets a few extra minutes of sleep). Her school is along the route we take to Indy, so it worked out wonderfully. The sky was still dark when we left, but with every passing minute, it grew a little brighter. Once the sun was up and shining in its fullness, God gave me a thought He'd never given me before. "Of course that's how God does a sunrise," I said aloud to Brian through mild laughter. "It's so like God that the sun wouldn't just turn on like a bright light in the morning when your eyes aren't yet adjusted. He slowly increases the light bit by bit, because in His kindness, He knows we couldn't handle it in its complete radiance all at once."

And just like that, it's as if God assured me that the reason He keeps me from knowing (that very thing I think I want) is not because He doesn't care, but because He does. He is my loving Father who knows everything about me (and that's not an exaggeration—straight from Psalm 139:1). He knows my thoughts (Ps. 139:2). He knows what I'm going to say even before I say it (Ps. 139:4). He watched me as I was being woven together in the dark of the womb (Ps. 139:15). He saw me before I was born (Ps. 139:16). And He also is aware of what is simply too much for His little girl to carry.

It seemed rather unfortunate that, of all cancers, I'd have a *blood* cancer... which meant lots and LOTS of blood draws. Besides their peeks into my marrow from time to time, their only way of knowing how things were going was by collecting blood. And my poor veins—the ones that barely had a fighting chance to begin with—were not only uncommonly small, but now incredibly scarred up as well. Before appointments, we consistently asked God to supernaturally bulk up my veins. Sometimes that happened, but most times they served as opportunities for me to experience the Lord for who He is...my *refuge*, my *shield*, my strong *tower*, my *hiding place*. What a gift that has been given to me. Before all this, multiple sticks plus "digging around" for a "good vein" would cause me to faint. Oh, but how He has held me up and given me endurance like I'd never had before!

Things seemed to be very slowly progressing when it came to my blood counts. My white blood cells remained especially low, which wasn't necessarily thrilling to my doctor (or to me). And with low white blood cell counts comes greater risk of infections and viruses, and a longer time to heal from sicknesses. I now joined ranks with those in the "compromised immune system" category, which wasn't necessarily easy for me to remember. Prior to cancer, I'd been blessed with a pretty boring health record, so it took time for my brain to adjust. Despite my diligence both in mask usage and hand washing, I ended up with the flu mid-January. And with it came all the classic symptoms—aches of every kind, nonstop high fever, abdominal pain, no appetite, lethargy, and coughing. In the beginning, it was the aches that were most prevalent. As time wore on, my cough turned into an uncontrollable *beast*, leaving me nearly unable to catch the next breath.

No one in the house had to question where Mommy was for the next three weeks. *Guaranteed,* I could be found on the chaise lounge in the family room with my pink fuzzy blanket and heating pad (for my tummy and rib cage). A couple weeks in, some of my limitations began to annoy our oldest daughter; I can't say I blame her. As they were getting ready for the school bus' soon arrival one morning, I realized I had forgotten to stick her water bottle in her backpack for lunch. Already planted on the couch—and with severe discomfort in my rib cage—I let her know she could get it in the fridge. In a huff she expressed, *"Boy!* I can't *wait* for you to be better!" Ha! You're tellin' me.

In the midst of all this, I had an appointment in Indy. The doctor wasn't pleased with how low my kidney was functioning, and said it could either be due to dehydration (caused by the diarrhea I was also experiencing), or a sign of graft versus host disease (which would ultimately result in kidney failure). Admittedly, the news troubled me but gave me new opportunity to focus my eyes and attention upon the Lord. Before leaving that day, they gave me a bag of fluids through an IV to hopefully help things along.

Just a few days later, we were back, and instead of feeling better, I felt worse.

A Near Malfunction

January 28, 2018

When the nurse heard that my temp clocked in at 102, there was an undeniable look of concern on her face as she told me very matter-of-factly, "You may not be leaving here tonight, so just be prepared for that."

As soon as all others had cleared out, I made eye contact with Brian and instant tears welled up in my eyes. My voice was shot (from all the coughing), plus I had the mask on, so there was no use trying to yell across the room. But I don't think any words were necessary in the moment. It may have been the first time I truly considered, "I may not make it through this."

I was sort of able to suck the tears back in my eyes before the nurse arrived with all the tubes and extra goodies for doing a blood culture. She started an IV easily, and even though the blood was a little slow flowing, she got what she needed for all the tests. And then, we waited...a very...long...wait.

Under normal circumstances, I may have grown impatient, but the lengthy amount of time worked in our favor this time. It was just seconds after the nurse left that I asked Brian if he could hand me my Bible, which was in my purse. I literally binged on the Psalms the rest of our time there—reading and praying them sort of all at once. There was absolutely nothing—and I mean, nothing—in me that was capable of thinking anything other than doom and feeling anything other than fear. I was desperate for His Truth to invade my mind. The Psalms proved to be the medicine I needed. Worries faded. Doubts departed. The enemy fled. There were countless verses that jumped out, this being just one of them: "Summon your power, O God; show us your strength, O God, as you have done before" (Ps. 68:28 NIV84).

Rewind with me for a moment to earlier that morning when I was getting ready. I was listening to "A Mighty Fortress Is Our God," and verse three pierced my soul:

"And though this world, with devils filled,

Should threaten to undo us,

We will not fear, for God hath willed

His truth to triumph through us:

The Prince of Darkness grim,

We tremble not for him;

His rage we can endure,

For lo! His doom is sure,

One little word shall fell him."[3]

I'm not sure there could be a more accurate picture of what took place Friday, January 26th, in Infusion Suite B. Yes, I am convinced Satan and his vile

---

[3] Martin Luther (1483–1546), "A Mighty Fortress Is Our God" (German: *"Ein feste Burg ist unser Gott"*), 1527–1529, Public Domain.

posse have been threatening to undo me. But we need not fear the darkness because the enemy has already been defeated through Christ's sacrifice on the cross and victory over the grave. And God's Word—yes, His Word—put those ugly lies of the devil to rest. His power is broken by claiming the Truth and rejecting him as the father of lies that he is.

They sent us down to the first floor to have a chest x-ray to eliminate the possibility of pneumonia. It was super quick. In fact, the thing that consumed the most time was me trying to figure out where the strings in the back of the gown were, so that I could maintain some bit of modesty. You'd think I would have that down by now. (Although now that I think about it, Brian was usually the one who did the tying.) I was outta there in no time, and when we got back upstairs, my nurse said that the blood work actually still looked good *(Thank you, Jesus!)*, and that though my kidneys were still functioning on the low side, things had slightly improved since Wednesday. *(Thank you again!)* They kept me for a bag of fluids, and as it turned out, the doctor decided I didn't need to be admitted overnight. My nurse was also convinced I was fighting a different virus, so they swabbed my nose to have it tested (I don't have the results of that yet). Oh, and the x-ray was clear—no pneumonia!

You talk about a complete 180. Now, this doesn't mean I've been magically made well again. I still have a fever, cough, aches, little to no appetite, and diarrhea. But to go from needing to stay at the hospital to being free to go after my fluids certainly lifted a lot of the concern that this was something bigger than we were able to conquer. And actually, it still is. But I know who is able. He is on our side.

Another sign of God's beautiful grace and foreknowledge was the fact that Brian's parents had already planned a fun weekend with the girls, and were having them stay with them in Upland for two nights. Now this was originally supposed to happen last weekend, but because of Clara's Friday stomach bug, it got bumped to this weekend. Couldn't have been more perfect. When the nurse said that I needed lots of rest and lots of fluids, I knew that this was actually possible since I could pause the "mommy" role for a couple of days.

While we continue to wait for complete restoration, He continues to be my *portion*.

After the long, hard fight with the flu, I was still left with what I described as a "bear hug" of pain. My ribs, man...they hurt *bad!* It wasn't until several months later when I had some sort of scan done that I figured out why...

I fractured two ribs! That tells you how intense my coughing was.

Once again, He was teaching me through it.

Signs of Life

January 31, 2018

I'm in the middle of the ever-exciting account of Moses in the Book of Exodus, and this time (as well as the last time I read through it), I was struck with this exchange between the Lord and Moses via the burning bush: "I have indeed seen the misery of my people in Egypt. I have heard them crying out because of their slave drivers, and I am concerned about their suffering. So I have come down to rescue them from the hand of the Egyptians and to bring them up out of that land into a good and spacious land, a land flowing with milk and honey" (Ex. 3:7–8 NIV84).

Wait a minute here. God says He sees, He hears, He's coming down to save...so do it! With one spoken word, the story could have ended. Many lives, livestock, and crops could have been spared, and the increasing abuse experienced by the Israelites could have been avoided. But instead, He sent Moses—a man who repeatedly questioned his ability and speaking skills—to approach a hard-hearted Pharaoh into letting the people go. Of course, as the story goes, Pharaoh won't allow this, which results in ten horribly destructive plagues, but which serve God's purpose of displaying His miraculous power and proving to all who saw that He is indeed Yahweh. Finally, they get out of there only to face an endless sea with no way around it or under it. The only way of escape was to go through it. You know the rest of the story. Moses stretches out his hand over the sea, and the Lord sends a strong wind that causes the waters to stand as walls on each side while they pass through on dry ground. As the waters meet back together, the Egyptians who were chasing the Israelites are all destroyed—drowning in the depths of the sea. "And when the Israelites saw the great power the Lord displayed against the Egyptians, the people feared the Lord and put their trust in him and in Moses his servant" (Ex. 14:31 NIV84).

The reason I share all of this is because in the midst of suffering, crying out to the Lord, and seeking His face as well as His favor, it can be incomprehensible why God wouldn't make things right already! I know He hears, I know He sees, and I absolutely know He cares. So make me better, for crying out loud! Believe me, there have been moments along this thirteen-day stretch that I've wept before the Lord, "I can't take this anymore! Please, God, I believe! See my faith. Heal me because of your great mercy." Yet sometimes it's only through the pain, plagues, and impossibilities in life that we come to realize what's always been true (we've just been too busy "handling life on our own" to notice)—how utterly powerless we are and yet how fully capable the Lord is. His patience is great—oh, so very great—and His timing always proves itself to be perfect. Always.

Fighting the Flu as Well as Lies
February 10, 2018

Thursday marked three weeks since the beginning of this influenza extravaganza, and I'm happy to report that we're seeing (and very near) the light at the end of the long, dark tunnel. On Monday, my fever finally broke, which was a welcomed sign. While the cough and rib/chest pains continue (Costochondritis perhaps?), they are showing noticeable improvements.

But it's just like our God to somehow—in only the way He can and knows how—produce good things out of a perceived wasteland. Last week in the midst of the desert, God began helping me recognize and articulate a lie I've probably been believing (without recognizing it) for quite some time. There's something about being "down for the count" that puts you in a convenient posture for listening to God.

I began articulating some of these stirrings to my mom when she was here helping with the girls on the day of our last appointment. By Friday, a week ago, I seemed to have more of a grasp on what it is that was bothering me.

In a nutshell, it began to really wear on me that my current life seems to be not much more than one big reminder of what I no longer have. I go to frequent doctor's appointments where I'm faced with this hard to get used to concept that my once stable health is now compromised and unsure. I attend church, and while I am still able to meet with God (and Him with me) in the midst of the company of believers, I'm continually bombarded with (and therefore, wrestle with) this lie that I no longer serve a purpose at our church. That I'm nothing more than a benchwarmer Christian, watching everyone else invest in their talents. That my gifts and passions are no longer compatible among this body of believers. I used to look forward to Sunday mornings. Now I pray on my way there that my flesh wouldn't overpower my willingness to follow the Lord.

So I cried out to God. Now, let me just pause here for a moment to say that one of the simplest yet most profound truths in all of Scripture (to me) is the fact that God WANTS us to cast ALL our cares on Him, because...get this... He CARES! Jesus actually cares! Do you know how monumental this is? First of all, that the God of the universe—who has an infinite amount of things on His plate—would have time for me. Mind-blowing! And secondly, that He truly desires to hear what's in my heart! He actively listens because He is fully invested in our relationship. I mean, let's be honest, we've all had times we poured out our hearts to what we later realized was a room full of crickets. What a waste of time and breath! Heart-wrenching. Or I think we can all admit we've been on the listening side when what's being shared is sort of...how shall I put this...less than moving. And though we've been taught better than to say it out loud, still the thought may cross our minds—*I really don't care.*

Wow. I got way sidetracked. So, what I was saying was that I began crying out to God. Casting this burden on Him, saying, "God, I don't get it. Is it your will for me that I lack enjoyment in life? That these Spirit-given gifts and passions go unused? Why do you take away things that are seemingly 'good' and that I feel 'made for' and instead call me into situations where I'm working in my weaknesses? Please, let me hear the truth about you to combat these lies I'm believing."

I listened. And I waited...aaaaaand waited. I searched the Scripture. I asked God again. I listened. And I waited...aaaaaand waited. I searched the Scripture. This pattern continued Friday night through Saturday night. That's when I felt prompted to read Psalm 37. "Trust in the Lord and do good; dwell in the land and enjoy safe pasture. Delight yourself in the Lord and he will give you the desires of your heart. Commit your way to the Lord; trust in him and he will do this: He will make your righteousness shine like the dawn, the justice of your cause like the noonday sun. Be still before the Lord and wait patiently for him" (Ps. 37:3-7a NIV84). It was good and right and healing in some regards. But there was more to learn. I woke up Sunday still with a low-grade fever, coughs, and aches. So I stayed home from church while Brian and the girls went. It was finally at around 11:30 that morning when I heard God's still, soft voice say, *Darla, I care about you. I am not against you; I am FOR you. There is just as much of my love and kindness in my taking away as in my giving.*

It took a little bit of time for this to sink in. There really wasn't anything "new" about what I heard, but yes...of course...that's it! God's taking away from me...or His keeping things from me that I desire and think are "good" is part of His loving (yes, *loving*) plan for me. He is my heavenly Father who knows exactly what His daughter needs and exactly when she needs it. Just like a parent sets limits and even purposely prevents his child from having certain things, so God in perfect love and wisdom does the same. He knows me (His daughter), and He has an unfaltering, all righteous understanding of what will grow me further into godliness as well as a greater fulfillment in Him.

I'm not sure what others' experience with life-altering news and circumstances has been. For me, there were aspects about it I expected and other things by which I was blindsided. I expected the hospital stays and treatments to be tough. I expected reentry (both times) to be hard. What I didn't anticipate was the difficulty of life after all of this. And that's where I am currently. While I wouldn't trade it in for anything (as I know it has served—and continues to serve—a wonderful purpose in strengthening my faith and drawing me closer to the Lord), I often feel alone, isolated, and perhaps slightly misidentified. There was the old Darla...now there is the new Darla. How does one relate to this one? What questions should I ask her and what should I refrain from saying? How do I still fulfill my purpose in the Body and for His kingdom? It's not quite as concrete as it once was. I told one of my sisters this week how life right now can be compared to a strange aftertaste. I can't really get rid of it, but I'm not sure I'm used to its flavor yet. From time to time, I also have this really crazy thought that maybe I will wake up tomorrow morning and all of this will be reversed. Like maybe this has just been one long dream. I know that sounds absurd, but perhaps it's some sort of coping mechanism.

But this is my new reality, and that is okay! More than okay. Because while I go through seasons of foreignness, there is a God who is familiar, real, and unchanged. He's the same One I cried out to when I was a little girl scared of the dark. He's the same One who met me at Camp Good News. He's the same One who orchestrated what college I attended, who I married, where we moved, and what my work looked like. He is the SAME! His love for me is just as unbelievable and unconditional as the day Jesus bled and died on the cross. With my Good Shepherd, I shall not want, for in Him is all that I need.

After finally healing from the flu, things seemed to look good with my kidneys. That was a huge relief. The road ahead appeared smooth until we hit a minor bump early March.

Reasons for Rejoicing

March 7, 2018

A week ago on Monday, I dropped Wendy off at preschool and used the kid-free hours to run a couple of low exertion errands. Upon time for pickup, I was walking across the parking lot per usual, but halfway to the door noticed what seemingly out of nowhere a bruise-like pain on the very lowest part of my right leg (if there's a "top part" to the ankle, that's where I would describe the location of the irritation). Though I couldn't recall any recent injuries that would have caused bruising, it seemed the best possible explanation. As soon as we got home, I took off my shoe and sock to check things out. Strange. No bruise, but a slight hint of swelling in the area where it was most tender. Then I began wondering, "Did I somehow sprain my ankle while running (I use that term loosely) errands?" I mean, I've never had a sprained ankle, but I figured the event would be more memorable, not to mention the result of something much more strenuous than a casual trip to Michael's and Target. Even though it was uncomfortable, I tried my best to simply ignore it and move on with life as a mom.

That plan worked well...for a few hours, at least. Later that day, after the girls and I headed to the park to meet friends for bike riding and playground romping (it was a gorgeous, spring-like day), the discomfort was hard to ignore. It was helpful to have Brian's perspective when he got home from work. He looked at my ankles side by side and noticed the swelling right away. He also felt warmth where it was swollen, which led me to my next concern: "What if this is a blood clot?" Time to make a phone call. I contacted the BMT (bone marrow transplant) doctor on call, and thankfully, she gave me some peace of mind. "Is there redness to your skin?" (No.) "Is there any pain in your calf?" (No.) "For pain management, you may take one ibuprofen." (Praise.) "If you do notice any changes, give us a call." (Will do.)

By evening, I could no longer walk using my right ankle. I was limping around the house to finish my "before bed" routine (note for Clara's lunch, meds, face, teeth) so that I could (prayerfully) sleep this absurd thing away. Finally, after tossing and turning in extreme pain (I described it to Brian as "labor pains" in my leg) for two hours (and this even after the one ibuprofen I was allowed), I fell asleep. The next morning brought hope, as I could actually walk relatively well again. Still, it hurt, but I figured no longer limping was an improvement. My mom contacted me to say she could head our way to help with Wendy and such, and even after my efforts at discouraging her from making the trip (especially since she was going to be in Muncie the very next day while Brian and I were in Indy for my appointment), she insisted on coming. I call that good "Mama instinct" right there, because as it turned out, we needed her.

We were having the piano tuned that morning, and Mom arrived in the midst of it. She took a look at my leg, and it was then that we noticed that along with the heat, there was definite redness to the skin, and the more time went on, the bigger the area grew and the higher up it reached (which was the most concerning part). I was praying for wisdom—"Should I call Indy or just wait to be seen at my appointment tomorrow?" It was when Bob was done tuning and I stood for a length of time chatting with him that I could almost feel the pain and heat creeping up my leg. Time for another phone call. In talking with the nurse, she asked if there was any way we could be evaluated at the Cancer Center at 2:00 that same day. The potential sticking point was Brian, as I wasn't sure what his schedule looked like at work; but when I texted him, he surprised me with the response, "Today is wide open for me so I can come whenever." Man! God's mercies continued to pour out. Mom was here to be with the girls, and Brian could drive us to the appointment.

When we arrived, we were called back by a nurse I didn't recognize. As it turned out, she was a "floater" from a different unit, which explained the unfamiliarity. She tried her best to stick what seemed to be a good vein, but after lots of searching (plus calling a regular nurse of mine over to help), they pulled the needle out. The "usual" nurse who knew the trickiness of my veins took it from there and got things started in my left hand. The fact that I was actually fully conscious at this point is such an act of God's grace. That whole "searching for a vein" thing really bothers me. If I choose to cast my thoughts on Jesus instead of on the needle lost in the somewhere between veins and God knows what, it really does make a difference. The fabulous RN who's performed three of my biopsies was the one who examined my leg, and by what she saw and felt, she guessed it may be cellulitis instead of a blood clot. But just to be sure (and certainly for all of our peace of mind), she got me in for (and even walked me to) an ultrasound downstairs. At one point, I asked the tech if it was a boy or girl. I mean, sometimes you've just got to make light of situations like this. It's actually quite amazing how similar the sounds in the leg are to that in the womb—you know, that unforgettable whooshing. When it was finished, I headed back upstairs (without the RN's help this time) and got just a tiny bit turned around until someone kindly pointed me in the right direction. I got back to the Infusion Suite B where my nurse was sitting at the computer with the ultrasound results. She warmly greeted me with, "Great news! It's not a blood clot. YOU HAVE AN INFECTION!" Is life hilarious or what? The fact that we were all genuinely cheering and excited about having an infection (I mean, who wants the alternative?) was such a hilarious and joyous moment. God...is...good.

Oh, and do you want to hear even more praiseworthy news from the day? Because we had blood work done and were seen by the RN, we DIDN'T need to return the next day. Instead, we were scheduled for the following Tuesday (that would be yesterday) to see the doctor.

I had to actually look up what "cellulitis" is because I wasn't sure. Apparently (and you all may know this), it's when an infection like staph or strep enters your body through either a small scratch or even a patch of eczema (which is probably more likely in my case). Anyhow, when I read that, I immediately thought of my sister, Dee Ann. When we were kids, she had strep in her knee one time, and I was so incredibly confused by that. A sore throat in your knee? Ha!

Surprise Seventh

March 14, 2018

A week ago on Tuesday, we walked up to the reception desk at Infusion Suite B to check in for our appointment. As the receptionist was printing my patient bracelet, she spoke somewhat quietly (as if talking to herself): "Looks like you have a regular checkup today, plus a biopsy." I looked at Brian with a puzzled expression—"Biopsy?!"—and then at her. "I don't have a biopsy today...at least not one that we were aware of." She said it's quite possible that information was put into the system incorrectly; we would soon find out if this was the case or not.

When we were called back to the labs, they confirmed that indeed it was a biopsy day. Ha! Brian and I looked at each other from across the room and literally started giggling while Brian mouthed the word, "Surprise!" Before they drew my blood, they asked if I wanted an IV started for sedation later. I opted to go without this time. It's always a bit of a toss-up, because while biopsies are no fun, neither is starting an IV on veins like mine. I was uncharacteristically calm, cool, and collected about the whole thing...and genuinely could not stop smiling.

Let's rewind for a moment, shall we? It was probably no less than an hour before this whole scenario that Brian and I were in the car on the way to Indy and I had my Bible open to Proverbs—"The prospect of the righteous is joy" (Prov. 10:28a NIV). I underlined those words, looked up from the page, and silently prayed: *God, gift me with joy in greater measure.* And as we were sitting in Exam Room 5, waiting for the nurse, doctor, and pharmacist to arrive, God reminded me of that prayer...which only caused me to smile more, laugh harder, and experience joy in greater measure (just as I'd asked, and just like He'd given). Isn't it astounding that we serve a LIVING God? One who hears us, sees us, and even answers us? Simply incomprehensible.

When the crew showed up, there wasn't a lot to talk about. My chemistry looked good, and besides my white blood cells count being lower (again), the doctor didn't have concerns. Apparently, I'm six months post-transplant (which explains why I was scheduled for a biopsy), so he said it's time to start weaning me off my immune suppressants. Also, unless something urgent comes up, he will see me in four weeks now as opposed to two. He does want me to get my blood drawn locally once between now and then just to check on how things are doing.

Another one of my prayers that morning (as well as most appointment days) is that we'd be the fragrance of Christ to those with whom we interact. I certainly saw evidence of that when the joy that was filling us bubbled over to bring smiles and laughter to all those in our room. I'm not sure how often hematologists laugh in a day...a week...a career. But I can't help but think a good, hearty bellow every so often is healing for their souls. The same RN who took care of my cellulitis came in the room with the consent form for the bone marrow biopsy (seventh and counting). "Let's get this thing over with, shall we?" she asked. In agreement, I said, "Let's." I lay down on the bed (tummy down), and with my face in the pillow, talked to God. Things like, "I need you; I trust you," and, "Keep my eyes fixed on you." And just as has been my experience every time (that I am aware of), God gave me a song to hum/song—Bethel Music's "Jesus, We Love You"—to help me endure the stinging of the needles and the sharp, deep pain caused by this whole process. As the pain intensified, I squeezed the pillow and hummed with more conviction.

After it was finished, they had me turn onto my back as usual to put pressure on the area. While I was lying there—so contented and relieved the hardest part was behind me—I noticed something on the wall opposite of me and asked Brian if he would be able to read what it said. They're gathering bone marrow transplant stories to later compile in a free booklet to "give future BMT patients and caregivers a sense of contentedness, strength, and hope." When I was on the fifth floor, there was a cart of books and information we could borrow, and I remember being so blessed by flipping through something like this is referring to…a collection of people's stories. And it did bring me a sense of hope. I would love to gift others going through this with the same. Which brings me to a couple of prayers requests: One, that God would give me anointed, inspired words to write out our story so that other patients may someday be encouraged as well; more than anything, I want God to be both magnified and glorified. And two, that as I wean off of immunosuppressants, my body would not reject my new stem cells. This is the time when graft versus host disease becomes more of a potential reality.

Now, for a HUGE praise! Last Friday, I received a phone call from my nurse as I drove away from dropping Wendy off at preschool…my biopsy showed no detectable leukemia! Oh, how undeserving I am of the Lord's continued grace and mercy, but oh, how grateful I am.

Unanticipated

Turning a Curse into a Blessing

April 10, 2018

This may be hard to believe (quite honestly, it is for me), but I miss being at the Simon Cancer Center every couple weeks. This was the first time there was a full four-week stretch between appointments, which from a health standpoint is a great sign, but from a community standpoint left me with an unexpected longing. One year ago, a hospital was somewhere I wanted to avoid, even for a brief visit. Just the "feel" and the smell of the place induced a for-real, no-joke queasiness. Now, I'm almost giddy with joy when it's time to be back. Isn't it amazing (and almost comical) how God can change a heart? I'm thankful for His presence and His grace at every uncertain turn.

At last Tuesday's appointment, they called me back for my blood draw, which proved to be without any issue—praise the Lord! When we were visited by the doctor, my nurse, and pharmacist, there wasn't a lot to discuss. They were pleased with my blood counts. Hemoglobin is the highest it's been since the day of my transplant back in September (the 12th to be exact). White blood count is still low...right at 2.0...but they didn't express any concerns. My chemistry results didn't come back until later, so when my nurse swung by the room to share how my kidney and liver functions were on par, she also handed me an immunization schedule. I knew this day would come but was both surprised and excited the time was NOW!

You may remember that the stem cell transplant completely started me over—a "rebirth," as it's referred to. This has several implications, one of them being that all of my previous vaccinations were deleted...eliminated...undone. So now it's time to walk in the shoes, crawl in the path of an infant for a while. A floater nurse entered the room with all my vaccinations. Since there were five (DTaP, Hib, HepB, Polio, PCV13), I was given the option of having a nurse at each arm administering simultaneous injections—I guess, to "get it over with" more quickly? I didn't have to think about that one long—No, thank you!

Just the good ole fashioned one at a time, please, for this non-multitasker by nature. Now you would think after all the blood draws, IVs, biopsies, and other procedures I've had that the idea of a shot would be no big deal, right? Wrong. Vaccinations feel like this new territory, so praying and clinging to God as my rock and my *fortress* was a must. Brian offered his thumb to squeeze, and I took him up on it. Starting with the right arm, she gave the worst three there (since it's my dominant arm, they knew I would keep that one moving more) and the other two in the left. They warned me that I would be very sore the next couple days, and boy, were they right! (My right arm is STILL tender a week later.) It required some creativity to figure out how to get clothed for a few days there, let me tell you.

The same day as my appointment, I was reading Deuteronomy 23, and the fifth verse jumped off the page at me. "The Lord your God would not listen to Balaam but turned the curse into a blessing for you, because the Lord your God loves you" (Deut. 23:5 NIV84). I sat on that for a while. Then a few days later, I was getting ready for the day and listening to a Tony Evans sermon and he starts mentioning Deuteronomy 23:5, and how God would turn your curse into a blessing. Wait a minute. Did he really say what I thought he said? He repeated it a few times, and since my short-term memory wasn't certain, I grabbed my Bible and looked up Deuteronomy 23:5. Sure enough, it was the same verse! Clearly it was a message God wanted me to hear...not once, but twice! I very much believe that being diagnosed with cancer could be considered a "curse," but I have seen God birth from it blessing after blessing. Oh, He is such a good God.

"He who dwells in the shelter of the Most High will rest in the shadow of the Almighty. I will say of the Lord, 'He is my refuge and my fortress, my God, in whom I trust.' Surely he will save you from the fowler's snare and from the deadly pestilence. He will cover you with his feathers, and under his wings you will find refuge; his faithfulness will be your shield and rampart."

(Ps. 91:1–4 NIV84)

As difficult and dry as the wilderness was, I was determined to hold on to the One who held me firmly in His grasp. He may not have spoken what I wanted to hear (a nicely packaged "remaining life plan," so I knew where this was headed and when), but He spoke what I needed to hear—consistently reminding me of His faithful presence and the value that comes from trusting Him in the waiting.

I'll end this chapter with the poem I ended up submitting. This journal entry explains more.

Rebirth: A Poem

April 28, 2018

Do you remember back in March when I mentioned that Be The Match (the leading bone marrow donor program) is looking for bone marrow transplant stories, poetry, or art? Well, I just finished submitting what I wrote—uncomfortably close to the May 1 deadline for my liking. I've been putting it off because I didn't have an obvious direction. This past week has involved much prayer, writing, rewriting, and starting again. In fact, what I ended up with was my third attempt. I'm thankful for Brian's wisdom, because when I started to share the second written retelling, he suggested a poem may be an easier outlet for my fragmented thoughts. He was right. So, here's what I sent.

Rebirth

"Would you like to hold them?" the nurse had asked.
My donated stem cells were here!
A perfect fit in the palm of my hand;

(Un)Becoming

I prayed with a few silent tears.
How could I not be moved in this moment?
A real hero in the making.
Why would a stranger care to sacrifice?
His own price and pain forsaking.
A rush of excitement, coupled with fear,
New cells intertwining with old.
The parallels to the Gospel of Christ
Indisputably must be told.
These stem cells increased my chances of life;
The remaining length is unsure.
But the blemish-free blood that Jesus shed
Is an absolute, guaranteed cure.
Not of the physical life you see now,
Time naturally withers and fades.
But my soul is secured for Heaven's Home,
Having trusted in Jesus who saves.
With much gratitude I say a huge thanks
To the man whose cells now are my own.
And with eternal thanksgiving and awe
To the One whom my sins did atone.

CHAPTER 9

UNFAVORABLE

Things seems to be mostly moving in a favorable direction. My platelets were in a healthy place and even though my white blood cells and hemoglobin appeared slower in recovering, the doctor didn't voice any concerns. I welcomed my hair back and bid a happy *adieu* to the caps, hats, and scarves. Spring had sprung, round two of vaccinations was behind me, and the girls' summer break was upon us. Though I still didn't have answers to all my questions, I chose to focus on what was before me.

Several years ago, I lay in bed struggling to fall asleep. Brian was still awake so I said, *"Man. I sure* wish that car would move on." He seemed puzzled and inquired, "What car?" I was surprised he wasn't bothered by it like I was. "The car that's stalled outside the house." His confusion had me curious, so I got up and looked out the window. There was no car. Turns out it was all in my head...rather, my ears. Unfortunately, it never went away. I hadn't had issues with my ears before, but now it seemed as if some form of chronic tinnitus had settled in. For probably a year after that, it was pervasive and unavoidable. Perhaps it was a case of "getting used to it" or things really did improve, but I reached a point where I didn't think about it so much.

During the spring of 2018, something seemed to reactivate something wonky with my hearing. This time, it felt like there was a cotton ball stuck in my right ear and all I could hear was a constant whooshing sound to the rhythm of my heartbeat. Other than being annoying, it hadn't caused much trouble until Memorial Day weekend. We were enjoying the outdoors with family when suddenly, I needed to come inside and lay on the couch. I was dizzy and motion sick. With my recent health history being what it was, it seemed only wise to get things checked out. Here's what I wrote at the time:

Planting in Tears to Harvest with Joy
June 16, 2018

On June 1st, I had an appointment at my local clinic. The doctor confirmed there was pressure behind both ears, so she ordered an MRA of my brain (which looks specifically at blood vessels) to be done the following Wednesday (June 6th).

It became quickly apparent why the question, "Are you claustrophobic?" was on the paperwork for the MRA. Eep! Needless to say, I was grateful for the headphones set to Christian radio (I was able to choose) to muffle out the loud sounds of the machine and help fix my mind on Jesus instead of on the fact that I was confined to a very tight space. After twenty to thirty minutes, the woman pulled me out of the tunnel-like tube to insert the dye. (This kind of test does a contrast to make blood vessels easier to see.) She couldn't see my face and I couldn't see what she was doing (since my head was still stuck in a cage-like contraption). I warned her that I'm not an easy stick, and three tries later, she understood why. (On her second attempt to start an IV—this time in my right hand—I actually yelled, "Ow!" That's when she apologized and said,

"Sorry, hun, I hit the bone. I was afraid of that." Yikes.) Back into the tunnel for the rest of the test. A week later, I received the wonderful news that all looked A-okay in the brain. Praise! This doesn't mean the symptoms aren't still there, but we're thankful a blood vessel issue was ruled out.

In the meantime, more anomalies were being discovered. As I was going to bed one evening that early June, a strange tinge of pain—one that left as quickly as it came—drew my attention to a very noticeable lump in my left breast. Since I'm not faithful in doing self-exams, the Lord was very kind to have alerted me. Again, my reasoning for not letting this slide under the radar was the same as the pulsatile tinnitus—my health history didn't exactly afford me the chance to ignore it.

I continued...

The other concern that has presented itself in the last couple weeks is a lump in my left breast. I scheduled to have a mammogram and ultrasound, which were done this past Thursday morning. The woman administering the mammogram could not have been sweeter or more perfect for the job. She was "easy" and made what could be awkward not awkward at all—that's a gift to all women! As she asked me routine questions for paperwork, she was a bit surprised when I answered "Yes" to having had a form of cancer before. Briefly catching her up, she called me a "miracle," which gave me an opportunity to give God audible glory and praise. She was in full agreement, and if I remember correctly, she followed it with, "Amen!" Across the hall, another woman did the ultrasound. When it was finished, the doctor came in to look at the pictures. Because the lump was solid (as opposed to being a cyst, which is fluid-filled) and slightly irregularly shaped, he said a biopsy would be a good idea.

They got me scheduled for the biopsy next Thursday morning there at the clinic, but I told them that I was also going to contact my hematologist/ oncologist in Indianapolis to make sure there wouldn't be any concerns or extra precautions due to where I am post-transplant. To make a longer and more complicated story shorter and easier (involving two days of back and forth calls to my local clinic as well as Simon Cancer), my doctor was faxed the tests/pictures and wants the mass to be removed (rather than a biopsy). Because I have formed a closer and more trusting relationship with those in Indy, I had them refer me to a general surgeon there. My doctor is also insisting the surgery be done before my next appointment (June 28th), so it will happen sooner than later. While I'm not particularly looking forward to another procedure, I'm thankful they aren't messing around.

Oh, I almost forgot! In between the MRA and mammo, I also managed to break a toe! Barefooted and unaware of a threshold at a friend's house, I tripped. There was an audible *Crack!* and it didn't take any time to realize it had been fractured. Taping it to the neighboring toe has helped and is really all that can be done until it's fully healed.

On top of it all, yesterday was my one-year anniversary of my initial leukemia diagnosis in the Ball Hospital Emergency Room. It was pretty moving when the girls and I were driving to Walmart for a few things yesterday morning and Wendy (unaware of the significance of June 15th) said, "Mommy, I'm thinking about when you were in the hospital. It makes me sad." That's when I was able to tell her that I was thinking about my time in the hospital too... but I wasn't sad! In fact, I was overwhelmingly grateful for the healing (both physical and spiritual) God has done in just one year. And because we've been talking about God's great love this whole week at VBS, I was able to incorporate that into my response as well. We parked the car, held hands, and started walking toward the store. Wendy looked up at me and said, "You know, I think God has healed you, Mommy." With tears in my eyes I looked at her and said, "I believe so too." She ended the conversation with a wonderful truth: "God is our healer."

I'm always thankful for God's Word, but maybe even more so when the season is desert-like. Recently, these words from Psalm 126 quenched my thirst. I've been sipping on it ever since.

> "When the Lord brought back his exiles to Jerusalem,
>> it was like a dream!
> We were filled with laughter,
>> and we sang for joy.
> And the other nations said,
>> 'What amazing things the Lord has done for them.'
> Yes, the Lord has done amazing things for us!
>> What joy!
> Restore our fortunes, Lord,
>> as streams renew the desert.
> Those who plant in tears
>> will harvest with shouts of joy.
> They weep as they go to plant their seed,
>> but they sing as they return with the harvest."

(Ps. 126:1–6 NLT)

Yet another journal entry...

Fixing My Thoughts
July 10, 2018

Our appointment two weeks ago (June 27th) was about as "short and sweet" as they come.

The biggest "red flag" from this visit was that my liver enzymes had elevated once again. I went into the morning hopeful (maybe even expectant) that I'd be taken completely off my immune suppressants (as I had been weaned down to just one of them at that point), but my doctor actually added a second back onto the daily meds. If things continue to rise these few weeks of increased immune suppression, next steps are steroids and a liver biopsy. To rewind for a moment, one of my biggest hesitations with the stem cell transplant was the realization I could be swapping one life-threatening disease for another. It isn't uncommon for major organs to be targeted post-transplant, which is why the doctor isn't going to sit back and watch the liver scores continue this pattern for long. Upon first meeting the doctor, he made it very clear what my options were: live twelve to eighteen months, or go through with the BMT in hopes of a longer life. Well, that cleared that up. Ha! God gave me a peace to pursue the risky procedure regardless of the potential setbacks. Just like those three friends of Daniel who faced the fiery furnace, my stance from the beginning has been, "Even if, God." *Even if it's the worst-case scenario, I will praise you and magnify you and glorify you.*

A week ago (July 2nd), we were back on the second floor of the Simon Cancer Center, but instead of turning "right" (as we usually do), we turned "left." This was the day I was meeting with the breast surgeon. After a whole lot of waiting, paperwork, waiting, and more paperwork, the doctor walked in. She gathered a brief history, did an examination, and then shared how things in the breast cancer world work differently than the blood cancer world. They aren't authorized to remove a suspicious mass before it's biopsied, so we're back to square one (my interpretation). And since there wasn't a radiologist there that day who could perform the ultrasound-guided biopsy, we will be back at Simon Cancer on Thursday morning. The comforting news amidst all this runaround is that the breast cancer surgeon isn't convinced it's cancerous.

This is the part of the story where I allowed Satan a foothold. Thoughts filled my head like: *Why didn't the doctors communicate with one another before we came all the way down here? I've wasted everyone's time—the doctors'/nurses', Brian's (for using a large chunk of his "day off" to drive me all the way there), my in-laws' (who had come down and watched the girls), and others'*

(I'm sure). Once I brought my thoughts to words when I met back up with Brian in the waiting room, he assured me that I'm not a "burden," and advised me to stop believing Satan's lie. Thankfully, I didn't allow myself to wallow in it for long (grateful for those of you praying). The lie was broken by the *truth* that God is FOR me, not against me.

Speaking of the enemy, I don't count it a mere coincidence that, as I was in the middle of typing this post, I received a call from my local clinic. The nurse wanted to let me know that my blood results—from my annual physical THREE weeks ago, mind you—came back normal "except your liver enzymes were elevated." There wasn't much more to what she said (except that the doctor would be checking on it next visit), but I know it was the enemy's attempt to distract and discourage me. The words "I will fear no evil, for you are with me" (Ps. 23:4b NIV84) rolled off my tongue as soon as I hung up the phone. I said it aloud again, this time with greater conviction. The result? Perfect peace.

> "Fix your thoughts on what is true, and honorable, and right, and pure, and lovely, and admirable. Think about things that are excellent and worthy of praise. Keep putting into practice all you learned and received…. Then the God of peace will be with you."
>
> (Phil. 4:8b–9 NLT)

Glorious Unfolding

July 17, 2018

Brian and I left bright and early Thursday morning to be at Coleman Breast Center for my 8:00 a.m. appointment last Thursday. The whole experience was much less predictable than our usual appointments have been—different waiting room, unfamiliar staff, and a new set of unknowns. I was first seen by a sweet nurse who asked questions and gathered some of my health history. Next came the doctor—a very young but humbly confident doctor who explained exactly how the biopsy would go. We walked across the room where I got to chat with the nurse quite a bit about my experience with cancer, etc. She said, "You seem to be in great spirits about it." That's when I explained to her my hope in Jesus, and the assurance I have because of Him. On the ride to Indy, I was telling Brian I have been asking God for greater boldness. Why edit "Jesus" out when He's the best part of the story?

When the doctor came in, she had me lay on my right side and raise my left arm above my head. As she prepped the area for the ultrasound-guided biopsy, I started talking to God (again), *God, I really don't like this stuff. I need you.* He said, *I know. I'm right here with you. I haven't left you.* Then, He gave me this vivid picture in my head of me as a little girl facing Him and holding hands. He was walking backward and I was just following His lead (as I couldn't see anything past His large chest). The more I thought of that picture, the more confident I was not only that God knew what was ahead (so much so that He didn't even have to turn around to look...He's the One who wrote my story and knows it from start to finish), but that if I kept my focus on Him, all would be fine.

And He was right, of course. His grace in that moment was indeed sufficient for me. Even to the point where I could "tolerate" (aka "not pass out") when the experienced doctor talked the student doctor (the one actually performing the biopsy) through the play-by-play of the procedure. Things like, "Yeah, once you go in there, you're going to twist and then pull the needle out." Yikes.

The following day (Friday), I missed a call at 5:08 p.m. As it turned out, it was my oncologist who asked me to give him a call back. Because I had never received a call from the doctor himself, I knew something was up...but quite honestly, I didn't expect the "something" he shared. (Especially given the breast surgeon's confidence that there was a slim-to-none-chance this was cancer.)

"Hi, Mrs. Peters. Yes, so the pathologist sent me the report from your biopsy yesterday. And the biopsy is actually showing it's leukemia. It looks like this is a relapse. I'm so sorry. I'm going to need to see you next week for a bone marrow biopsy. Does Tuesday work? Also, do we still have you on immune suppressants? Yeah, stop taking all of those. I will see you then."

Today was the "Tuesday" to which he was referring. Besides the obvious, I was praying (and asking others to join me in it) that I would be prepared to give a reason if anyone (my doctor included) asked how we could have hope/joy/peace at a time such as this (see 1 Peter 3:15).

When I was called back for labs and seated for vitals and blood draw, the nurse walked over and gave me a huge, long hug. No words. Just this incredibly warm embrace; and when she pulled back and looked at me, she had tears in her eyes. She's told us before how the patients there become like a second family, and I can understand what she means. It's a unique community, that's for sure.

My oncologist and nurse walked in the exam room. There was the usual smile, handshake and "How are you?" but it felt different this time. To them too, I think. The doctor then sat down and asked in a more intentional, "I really want to know" way how we are handling the news. Praise the Lord for answering prayers, as I was able to tell him that we are doing well because our hope isn't in the medical advances or statistics, but our hope is built on Christ. Both Brian and I sensed that the information shared with us after that we need to shield from others' ears for now. Because of the unknowns regarding the marrow (at this point) we'd rather not jump ahead of ourselves and weigh you down with an unnecessary burden.

The room cleared out and Brian and I remained. We let out the tears we'd been holding in (perhaps unknowingly) those past several minutes of exchange with the doctor. Heads bowed and hands held, we started praying and audibly declaring every truth from Scripture God gave us in that moment. By the time the doctor walked in, we were ready for the next part of this battle—bone marrow biopsy #8! (And yes, the doctor was the one to do it!) Those are never a "breeze" by any means, but God's grace was sufficient once again. And this time around, when we reached the part of the procedure where I think, *How much deeper can that needle go?* I thought of how excruciating the nails must have felt being driven into Jesus on the cross...all because He loves me. Before I knew it, the biopsy was done.

On Friday (hours before I'd received the call from the doctor about the cancerous biopsy) while I was driving our girls to Walmart for back-to-school supply shopping, the song "Glorious Unfolding" by Stephen Curtis Chapman came on. I think maybe I had heard it before, but there was something about it this time...like God was singing the song over me. (Fast forward.) Yesterday, as I was driving to ALDI, the same song came on the radio. Once again, I felt this "tug" on my heart like it was being sung specifically for me. At the same time as I'm listening to the line in the song about clinging to God's promises, I look up (while I'm at a stoplight) and see a RAINBOW! I'm trusting God that this entire journey is leading toward some sort of glorious unfolding.

Unlike my initial diagnosis a year prior to this, I was surprised by the news of my relapse. No one in the medical field seemed concerned or convinced this was anything cancerous, let alone that it was AML (a blood cancer, mind you) in *solid* form. In fact, I didn't even know such a thing existed! Oh, how I continued to defy the odds. Maybe just not the odds I was hoping for.

Three days after Brain made public our most recent news, I wrote...

Unfavorable

Praise!

July 16, 2018

I don't want too much time to pass between Brian's latest post and the next update because I sense a need to reassure all of you...

God is hearing and answering your prayers!

We are full of PEACE, HOPE, and JOY. (I've even gone so far as using the word "excited.") We are confident that God is ABLE—nothing is impossible with Him! (As my Bible app "verse of the day" so providentially reminded me of today.) The taunts of the enemy are no match for the reassurances of the Father. God is FOR us, not against us.

I have more to share but will do so when I have a greater pocket of time. For now, I leave you with this—Psalm 103 is the treasure God gave me on the night we first found out the news. A call to PRAISE! Join with me.

"Let all that I am praise the Lord;
    with my whole heart, I will praise his holy name.
Let all that I am praise the Lord;
    may I never forget the good things he does for me.
He forgives all my sins
    and heals all my diseases.
He redeems me from death
    and crowns me with love and tender mercies.
He fills my life with good things.
    My youth is renewed like the eagle's!
The Lord gives righteousness
    and justice to all who are treated unfairly.
He revealed his character to Moses
    and his deeds to the people of Israel.

(Un)Becoming

The Lord is compassionate and merciful,
> slow to get angry and filled with unfailing love.
He will not constantly accuse us,
> nor remain angry forever.
He does not punish us for all our sins;
> he does not deal harshly with us, as we deserve.
For his unfailing love toward those who fear him
> is as great as the height of the heavens above the earth.
He has removed our sins as far from us
> as the east is from the west.
The Lord is like a father to his children,
> tender and compassionate to those who fear him.
For he knows how weak we are;
> he remembers we are only dust.
Our days on earth are like grass;
> like wildflowers, we bloom and die.
The wind blows, and we are gone—
> as though we had never been here.
But the love of the Lord remains forever
> with those who fear him.
His salvation extends to the children's children
> of those who are faithful to his covenant,
> of those who obey his commandments!
The Lord has made the heavens his throne;
> from there he rules over everything.
Praise the Lord, you angels,
> you mighty ones who carry out his plans,
> listening for each of his commands.

Yes, praise the Lord, you armies of angels

who serve him and do his will!

Praise the Lord, everything he has created,

everything in all his kingdom.

Let all that I am praise the Lord."

(Ps. 103 NLT)

Since I documented most of this portion of the journey via my *CaringBridge* account, much of this chapter's content will come from there.

Turbulence

July 24, 2018

If you've spent any amount of time as a passenger on an airplane, chances are good you've heard an announcement at some point similar to this: "Ladies and gentlemen, this is your captain speaking. We're about to experience a bit of turbulence, so please return to your seats and fasten your seat belts."

I don't enjoy flying, and I especially don't prefer bumps and jolts 35,000 feet above ground. But when the pilot gets on that intercom with his notably untroubled voice, a peace washes over me. It's as if he's saying, "Don't worry. I'm still here...flying the plane. I see what's ahead, I know how long it will last, and we'll get through this...together. For now, rest."

Yesterday afternoon as I bowed face to the floor in my living room, I heard the Lord gently whisper the word "turbulence," and it brought immediate reassurance. He isn't promising an easy ride—"In this world you will have trouble..." (Jn.16:33a NIV84)—but He is my captain—"Take heart! I have overcome the world" (Jn. 16:33b NIV84). I can trust Him. He knows what He's doing and how (not to mention, when) to land this plane.

What's even better is that the word picture has parallels with a New

(Un)Becoming

Testament story that has been on my heart near-constant this year. Here's the scene:

> "As evening came, Jesus said to his disciples, 'Let's cross to the other side of the lake.' So they took Jesus in the boat and started out.... But soon a fierce storm came up. High waves were breaking into the boat, and it began to fill with water. Jesus was sleeping at the back of the boat with his head on a cushion. The disciples woke him up, shouting, 'Teacher, don't you care that we're going to drown?' When Jesus woke up, he rebuked the wind and said to the waves, 'Silence! Be still!' Suddenly the wind stopped, and there was a great calm."
>
> (Mk. 4:35–39 NLT)

Now let's get one thing straight here—if I ever found out that my pilot was the one snoring in the back row of the plane, I would have real issues. But not when Jesus is my captain. It's not that He's lazy, inactive, disengaged, or uncaring. It's just that He is both the Alpha (beginning) and the Omega (end), not to mention the author and finisher of my faith story. He doesn't have to see what's ahead, because He IS what's ahead. He wrote the story, and He knows the exact moment when to speak silence over the winds and waves. And He's inviting me to join Him in resting. "He who dwells in the shelter of the Most High will rest in the shadow of the Almighty" (Ps. 91:1 NIV84).

Did I mention how much He loves me? So much so that there is neither a "what" nor a "who" able to sever me from His unconditional affection.

> "Yea, though I walk through the valley of the shadow of death,
> I will fear no evil; For you are with me..."
>
> (Ps. 23:4a NKJV)

Unfavorable

News

July 25, 2018

As we drive away from Simon Cancer Center, I wanted to give you a brief update. You all have been such necessary troops in this battle; we cannot thank you enough for all your love and support. Since it's not always feasible to respond to everyone's individual texts and emails, we thought this would be the quickest way to share our latest news.

First, the good news. The bone marrow biopsy came back leukemia free! Praise the Lord for His undeniable mercy. My doctor said had it been found in the marrow, we are talking mere weeks of life left. Also, unrelated to the biopsy situation, my blood work was the best it had been in weeks! Praise.

Second, the not as favorable news. Chances are good that this myeloid chloroma (the leukemic tumor found in the breast) will eventually work its way into the marrow if left untreated. Hence why they not only did a PET scan today (to detect if there are other tumors), but are referring me to a radiation oncologist next week as well.

Third, the least favorable news of all. Even if the cancerous tumor is treated with radiation, chances are good my leukemia won't sit quiet for long (AML by nature is fast and aggressive) and soon work its way back in the marrow.

Fourth, the news to pray over. The doctor went on to share "options." After radiation, they can do another stem cell transplant, this time, using a "half match" to one of my siblings. Since both of my sisters have had children, that makes my brother the most favorable candidate. Depending on what we find out from today's scan, these will be the next decisions for which we need prayer and wisdom.

(Un)Becoming

Walk Through It

July 28, 2018

Because I typed the previous post from my phone in the car, I wasn't able to speak much "life" into the words. What we heard at this week's appointment is similar to what we heard last week...with the added benefit of knowing my marrow is leukemia free. (Huge praise.) Plus, I'm not sure if my doctor used different words this time or if I had different ears hearing them, but everything sounded more promising somehow. (Actually, now that I'm thinking out loud, my guess it was simply God's grace.) I'm so thankful that there's no amount of weight God's not able to carry—we just have to give it to Him! There have been stretches of time when it seemed as if on the hourly, I was again on my knees with hands raised, saying, "God, this is too heavy for me...please take it." He always answered.

At one point on Wednesday morning, as the doctor replayed all of the "options," he stopped and asked, "So, how are you feeling about all of this?" I actually smiled and let out a light chuckle, one part joy and the other part curiosity. How is a thirty-five-year-old mom of young children supposed to exactly "feel" when words like "months left," "another stem cell transplant," and "10%-20% chance of cure" are used? So I answered, "Well, ya know, ever since meeting with you last week, I've sort of pictured myself inside a large box. I see the walls around me, but I don't see a way out yet."

Yet.

After our appointment and PET scan, we headed home. Brian dropped me off at the house while he drove to work, and I had some "quiet" before the girls got back from being with Grandma and Grandpa. ~~Something~~ Someone prompted me to open up the cupboard where I had kept this devotional written by Joni Eareckson Tada (Google her name if you don't know who Joni is... you'll be blessed and inspired) that my mom had given me a while back. It's called *A Spectacle of Glory.* What's funny is when I opened it (on July 25th), the bookmark was on July 23rd (where I had left off an entire year ago).

Anyway, as I read these words, I was blown away—though should I really be surprised at God showing up again?

"Ever felt like you were up against a wall? Stuck? Stalled? Smack-dab against an unyielding barrier?" (Pause. Yes, yes, and yes. Remember the box analogy?) "You can't go back, sideways, over the top, or underneath, and there are no detours. What do you do? *Walk through it*....When we face a wall—whatever it may be—God wants to walk us through that wall. As we take that first step into the impossibility, we will find Jesus there, in the most unlikely place in the most unbelievable circumstance. And then we will walk hand in hand with Him through that wall to the other side."[4]

I repeated the words, "Walk through it," and a similar "feel" washed over me that came when I heard God whisper, "Turbulence." Supernatural peace... joy...hope—can I say an "excitement" over what God is going to accomplish? He is walking hand in hand with me through this valley of the shadow of death. Fear isn't invited. I woke up Thursday morning (the next day) with this gentle reminder in my spirit that while I have defied the odds on the negative end of things (the likelihood of someone in my age/gender having AML...an extremely rare form of leukemic relapse...etc.), God can just as easily defy odds on the positive side. Having another stem cell transplant offers a 10%–20% chance of curing my disease, but statistics make no difference in God's kingdom! Remember the story of the boy who gave Jesus his little lunch—two fish and five loaves of bread? Jesus blessed the few crumbs offered and created a feast that fed thousands of hungry people...with leftovers to boot!

That is our God!

Oh, and more great news! My nurse called Friday morning to let me know my PET scan showed no other cancer besides the one spot in the breast we knew of. Praise the Lord that it hadn't spread elsewhere (especially given all

---

[4] Joni Eareckson Tada, *A Spectacle of Glory: God's Light Shining Through Me Every Day*, (Grand Rapids: Zondervan, 2016).

the time that has passed since I first found the lump to now)! Secondly, I asked if there was a chance we could do radiation locally, and she said yes! We do still need to meet with the radiation oncologist Monday in Indy to come up with a "plan," but the treatment we can most likely have done at Ball Hospital.

His blessings are flowing! THANK YOU for your continued prayers. God is listening...God is answering...God is being magnified.

> "Do not be afraid! Don't be discouraged by this mighty army, for the battle is not yours, but God's. Tomorrow, march out against them... you will not even need to fight. Take your positions; then stand still and watch the Lord's victory. He is with you.... Do not be afraid or discouraged. Go out against them tomorrow, for the Lord is with you!"
>
> (2 Chron. 20:15b–17 NLT)

Even though this whole thing could have had a very *déjà vu* kind of feel to it, it all felt strangely unfamiliar. Especially the road leading up to my second transplant.

CHAPTER 10

UNFAMILIAR

Newest Development

July 30, 2018

It's funny, with as many times as we've been to Simon Cancer Center, today felt like we were in a whole new world. We had been told that the radiation department was in the basement, so that's where we headed upon arrival. However, as we approached a waiting room labeled "Surgery," I thought (or hoped), *Surely this isn't it*. And sure enough, it wasn't! (Phew!) The exceptionally kind receptionist actually walked us to where we needed to be. She said it was almost too confusing to explain (Boy, was she right!), plus she liked having a reason to walk.

After a long wait (we're getting a lot of practice with that), the nurse called us back. She went over some brief questions and vitals, and then left while I changed into a gown. Next to come in was a resident doctor, and finally the radiation oncologist we were scheduled to see. As it turned out, he reviewed my PET scan and had concerns with something showing up on my right breast. After consulting with a radiologist, he, too, was in agreement that an additional abnormality was there. He examined the area today at our visit and found a definite lump. That means our first "next step" is to sched-ule another ultrasound-guided biopsy—this time on the right side. If it comes back as cancerous, the radiation treatment will be done on both breasts, as opposed to just the one. I went ahead and called my usual oncologist's office, and they are in the process of coordinating with the radiology department.

The radiation oncologist also confirmed that we should be able to have the radiation done locally. He is going to call Ball Hospital and get something set up with a radiation oncologist here. After finding out that the treatment for this myeloid sarcoma spans twelve business days (each treatment involving a low dose of radiation for thirty minutes), we realized the time to travel to Indy and back for so many consecutive days could become pretty taxing (espe-cially given this is Brian's busy season at work and the girls start school next week). At the end of our visit, the doctor apologized in case he "ruined our day" with the surprising news about the second lump. I smiled and reassured him, "You haven't ruined our day at all...we're used to hearing 'bad news.' We're very thankful you used good wisdom and inquired further about the area."

On our drive home, we were thanking God that He is not concerned with—or bound by—time. What we can worry is a "waste of time" or fear as "time running out," God sees as opportunity to fan the flame of our faith and reveal an even greater measure of His glory. The road ahead continues to increase in fogginess, but we will not back down in praising the One who is walking alongside us. He is good, and His love endures forever.

Take Two!

August 9, 2018

Yesterday, Brian and I made our way toward Indy for my back-to-back appointments. We checked into the Coleman Breast Center, and before long, my name was called. (Actually, the nurse called for "Darla Jo" which made me smile—reminded me of my childhood.) After changing into a gown, I sat in another waiting room until a different nurse came for me. She settled me in an exam room, asked a few questions, and then went to get the doctor. I heard a soft knock-knock, and in came the same physician who performed my last biopsy.

Because we didn't have an actual picture of this lump like we had for the other, the doctor first did an ultrasound of the area. For whatever reason, it was absolutely fascinating to me. Watching the screen, I was able to appreciate a small taste of the intricacies of how we were made and even to recognize with my untrained eyes that something didn't belong there. (That totally just reminded me of that old school Sesame Street song, "One of these kids is doin' his own thing.") She said, by picture alone, the mass looked identical to the left side. Needless to say, I'm glad they're getting it checked! Next, it was time to get my bed rearranged and the area prepped for the procedure. To prevent from thinking too much about it or getting lightheaded (this time, the ultrasound screen was directly in front of me, so if my eyes caught a glance, I saw the needle going in and such), God kept steering my mind to a visual concept of being covered with His "feathers" and finding refuge under His "wings" (see Psalm 91:4). It worked. For whatever reason, this one ended up being more painful—especially when the needle aspirated. Even still, I'd probably choose this over a bone marrow biopsy. Ha!

By the time the biopsy was finished and we walked to our usual stomping ground (second floor, Infusion Suite B), we were forty-five minutes behind schedule. Thankfully, they were aware of the likelihood of this (given the time between appointments), and weren't upset in the slightest. In fact, when the doctor, nurse, and pharmacist walked into the room and we apologized for showing late, the doctor laughed and asked, "Have I ever been on time?" He recognizes (as we have also grown to understand during the course of this year) that the world of post-transplant is not predictable; you accept it, remain flexible, and extend grace on either side.

The discussion mainly revolved around next steps after radiation. The fact that we can say, "Let's go through with the transplant," with peace gives us an assurance that God is in this decision. A couple weeks ago, the Lord resurfaced the story of the three friends (Shadrach, Meshach, and Abednego) in the fiery furnace...not just once or twice, but FOUR times in four distinct ways! I'm so thankful to serve a God who speaks! Nothing can compare to the peace that comes from the Father's assuring voice. He used this powerful story to prepare my heart and mind the first time we had to make a decision about the transplant—with all of its frightening potentials. And here we are again...facing this even scarier than before reality in front of us...surrendered to His will and committed to "Even if." Perhaps round two is comparable to the "furnace heated seven times hotter than usual" (Dan. 3:19 NIV84).

I wish I could better communicate what we heard from the doctor, nurses, and pharmacist yesterday concerning this particular transplant. It's difficult for me to translate some of the medical aspects. What I do know is that this "half-match" transplant is formally known as a haploidentical stem cell transplant. There will be some similarities to last time (tests beforehand, hospital stay, etc.), but several differences (given the fact that it's "half" versus my previous "full"). There is a total body radiation beforehand, different doses and makeup of chemo, and an added dose of chemotherapy a few days after I receive my brother's stem cells. All in all, it will probably add an extra week to my hospital stay.

As far as "how to pray," I think our biggest prayer need is time. The doctor expressed some concern with the time between now, radiation, and transplant. We don't know how long it will take before this leukemia could seep into the marrow, but we do know time is not on our side. Please pray that after our consultation next Tuesday with the local radiation oncologist, we can get this radiation show on the road! Again, I go back to the fact that time isn't a factor for God...and He can set boundaries as well. ("Leukemia, you're not going any further!")

The other prayer concern involves decisions that will need to be made once it's transplant time. Mainly for Brian really as he discerns how best to juggle work, home, and hospital.

We've seen the Lord move mountains before, and we can certainly see Him do it again. Amen?

Amen.

A Mountain Moved

August 15, 2018

Yesterday, Brian and I had the pleasure of meeting a local radiation oncologist referred to us. She informed us that the results of last week's biopsy confirmed that the right breast lump is, in fact, a myeloid sarcoma and proceeded to talk us through the radiation process. We appreciated her thoroughness, complete with a picture from my PET scan and a ruler to help visualize how they'll angle the beams of radiation on either side of me. After she finished with her explanation, she asked if we had any questions. I had just one: "How soon can we start treatment? We aren't pushy people, but we are sensing an urgency in the timing of all this given the nature of these kinds of tumors as well as our future transplant plans." Thankfully, she heard our request through gracious ears and expressed an understanding. Shortly after the doctor left the room, her assistant walked in and asked, "Can you be here tomorrow for simulation?"

Sure can!

Today, after a brief wait, I was approached by a woman who walked me back to the changing area. Once robed, I followed her to where the CT simulation would take place. I answered a few questions, signed a couple papers, met another tech who was helping, and away we went. In order to "stage" upcoming radiation treatments, they had me lay flat on the table with my hands folded and arms above my head. Because positioning is an important part of an accurate radiation treatment, they formed a mold around my arms and head to sort of "lock" me in place for each round of radiation. Once that piece was set, there were various measurements taken, several trials of breath holding, markings (with a purple Sharpie), taping, and finally pictures. Before I knew it, we were done.

I wish I could remember exactly how the conversation started—something having to do with healthy cells reforming after radiation—but one of the techs said, "It's amazing how God formed our bodies." Of course, I couldn't keep silent on the matter. "It absolutely is!" Before I knew it, all three of us were giving verbal praise to the God who is so far above us and who created our bodies so wonderfully and intricately. All praise, awe, and glory be unto Him! It was for sure among the least expected (Yet most welcomed!) moments I've had this year with medical professionals. While it wasn't a Sunday morning and there was no band on stage in front of me, it was undeniably one of the most authentic (not to mention, spontaneous) worship services of which I'd been a part and attended.

After changing back into my normal attire, I was led to a consultation room for one last larger than life surprise. Handing me a half sheet of paper describing "Step 1" and "Step 2" of the radiation treatment, she explained, "Now, normally it takes seven to ten business days (pointing to the words on the paper as verification) before we can move on to the next step, but in your case, we are having you come back tomorrow. The doctor will finish simulation by marking the precise areas that will be treated. Once that's finished, we will go ahead and give you your first dose of radiation."

I walked out of the Cancer Center wanting to SHOUT to the world about how awesome our God is! How we went from seven to ten business days to TOMORROW is nothing short of a miracle. When I got to my car, I started thanking God through laughter and tears for His various blessings, and He left me with this thought: *A mountain moved.* That phrase stuck with me and has been on the back burner of my mind all day. It wasn't until tonight as I started typing it out that God reminded me of how I ended the last CaringBridge post: "We've seen the Lord move mountains before, and we can certainly see Him do it again. Amen?"

He did it again.

"I will extol the Lord at all times;
   his praise will always be on my lips.
My soul will boast in the Lord;
   let the afflicted hear and rejoice.
Glorify the Lord with me;
   let us exalt his name together."

(Ps. 34:1-3 NIV84)

Radiation so Far

August 22, 2018

I'm nearly halfway through radiation already! Five treatments down, only seven to go.

Things I have learned this particular chapter of the journey:

1) Simple items—Sharpies, tape, and washcloths—can be used to accomplish great things.

   Between last Wednesday and Thursday's simulations, I was one marked-up woman! The unspoken (sometimes spoken) "rule" for marker usage ("Do not color on your skin!") doesn't apply when it comes to ensuring accuracy in radiation. I came home with black, purple, and blue Sharpie from my chest to my belly button, as well as down my sides. Clear, circular pieces of tape (each about the size of a quarter) cover the areas that are especially crucial to consistent radiation. When it comes to actual treatment, they place a wet washcloth (warmed from letting it run under hot water) over the area to "trick" the machine into thinking there's more membrane to get through than there actually is. The doctor explained how, since both tumors are so close to the surface, this is a way to ensure the right amount of radiation is hitting the area. Fascinating.

2) The Cancer Center gets to know their patients quickly. Eerily so.

The second day I walked in, I hadn't said anything more than "Hi!" to the woman at the front desk. Clicking around on her computer she asked, "Just radiation, right? Got you checked in!" I walked away like I knew that was going to happen, but in my head, I was thinking, *How did she know me already?* Then, as I made my way down the hall to the radiation portion of the building, a woman I had never seen in my life said, "Hi Darla!" I smiled and said "Hello" in return. Honestly, I figured she said "Darlin'" and it just sounded like "Darla." Wrong. When I came the next day, there was no doubt about it, she knew. So I said, "How do you know my name?" She replied, "We like to get to know our patients here." I guess!

3) Taking "normal breaths" on command makes breathing abnormal.

When they said treatment would only take about five minutes, they were right! On average, it seems I'm in the building a total of fifteen minutes. (This includes robing, waiting briefly in the private waiting area, setting up, radiating, and changing back into clothes.) They target one tumor at a time, but the routine on each side is the same. I hear one of their voices through the speaker, "Take two normal breaths." (Breathe. Breathe.) "Now take a deep breath and hold." (Big breath.) "Breathe." (Exhale.) This is how it goes every single time. Two times per side since they radiate from two different angles. But there's something about when you're told to breathe normally...it just becomes awkward. Like, I think I'm taking a normal breath? But thinking about something that is meant to be automatic—breathing—is just strange.

4) Having this same treatment done in Indy would have been stretching.

As I've gotten into a routine of driving myself to these appointments and being there for such a short amount of time, I have come to appreciate all the more that we've been able to do this phase locally. When discussions about radiation were first happening, I had no idea how in and out these treatments would be, nor how "every day, Monday through Friday" would really feel. Needless to say, this has been a huge blessing.

5) Aquaphor lotion removes permanent marker and stains your clothes.

Even though I'm receiving a lower dose of radiation than breast cancer patients do, there's still a chance that my skin can/could become irritated from the treatment. So the doctor advised I rub Aquaphor from the neck to the belly button, from the armpits down the sides three times every day. I guess I've never used this particular brand of lotion before, and now I understand why. It has mineral oil in it, so it's super greasy (enough to remove most of the lines they drew on me last week) and it leaves stains on cloth. My advice to others out there who are asked to use it: Wear older clothes, and don't assume a normal wash will remove the blotches. I learned the hard way. And hey, if you're looking for a way to get Sharpie stains off your hands (or your kids' hands), give Aquaphor a whirl. Ha!

6) Going this long without deodorant isn't as bad as I thought it would be.

Of course, I've never asked others what it's like to be on the "receiving end." Hmm. Word to the wise: Err on the side of caution... don't get too close!

7) Doctors need God, whether or not they recognize or acknowledge it.

I was floored when the radiation oncologist himself from Simon

Cancer called me last Friday morning, shortly after 8:00 a.m. He just wanted to check in and make sure radiation was going okay in Muncie. I told him it was and thanked him again for setting it all up. He also apologized that the right side indeed was cancerous as well. I reiterated our gratitude that he inquired about the area in the first place. He responded with, "Yeah, it was just kind of dumb luck that I found it." Oh man...I couldn't let that one go. "Doctor, it wasn't 'dumb luck.' God was involved in finding this." My words still came from a place of reverence for the doctor, but I couldn't miss the open invitation to acknowledge the *great(est) physician* responsible for the discovery.

8) My oncologist cares.

When I met with the radiation oncologist after my first treatment last Thursday, she mentioned how she talked to my oncologist on the phone. He asked her, "Will this give Darla ulcers?" She kind of giggled (perhaps implying that in the radiation world of cancer, this was an easy question) and said, "Oh no...no." I don't know why my doctor asked her that particular question, and I'm not even sure why the radiation oncologist shared the exchange with me. But the entire thing went straight to my heart: My oncologist cares. It just felt like a father checking in on his daughter, making sure she was in good hands and being treated well. Which, of course, got me thinking about my heavenly Father...how much MORE will He give me good things? (Matt. 7:11).

"My times are in your hands..." (Ps. 31:15a NIV84)

Another Chapter Ends

September 1, 2018

Yesterday was my final radiation treatment. I said my goodbyes, unstuck all twelve pieces of tape, and walked out to the parking lot for the last time. An uncontrollable stream of tears began, and I drove home giving God audible "thanks" through sobs for His undeserved, very personal love to me. These twelve days of radiation have proved to be an unexpected retreat—an oasis in the desert. One specific radiation therapist was my "constant," daily making sure I had a warm blanket in the chilly room and setting me up for accuracy. It cracked me up every time she said, "You're so good at this." My response was always, "I'm not doing anything...you're doing all the work!" as she pulled me one way or the other on the table to line my marks with the beams. Her enthusiasm to see me each day was sweet. ("You're the bright spot in my day.") And the relationship with Jesus we share sealed the deal. She was also my advocate, making sure I was okay with ("Has anybody asked Darla about this?") three visitors from Reid Hospital in Richmond (One who happened to be a high school classmate of mine!) watching how the breath-holding method of radiation works. Already anticipating my soon completion, my go-to radiation therapist and I spent some moments in the hallway after my treatment on Thursday...crying together (I'm going to miss her!), and reminding each other that God's plans are always good and His power goes beyond what's humanly possible. I knew that I wanted to get her a little something (and turns out she had the same idea), so we ended up swapping gifts on Friday. Also, an unexpected "Certificate of Merit" for my completion.

It had been a long time since I'd received any sort of "award" for anything. It read:

(Un)Becoming

Radiation Oncology Department

DARLA PETERS

Having complete the prescribed course of radiation therapy with a
high level of proficiency in the Science and Art of being
cheerful, outstanding in courage, tolerant and determined
in all orders given.
We appreciate the confidence placed in us and the
opportunity to serve you.

It became almost comical to me how many friends, family members, acquaintances, and even people I didn't know (but heard my story through the grapevine) began using this one specific word to describe me: "You are so *brave*." And the reason it made me chuckle inside was because I know that's not who I am by nature. It had been only a year ago, as I prepared for the first transplant, that I wrote...

Only a Girl Named Darla

August 17, 2017

I woke up this morning thinking of a tune from my childhood—"Only a Boy Named David." Perhaps some of you are familiar with it as well. The song gives the cliff notes version of the famous "David defeating Goliath" story. Here is this kid who chooses five stones from a nearby brook, and with the first pebble that he slings toward the giant, the battle is won. Even though there are many contextual details missing from the lyrics, I appreciate the songwriter's choice of the words "only" and "boy." David was no action movie hero; in fact, he wasn't even a trained soldier. We're talking about a teenager who looked after sheep for a living—a "nobody" who wouldn't have even known about this

Goliath guy had he not shown up one afternoon with lunch for his three older, more experienced brothers.

So, from where did his courage come? Clearly not from his stature or natural abilities and certainly not from his weapon of choice. His heroic bravery came from the Lord—the same place from which any authentic courage is derived. As a shepherd, God had helped David fight off many lions and bears which had come to attack his sheep. He recalled how the Lord provided for him then, so surely He would prove faithful against this giant as well. David spoke confidently to Goliath: "You come to me with sword, spear, and javelin, but I come to you in the name of the Lord of Heaven's Armies—the God of the armies of Israel, whom you have defied. Today the Lord will conquer you.... And everyone assembled here will know that the Lord rescues his people, but not with sword and spear. This is the Lord's battle, and he will give you to us!" (1 Sam. 17:45–47 NLT).

There was a day during that first stretch in the hospital when my entire immediate family was with me in the room. I looked around the hospital bed at my three older siblings and thought to myself, *God, you got the wrong person for this.* My brother and sister, Dee Ann, are both in medical professions—needles, blood, and the like are commonplace (not bothersome) to them. And Dana, my oldest sister, seems to be fearful of nothing; in fact, she is the sibling I would visit during the middle of the night when I was scared and needed comfort. I still remember fondly the Christian Evangelism Fellowship song she would sing to me: "Don't be afraid, Jesus is watching you. In the dark night, He is protecting you. Talk to the Lord, ask Him to make you brave. Jesus will hear when you pray."

And then there's me. Skittish. Timid. Second-guessing. Non-risk-taking. The definition of a scaredy-cat, especially regarding medical things: Needles, the sight of blood, foreign things inside of my body, the smell of hospitals, etc. You really could not write a story for me that is more in opposition with who I am by nature. And since I have a blood cancer (of all types), that means blood draws—lots and lots of blood draws—also, blood transfusions, platelet transfusions, IVs, PICC line, and a future port. Oh, and on top of it all, there's the fact that, apparently, I have the tiniest, toughest veins that test every technician's and nurse's skill. Brian and I have watched the humbling of many a proud expert claiming, "I got this..." and let me tell you, they don't. I have endured more "chasing" of veins and retries than I ever cared to experience in my life.

So naturally, there's the question, "Why, God, did you pick me (of all people) for this battle?" The same reason God chooses any unlikely candidate: To MAGNIFY His name. When our night nurse says I am such a courageous person, when our student doctor daily calls me "Champ," and when another leukemia patient on the floor refers to me as her "inspiration..." do you think I can sit there and take credit for any of this? Absolutely not! I know that ALL glory goes to God. In fact, I realize I'm "only a girl named Darla." I am well aware that there is nothing worth commending or immolating in my life apart from Christ. I would be lying if I said any of this was "easy." I would also be untruthful to pretend I'm relying on any of my own strength. Rather, every step along the way, I am clinging to God as my shield and refuge and claiming His truths as I endure uncomfortable procedures. YOU will supply all of my needs. YOUR grace is sufficient for me. YOUR power is made perfect in my weakness. When I am weak, YOU are strong. Nothing can separate me from YOUR love. YOU will never leave nor forsake me. YOU are my ever-present help in time of need.

"But we have this treasure in jars of clay to show that this all-surpassing power is from God and not from us"

(2 Cor. 4:7 NIV84)

While I was quick to shut down all this "brave" talk with a firm, *"No! I'm not brave,"* I began to sense the Lord challenging me to think differently, and to see things from *His* vantage point...not mine. He wanted me to receive what He was graciously offering: *Darla, I'm making you brave. Accept my gift of courage to you.*

Radiation was behind us. Now it was time to prepare for the soon stem cell transplant, part two.

Workup

September 8, 2018

Wednesday was our pre-transplant "workup." We knew it was going to be a full day, but it proved to be even more jam-packed than anticipated. The schedule we received via email had neglected to mention a 4:00 CT scan, which we were thankful was "caught" at check-in! When we got to our usual stomping ground, my twenty-four-hour urine sample was collected, labels were printed, and a pile of empty vials were gathered. My "go-to" nurse for blood draws saw me from a distance and asked the nurse helping if she'd like her to take over. Knowing I was a hard stick, she gladly accepted the offer. Because I would need an IV for the dye contrast (part of the CT regimen), I asked if she would go ahead and start one. She warned me that I would feel a whole lot of pressure due to the size of the needle, aaaaaand she was accurate. Ha! The right arm didn't cooperate and the left arm had nothing, but thanks to the "vein finder," she discovered something potentially workable in my left hand! It wasn't necessarily a "breeze" (For me OR for her!) even after a successful stick. But through what seemed to be a continuous finagling of the needle as well as tourniquet (on again, off again), all fifteen vials were filled! No small feat. Praise Jesus who proved to be my refuge once again. And thank God for the nurse, who didn't back down from the challenge or give up when things appeared less than promising.

We headed across the hall to meet with my oncologist (along with two med students) and nurse. After the usual questions and exam, he inquired about the lump on my lower back I had called about earlier. I'd almost forgotten about that! But yes, last week, I sort of tweaked my lower back, which—in God's kindness—prompted me to feel a suspicious mass. I was hopeful it was only scar tissue from all the bone marrow biopsies, but he said it wasn't in the same area. Not liking what he felt, he ordered my nurse to schedule me for an ultrasound-guided biopsy with the radiology department that same day. He also asked for the phone number of the radiation oncologist in Muncie, so he could ask her what kind of time frame for radiation treatment would be needed if this proved to be cancerous.

Everyone cleared out, and Brian and I started praying. When they returned to the room, a biopsy had been added to the afternoon schedule, and a doable radiation plan was mapped out (five days of concentrated dosage) just in case. I sensed that the doctor felt more relieved than he did just moments before, but there seemed to remain a hint of despair. He didn't have time for a well-thought-out plan of action; instead, we had the rare opportunity of seeing him work under the stress of the unexpected. "You've got to stop making these tumors," he joked. We all had a good laugh, which is a blessing we can do that. I will never know the full weight of his load—the pressure he experiences dealing so closely with grave illness on a regular basis—but I know it can't be light. I certainly don't envy his call, and I even feel a strange sort of gratitude to God for not gifting me with that sort of intelligence. Wanting to reassure him that, no matter where all this ends up, we're still thankful for him and the team, I looked at the doctor and said, "We still believe we're in good hands." He sort of stumbled over his words and for a brief moment stepped down from his lofty oncologist role. "Yeah...well..." he fumbled. That's when he looked at me and spoke words I never thought I'd hear him speak, "We know you're in good hands because you're in God's hands." I haven't been known to have much of a poker face, so I can't help but think they picked up on my surprise when he admitted this. But I smiled and said, "I absolutely am! And I can't help but think of the story when Jesus took the little fish and bread and multiplied it to feed thousands. He can do more with the mere 10% than we can know."

When the RN who would be doing my bone marrow biopsy walked in with the consent form, she asked if I'd like to have sedation since I had an IV started. Without hesitation, I said, "You know, I figured for biopsy #9, that would be a nice treat." She was in full agreement. The calming drugs were administered, which helped to take the edge off of the experience. What...a... blessing. The rest of the day was pretty much just keeping to the schedule; going from one floor to the next, making sure we checked everything off the long list. Having the biopsy on the back mass was the only true "new" thing I had, and besides the initial sting and burn of the numbing medicine, it was pretty easy.

By the time we were leaving the hospital, Brian and I both were dragging under the weight of exhaustion. I'm so thankful Brian was alert enough to get us home because I dozed off pretty quick into the trip. Also, it was surreal to be pulling into the garage at 6:41 p.m...exactly twelve hours after we left for Simon Cancer.

Yesterday, I got a call from the transplant coordinator nurse with two pieces of good news: 1) My bone marrow is still clear of cancer! Praise the Lord for the boundaries God has placed on these leukemic tumors. And, 2) The aspirate from the other mass proved to be non-cancerous! It was also the day of my brother's workup. From both his end and theirs, it sounds like it was a smooth experience. Daniel had good things to say about them, and the nurse emailed me later saying, "Your brother is a super nice guy!" (I would agree with that assessment.) He discovered from an x-ray that he, indeed, had fractured some ribs from an earlier injury (on the mend), and I was surprised to find a similar report from my CT scan this time around. The only event I can attribute to fractured ribs is the flu; the aggressive (and incessant) coughing did some damage.

A couple things on the horizon...

*September 12th (next Wednesday), I am scheduled to meet with a radiation oncologist. Part of the regimen for this transplant is a TBI (total body irradiation). In order to be ready for it on "Day - 1," they need to get things set up. Wednesday won't be my actual radiation treatment, but rather a simulation.

*September 20th is my tentative hospital admitting day. Similar to last time, I'll start by having a small bore catheter placed, and from there will follow the schedule for chemo days, rest days, and TBI...all leading up to the "rebirth" September 26th.

Almost There

September 14, 2018

On Wednesday, we were back at Simon Cancer for my TBI (total body irradiation) simulation. It was a packed house in the waiting room, and we even got to catch up briefly with some friends from church who were just finishing up treatment.

I love "small world" moments like that.

Before having a chance to use the restroom or complete forms, the nurse called my name. Standard questions and answers were exchanged before the radiation oncologist entered. He was able to articulate things in a very clear and concise manner, which we appreciated. Contrary to what I assumed, the dose of radiation given for this is extremely low. In fact, to put it into context, it's less radiation than just one treatment (of the twelve) I had for the myeloid sarcoma tumors.

A couple of radiologists and a different doctor took us back to a dimly lit room for the actual simulating. Lying on one side facing the machine, they cushioned the pad around me until it was where they wanted it, then increased the air to lock it in place. Next, they measured from my ankles, bellybutton, and forehead to the machine to see if I was roughly parallel. Before repeating on my other side (facing the wall this time), they took dimensions from my head to ankles. Since our bodies are made of varying depths, radiation is adjusted depending on where it's entering to keep everything equal.

In the midst of all this, my transplant coordinator nurse sent me my official transplant schedule. Bright and early on Thursday morning (7:00 a.m.), I will have my central IV catheter placed. From there, I'll move into my fifth floor room and start chemo. Five days of chemo. Radiation. Stem Cells. She also wrote, "I'm praying for a complete cure and know you are in God's loving arms through this journey. 'May the God of hope fill you with all joy and peace as you trust in him, so that you may overflow with hope by the power of the Holy Spirit' (Rom. 15:13 NIV). 'When I am afraid I put my trust in you'" (Ps. 56:3 NIV).

I read her email through tears. God is so good to me. His grace, each step along the way, continues to astound me.

Specific Prayer Requests:

*The girls. Each of them has a different way of coping with the upcoming stresses. Clara puts up walls and does all she can to avoid "feeling" or admitting the hurt. She would prefer to avoid any extra contact with me to make the separation less painful. Then there's Wendy, who is overcome with sadness and fear when (as she puts it), "I couldn't see you." She's also slipping back into thumb sucking, which is most likely a way to comfort herself amidst all the uncertainty around her. It breaks my heart that the girls have to go through this again. Please pray for healthy ways of expressing their grief, for God's presence (Immanuel, God with us) to be increasingly noticeable in their lives, and that the enemy would not use this to harden their hearts (rather, that God would use this to help them press into Him all the more).

*My brother. I'm so thankful for Daniel's willingness to go through the pain and inconveniences to be my donor. Please pray that God graces every step and relieves any nerves surrounding the unknown in all of this. He starts Neupogen injections (Saturday, the 22nd) to "trick" his bone marrow into overproducing stem cells so they can be collected on the 26th. It's hard to know what he will experience that week leading up to donating, but some people feel achy and unwell because of it. Pray that God sustains him through his various commitments that week (job, ministry, family) and keeps him healthy between now and then.

*Brian. He's juggling work (in its busy season), the girls, and a sick wife. Need I say more?

*Family and friends. That God would protect hearts and sustain. (Parents and in-laws will take the brunt of back-and-forth help with the girls.)

*Me. Pray that I would use well my last days before hospital stay. Pray that I would keep my eyes fixed on Jesus; that God's light would shine through me in a very dark place; that He would give wisdom and precision to nurses and doctors involved in the stem cell transplant; and that a miraculous healing would unfold.

This junction of our journey was unfamiliar for obvious reasons. Cancer in tumorous form was new, as well radiation and the people and places it brought with it. But where we were headed was familiar. Besides the patients, not much had changed on the fifth floor BMT unit in a year's time. The biggest difference would be with Brian's lack of physical presence. Due to various circumstances, he would be staying home and traveling to the hospital to see me after work most evenings.

I was about to end the chapter with, *Ready or not...here I come!* But then I realized it wasn't accurate. There was no doubt about it, by God's grace, I *was* ready! In fact, I was actually *excited* to see what the Lord was about to do as I walked through it with Him...a second time.

CHAPTER 11

UNHARMED

God's grace continued to blow me away. Those last couple of weeks before my second transplant were permeating with the Father's rich love for me. I wrote of all the ways He showed up:

1) There was a recent weekend which was an absolute rain in. Clara's first soccer practice and game were cancelled, and we were pretty much homebound. I had already asked Clara which she would prefer: celebrate her birthday early (before I went to the hospital), or have all the family over on her actual birthday (Saturday, October 6th). She picked the latter, which gave us an opportunity that wet weekend to prepare all the sweet treats for her "sports birthday" (a theme which she had been talking about and planning for months). Football brownies—check. Baseball cookies—check. Soccer ball cake—check. Our freezer is full, but our hearts are even fuller to have experienced it together.

2) It was Clara's first Friday night of soccer practice (after the rain out) and we were all packed in the car headed there. That's what I thought, at least. Brian had kept a really big secret from me, which still wasn't fully revealed to me even when he dropped me off at Olive Garden. My small group friends had surprised me with dinner out, followed by dessert at the church where a couple dozen women were waiting to bless me with their life, their love, and their prayers. To say I was overwhelmed by their outpouring of love (by God's outpouring of love through them) is an understatement. It was incredible.

3) We were sitting together on the sidelines of Clara's soccer game the following Saturday morning. My parents and Brian's parents were there as well, and as we were talking and watching, the director of the soccer program approached me. "Are you Wendy?" he asked. "No, I'm Darla, but Wendy is my daughter and our other daughter Clara is out on the field." He smiled and handed me an envelope. "Someone reimbursed you for your soccer fees." I barely had words to say, but through tears got something out like, "Wow. That's amazing. Thank you."

4) I've had this ongoing eyelid situation, and my nurse at Simon Cancer suggested I see an eye doctor before transplant. It was scheduled on last Wednesday (the day before we left for Indy) at 1:45 p.m. I had two telephone confirmations of the time and date. Then, the day before the appointment, I get a text to confirm an 8: a.m. appointment. I made an immediate phone call to sort out the time discrepancy, and she said it was absolutely at 8:00. (And explained that the doctor took his lunch break at 1:45...ha!) It was actually a more ideal time since I wouldn't have concern with the girls' afternoon bus drop-off. So as I sat in the waiting room, 8:00 a.m. Wednesday, filling out some forms, I look over and see one of my best friends from college walking in the

door! NO WAY! She doesn't even live in Indiana but happened to be visiting her sister (who lives in Muncie) who had asked her to come help her pick out glasses. It was hilarious and yet another form of God's grace and goodness.

5) The night we dropped the girls off at a friend's house (since we would be leaving around 5:30 the next day for the hospital), the sky was particularly spectacular. Above the gently blowing Indiana corn were splashes of color arranged in such a way that reminded me: "O Lord, our Lord, your majestic name fills the earth! Your glory is higher than the heavens" (Ps. 8:1 NLT). The sky always serves as a reminder to me of how BIG God is, and how if He can create such beautiful masterpieces day after day, nothing is too difficult for Him.

Could there be any better lead-in to what was about to take place? The closer we got to my next hospital stay, the more convinced I was of the Lord's presence. To say that God was overwhelming me (in the best possible sense of the word) by His love is an understatement. And while I wanted so badly to repay everyone for all they had sacrificed on our behalf, God kept saying, *Just accept it as my grace.*

With a God like that on our side, who wouldn't be ready to walk through this with utter confidence?

Day - 6 (Again)

September 20, 2018

We arrived at the University Hospital main registration at 6:45 this morning, and from there, took the elevators to the basement for my small bore catheter placement. After updating health history, signing consent forms, and getting an IV started (Thank God for sending a man who got it in one stick!), it was time to be wheeled into surgery. In making small talk with the surgeon, I found out he was a Ball State grad and a former frequent of Minnesota thanks to a family-owned summer cabin. (That's one of my favorite parts of this whole medical journey—all the people I get to meet and discovering those random connections in our stories.) Even though I was given sedation through my line, I could still feel the classic sting and burn from lidocaine, as well as the pressure of the catheter being pushed and pulled into place. But before I knew it, the procedure was done and I was being wheeled to a recovery room.

This is where the story gets kind of murky. Apparently, the fifth floor room wasn't ready, so we ended up in the basement for five more hours. I was able to rest for the first half and catch up on texts and emails for the second. Twice, I received a call from the BMT nurse practitioner asking where I was. "In the basement" is the only information I knew to give her, and I was somewhat confused why they weren't aware. Once we were finally discharged, we were told to go to the fourth floor, which we assumed would be another "holding place" until our actual room was ready. But after giving my name at the desk and the reason I was there, it became apparent I wasn't in the right place. Their charge nurse made a phone call to find out where I should be—lunch, followed by the second floor.

We headed to the cafeteria for a bite to eat, and then to our normal BMT Infusion area. The nurse called us back for weight, height (we had a good laugh together when she said I was 6'2" instead of 62"), vitals, and labs—through my new catheter! The NP I spoke with on the phone earlier met with us, and we shared more hearty laughs over the basement fiasco. "We were just doing as we were told," I explained. She also said that since the room still wasn't ready for us, we were free even to take a walk outside. If we didn't hear from her before 5:30 (which was another two and a half hours away at that point), we were to go on up to the BMT floor.

Making our way toward the stairs (so we could go outside), we ran into my doctor. Briefly catching up, he said he'd visit me tomorrow. We enjoyed our walk as well as time to cool off again in the air-conditioned hospital. As 5:30 was approaching, we decided to go to the car and gather my stuff to take to the fifth floor. We camped out in the lobby until they were ready for me a little before 7:00 p.m. Since it was time for shift change, Brian and I had time to get my room set up with my pictures, posters, cozy blankets, etc. Feels more like home already. Somewhere around 8:00, Brian left to go back to Muncie, and I started typing this post (which I lost, and decided to go ahead and attempt to retype tonight). Chemo was supposed to start at 10:00, but actually didn't until after 11:00 p.m.

All in all, it was an unpredictable day mixed with all sorts of unforeseen blessings. Rest. Lunch date. Laughter. Fresh air. And the remembrance/recognition of being, "Oh yeah! The one who had a really strong faith," by the BMT nurse who checked me into my room.

God's favor continues to astound me.

Day - 5

September 22, 2018

It's been a change to have my chemo in the middle of the night this time around (since I was admitted late Thursday), but I've slept soundly the last couple of days. The interruptions in the night have been hazy memories, and I've had no trouble at all falling back to sleep. Praise be to God for this amazing gift of rest! So far, I've been spared of chemo's less than pleasant effects, except for a significant drop in my blood pressure as I was going to bed last night—80/40 range. They ordered a bolus (which is a bag of IV fluids they run rapidly through me), which seemed to help increase things to a healthier place. It hasn't been a concern since.

Yesterday morning, I did some walking in the hallway, praying for each of the patients (I still have yet to see/meet any of them) as I passed their rooms. Running into so many familiar faces has been sweet as I've genuinely enjoyed catching up with nurses and techs. One of the highlights of my morning stroll was seeing the woman who took care of our food service on the third floor through the windows of the door leading out of the unit. I waved her down, and she parked her big food tray to come through the doors and give me a hug. She then asked if she could come to my room to pray...absolutely! Holding each of my hands, she prayed a beautiful and powerful prayer of healing over me...over this room...over my family. After she finished, she looked and me and said, "Sorry, I got a little carried away." There's never an apology needed when the Spirit moves, as He did so evidently through her.

My doctor stopped by for a brief visit. He won't be the rounding doctor next week, but he said he'd try to swing by then as well to see how I'm doing.

The rest of my day was blessed with visitors. Both my sisters and their families were in town, and my parents swung by as well. At one point, it was just my sisters with me in the room, and—thanks to my brother-in-law for bringing along his guitar—we were able to play and sing a variety of favorite hymns and Christian songs from our past. It was enriching. Brian visited too and stayed long enough to go on a walk with me, play Password, and help me clean up for the night. Also, I wanted you to know that your prayers are continuing to be answered. I can say with sincerity that I have felt nothing short of peace and joy since entering the fifth floor walls again. Just as He promised, God has (again) been with me in this fire, shielding me from the full effects of the heat.

"Shout with joy to God, all the earth!
　　Sing the glory of his name;
　　make his praise glorious!
Say to God, 'How awesome are your deeds!
　　So great is your power
　　that your enemies cringe before you.
All the earth bows down to you;
　　they sing praise to you,

they sing praise to your name.'

Come and see what God has done,

how awesome his works in man's behalf!

He turned the sea into dry land,

they passed through the waters on foot—

come, let us rejoice in him....

Praise be to God,

who has not rejected my prayer

or withheld his love from me!"

(Ps. 66:1–6, 20 NIV84)

Unlike before, Clara no longer carried with her those walls of protection around her. Rather, she was willingly expressive of the difficulty of their situation, relayed through many tears and an admission of "I miss you." As much as it pained me to see *her* pain, it was an answer to prayer that she didn't feel the need to hide this time around. In fact, what a *joy* to see three sweet visitors peek their heads in my room just a couple of days into my stay—Brian, Clara, and Wendy! We sat on my bed playing games, coloring, and catching up on school, home life, and soccer. At one point, Wendy whispered, "Can I snuggle with you?" Of course, I didn't turn down the offer. I had been praying that God would anoint and cover their visit, and He absolutely did. Everything about their time on the fifth floor felt natural, which was a God-given gift. Saying goodbye to the girls was just as authentic as their visit. Wendy wanted to give me ten cheek kisses followed by ten hugs, while Clara wiped tears from her eyes as Brian helped her get her shoes on. God certainly had His hand in all of our lives.

All my rounds of chemo went well. Next, it was time for one last blast before the stem cell transplant—total body irradiation. (Can I just say the first time I heard about the TBI, all I could picture in my head was an old cartoon character being electrocuted, revealing his insides all aglow? Thankfully, it wasn't nearly that dramatic.)

Day - 1

September 25, 2018

At 7:30 this morning, transportation was outside of my room ready with a bed to wheel me downstairs for my TBI. It wasn't long before two techs came and wheeled me from the hallway "holding place" down to the radiation room. There, they and a doctor worked diligently and strategically to get all the nodes taped where they needed to go, which was by far the longest part of the procedure. Once things were in place, they turned up my speaker and I was blessed to worship along with all the wonderful songs you sent my way. At the halfway mark, they switched my molding and had me face the wall instead of the machine. They unstuck the first set of nodes and replaced them on the other side of me and positioned me "just so" for one last blast.

When I was wheeled out, they left me in the same hallway "holding place" as before until a doctor came by to discharge me. She said the symptoms that may be most noticeable from the radiation were fatigue and nausea. Within a few moments of that brief interaction, transportation was there to take me back up to my fifth floor room. It was 10:30 by the time I returned, so there was "catch up" to play with vitals, meds, breakfast, etc. My nurse went ahead and gave me some anti-nausea medicine, which must have worked (since I never did feel sick). Fatigued, however, would pretty much define me today. There was a noticeable decrease in my activity and energy level, and I allowed myself several moments just to "nod off" in bed to ward away some of the lethargy.

Brian asked me how I was feeling about tomorrow's stem cell transplant. Honestly, I feel very similar to last time. So many unknowns around what it will look like...again. While I have full confidence that God called us back in this furnace (and is with us in it), who's to say I don't come away with a very different set of circumstances (or "quality of life")? Anyway, these are the things I have to continue to lay at the Lord's feet. He can carry it...I cannot.

For those of you who are married, think back to your wedding day. No doubt, you'll recall the unique feeling when you woke up in the morning of your "BIG day." A fine blending of one part *excitement,* the other part *fear.* As all the preparations were being made that day for your climactic walk down the aisle, you tried not to let your mind ruminate too long on thoughts of how this one moment would forever change the course of your life. *'Til death do you part.* Minus the pretty dress, guests, and cake-eating, this is what it felt like to wake up on September 26, 2018—the day of my ~~rebirth~~ second rebirth. I woke up around 7:00, washed my hair, put on makeup, and then dove into the Word and prayer. And similar to a bride's curiosity as to how the groom was doing, I texted my brother at 8:00 a.m.—he was in the building being prepped for his donation!

Brian took off work to be at the hospital that entire day. It was wonderful, of course, to have his company. He was even able to visit my brother (and wife) in the room where his cells were being collected. Donating seemed to be slow-moving at first, but finally—by 4:00 that afternoon— my brother's part was done. *Phew!* I felt a sense of relief for his sake when I heard the good news. Despite the long day, they came upstairs to say "hi" before leaving the hospital. It was so good to see them, to see he was doing okay, and to let him know (again) how grateful I was for his selfless sacrifice. It was then that I inquired as to how all the prep work was for my brother. Not only was it moving to find out Daniel endured significant discomfort for several days (the kind that resonated with my leukemia beginnings) and restless nights (propping himself up on a couch in attempts to ease the jabbing chest pains...again, relatable), what touched my heart most was that he had kept these things from me. He was shielding my heart, which only added to how genuine and sacrificial the whole act was.

A little after 5:00 p.m., the same man as my first go-round walked in my room, delivering my stem cells in that same purplish/bluish cooler. By 5:30, the bag was hanging up on my IV pole and ready to infuse. Brian and I prayed, read Psalm 103 aloud in the room, and then turned on the music mix compiled of all the worship songs my friends and family sent me. There were tears, prayers, and praising exchanged between Brian and me until by 6:30, my infusion pump started to beep: Transplant was complete.

Convinced

September 27, 2018

This morning, in the quiet moments before shift change, I listened for the sound of my Savior's voice. And through the piercing silence, He delivered this one-word message:

Convinced.

In two syllables, He managed to minister to the very depths of my heart: *Darla, I love you. You can be absolutely certain of this! Nothing can sever you from my rich supply of love found in Christ Jesus.*

The layers of His love are interwoven throughout this story. With each next step of faith, the Lord seems to enlarge the very path of His grace and favor under my feet. It's a story that encompasses an army of family and friends (Even some strangers!) who are committed to fighting this battle with us. Every person is playing a crucial role, and somehow God has given me a front row seat.

My brother's selfless donation was yet another broad brushstroke of His love. Several days of shots and sleepless nights, plus a full day of donating... all to help save his sister.

Unharmed

"Greater love has no one than this..."

(Jn. 15:13a NIV84)

Rest Days

September 28, 2018

"Let us hold unswervingly to the hope we profess, for he who promised is faithful."

(Heb. 10:23 NIV84)

Yesterday and today have been providentially timed "rest days." After the initial spike of white blood cells (thanks to the influx of new stem cells), my white blood plummeted today (as expected). I've been experiencing a progression of aches and chills and have been in and out of sleep more often. As it turns out, my temperature has been steadily increasing all day and finally reached their "magic number" tonight. It's something they anticipate will happen (at least once) to every patient here, given the layers of treatment and compromised immune systems. My nurse just took several blood cultures, and another nurse is currently hanging a bag of antibiotics. I'm so thankful for the BMT nurses who are specifically trained for these things.

Tomorrow and Sunday, I have two more blasts of chemo. I remember this particular strand being more intensive from my first stay here. They will be forcing IV fluids through me rapidly over the course of its use to protect my bladder, which last time wreaked havoc on my electrolytes. I still remember my night nurse flipping the lights on at 4:00 a.m. to get me to drink a double dose of broth. Ha ha ha. The girls and Brian will be spending the weekend nearby, so I'm looking forward to lots of cuddles and interactions with them.

Brian and the girls were coming to visit the next day, and as much as I wanted to feel like "myself" and give them "my all," the overall ickiness I was experiencing couldn't be denied. My fever had been steadily creeping up as the day wore on, and by the time they arrived, I didn't have a whole lot to offer. But oh, how I welcomed the hugs and cuddles! Clara even brought me a surprise—a manila folder stuffed full of homemade cards by all her classmates and teacher! Incredibly moving. Attempting to work on a word search puzzle with her proved to be quite the challenge. It was then that I realized my brain was nearly fried. And I certainly didn't have the concentration ability needed to play a round of Memory either (the girls' next activity of choice). For a brief moment, I contemplated turning the TV on but felt a strange guilt about it. I mean, I'd never turned it on either of my other stays. I liked it that way. But that's when the Lord gently spoke these words to me: *Darla, you have nothing to prove.* I let it sink in for a moment, smiled, and then asked if the girls wanted to snuggle next to me while I turned on the Food Network.

There were no objections, as you may imagine.

Unfortunately, the fever wasn't letting up anytime soon. Rather, it reached an all-time high, which I found out shortly before Brian and the girls returned to my room (after grabbing a bite for dinner). When the nurse read off a temperature dangerously close to 104, she instantly put me at ease with her soothing words. "If your fever gets any higher, your brain cells will be permanently fried." (You know, I figure some things are better left unsaid.) I had the shakes like crazy, but was told I couldn't cover up... that would only trap the heat in and make my fever worse. When the nurse uttered the words "ice bath" if things didn't soon improve, I threw off my covers. As miserable as this uncontainable shivering was, the thought of an ice bath was enough motivation for me. Late that night, the fever had dropped to 100.9—praise the Lord! When it went back up in the middle of the night, it was time to shed the blanket again. Fortunately, this little game didn't last but a couple days. I was also thankful that there was no source of infection linked to the fever. One of the doctors was able to explain to me that half of the time there is no known cause for the fever. Just some phenomenon that can show up when you're white cells are sitting at ground bottom.

I couldn't help but think of Shadrach, Meshach, and Abednego through this whole ordeal. The heat (in fever form) was blazing, but the Lord shielded me from its full effects. In fact, it brought me assurance when God brought the story to my mind again. Not only that He was walking it out with me, but I trusted that He would eventually bring deliverance as well. At one of the last soccer games we attended before our hospital stay, we sat uncomfortably in the 100-degree weather—sun intensely beaming against our backs—until God moved a timely cloud to cover it. The relief was immediate. I thought of this during my high fever, and wrote:

Shield and Deliverer

What did you feel

When you were thrown Into the furnace?

Were you too busy Worshiping to notice?

The fourth Person in the fire,

Was He like a cloud

That hides the sun

And brings relief upon

A sweltering soccer field?

Surely He was a shield around you.

You went in bound

But walked out with heads lifted high.

Delivered.

Now would be a good time to give this stem cell transplant its proper name: A haploidentical stem cell transplant—*haplo* for short. This modified transplant was basically created to give patients more options. It's not always easy to find a donor, and there may not be time to hunt down a "perfect match" (given how quickly cancers like AML take over). So while none of my siblings' HLA perfectly matched mine, they were each guaranteed to be at least half of a match...which made them all likely candidates for being my donor this time around. Talk about something that could become potentially divisive! How was I to choose between my three siblings? Oh, but God took care of that. I never had to make the decision; the doctor made it for me. Since my sisters have both had children (somehow this made them not as strong of candidates), he whittled it down to my brother before I even had a say in the matter. The chemo leading up to this haplo transplant was the same as the first, but in different doses. The TBI was a new animal, as were the two extra days of chemo *after* the new cells were infused (to kill off my brother's T-cells). It wasn't, however, a new concoction. I remembered this one well since it was the one I was on when I passed out without warning. The same message the Lord spoke to me about turning on the TV—*You have nothing to prove*—stayed with me those next couple days. As a precautionary, I paged the nurse anytime I was going to get up to use the bathroom. I wasn't taking any chances this time around.

Learning to Mitigate

October 2, 2018

It was wonderful waking up yesterday to the sound of normal temperature readings (and sodium levels) once again! Oh, what glorious news to start a Monday...to start a month! In fact, the jump that the sodium took in such a short amount of time was nothing short of miraculous. The nurse was shocked and said it was unheard of that it made such a quick recovery. I was able to share with her, "Well, lots of people have been praying." That's our God!

As I waited for a friend who was coming to visit, I decided to clean out my little hospital fridge. I know it sounds like a funny thing to focus on, but there were three good reasons for it. One, I felt well enough to do it. Two, several days of high fever also translate to lower appetite, which means a lot of food got sent to the fridge. And three, given the fact that some of these foods were partially handled while I had said high fever (plus being neutropenic on top of it), there was no way I was planning to revisit any of the items again.

In the midst of the autumn cleaning, my friend arrived (soon followed by another friend)! It was great spending time with them, even walking a few laps in the horseshoe-shaped hallway and then seeing my parents walk into the unit as well! What a blessing a support system is.

There have continued to be little differences along the way with this "haplo" transplant experience. Take last Monday when my nurse plopped down an orange syringe with what I thought was a little pumpkin on top and said nonchalantly, "There's your vitamin K." I picked it up, examined it, and honestly questioned whether I was supposed to feed this through one of my IV lines. Of course, I didn't proceed with any of my assumptions before asking, "What do I do with this exactly?" He sort of chuckled and said there was medicine in it to take orally. I could either use the syringe or squirt it into a medicine cup first. I chose the latter, because I somehow felt better if I could at least see what I was about to send down the hatch. He said they started giving patients vitamin K on Mondays; so yes, yesterday, I had another one and took a picture of it this time.

Also, I didn't even know our bodies needed phosphorus, let alone I could have a shortage of it. But the last two days, the nurse has brought supplement in powdered form of the mineral to mix into my water. I'd definitely choose the vitamin K to this any day of the week.

The other surprise yesterday came when the nurse said, "Oh, and the Neupogen shot in your belly." I actually thought she was joking at first, but she wasn't. Turns out I could barely feel it. Praise. Plus, it will get my white blood cell counts bumped up a bit, which is a good thing.

All in all, I felt great yesterday and much more myself. Without the fever, my head felt less heavy and I could think more clearly. I went into today assuming more of the same, but it's not exactly the experience I had. I really can't pinpoint it, but I just felt "off"—lightheaded being on my feet, groggy, tummy grumbles, and just overall feelings of lethargy. When the doctor made his rounds, he made sense of what confused me. "That's just the nature of transplants." Having brand new stem cells trying to find their way in your body, that's nothing short of complex. You're going to have good days, and you're going to have not-so-good days. As he was walking out he said, "Try to mitigate some of the expectations." I laughed heartily out loud and said, "That's exactly what I needed to hear, Doctor. Thank you for your timely advice."

His advice, in fact, was the very answer from God to a question I'd been waiting to hear the answer to. I was talking with the Lord this morning that while I know there's nothing in my own strength that is going to win this battle, what does it look like to fully rely on Him through it? Is there any of it that is my part? The doctor's words spoke into that—"Darla, you have nothing to prove."

It was a lesson I seemed to be slow in learning. Thankfully, the Lord is patient and gracious to keep reminding me.

Burnt Toast

October 3, 2018

I woke up this morning with the same gnawing feeling in my stomach I've had since late Monday night. There's usually not one "culprit" to blame.

Chemo, new cells, antibiotics, meds, and a steady diet of hospital food all join forces to leave your tummy with no other choice but surrender.

So when I was asked at 7:30 this morning what I'd like for breakfast, I went with the only thing that sounded relatively good—toast and peanut butter. By 9:30 (two hours later), the bread and packet of off-brand peanut concoction finally arrived. I did the spreading, took a bite, and instantly realized the toast had become nearly inedible—almost like, as I'd imagine, a Styrofoam. It was so tough that I was still mid-chew when the brand new tech came in to check on me. With one question, "How are you doing?" I lost it. An involuntary flood of tears began rushing down my cheeks, and I answered with the only thing I could think to say, "Eh, okay." Handing her my tray with the remaining toast, I explained I was finished with it.

I sat alone in the room, crying to God. Of all things, why was this so hard? Maybe because I was counting on the nourishment. Maybe because I had waited so long for something that was really my only option until lunch time. Maybe because I thought, surely, I'd let God down. I mean, seriously, crying over breakfast in front of a new tech? But sitting in His presence a little longer, I realized God wasn't disappointed with me. He knows all of this is hard, and He's actually delighted I would care to tell Him, "This stinks." And besides, that's why He promised to be here with me...because I can't do it alone. Then the day just kept getting better.

I was in my room typing the beginning of this post when my nurse walked in to change a bag of tacro on the IV. Without me even saying a word to her, she said, "There's always such a calm feeling when I walk into your room. I don't know if it's the way you're sitting or your faith. But it's not the like in any other room, believe me." And with that, she walked out.

Once I picked my jaw off the floor from such an unexpected, out-of-the-blue exchange, I started laughing and thanking God for His sweet reminder. He was making sure I got the message about the whole toast thing earlier. His presence isn't dependent on me having a "good day" or "bad day." He is in this place, and it's noticeable. Period.

When Brian arrived, we decided to go out into the hallway for a little walk. Looking up—who is coming toward us but my oncologist! "Just who I wanted to see! How are you?" he greeted us with a smile. He wanted to know how I was doing and how it's compared to my last transplant. And that's when he told us the most shocking news of all, "Depending on how quickly your counts go up, you may be looking to go home end of next week." NEXT WEEK?! Well, that would be fantastic! Praying toward that end.

Brian and I continued our walk, and then stopped to work on a puzzle. In the meantime, the unit's nurse practitioner saw me and said, "Did your doctor find you? He was wanting to see you." Yep...just did! That's when Brian reminded me, "Man. He cares about you."

And the day ended with a visit from a dear friend.

God sure made it easy to forget about some burnt toast.

"We thank you, O God!
We give thanks because you are near."

(Ps. 75:1 NLT)

Besides God's continual reminder to lower the ridiculous expectations I placed on myself, the most notable aspect of this hospital stay was how relational it was.

Relating

October 10, 2018

God has given me a genuine love for connecting with people. And while it's not a population I ever thought (or even hoped) I'd identify with, it's hard not to appreciate the unique community that forms over something crazy like stem cell transplants. A concept that was completely foreign to me a little over a year ago.

Yesterday, I went out for my usual after-breakfast stroll in the hallway. When an older fellow two doors down popped out of his room, I asked how he was doing. "I never thought it would be this hard." I was able to express my sympathy and let him know that I pray for him and the other patients as I walk by rooms. He was appreciative. Then we walked the hallways together for a good twenty minutes, discussing how we can trick ourselves into thinking we have some sort of control over our lives. Then something like this happens, and you realize what's been true all along—our lives are in God's hands. We aren't self-sufficient (though we'd like to think we are), and truly, He is our only hope. Later in the day, I ran into him again. He was sitting at the puzzle table and joined me for a few laps before calling it a day. "Let's do this again tomorrow," was the last thing he said. Sadly, he's been too sick today for being in the hallway, but it was great to see he had a friend visiting his room all day.

No sooner had I gotten back to my room that night when a "code blue" announcement came over the loud speakers. Again, a patient on this floor. I knew exactly who it was—I had just walked past his room! Through weeping, I prayed mercy over this man and his family. Also, today I found out that the young man a couple doors down who coded last week didn't make it. It tore me up. Continuing to pray for his family.

Another stem cell patient two doors down in the other direction is someone I enjoy connecting with any time we get a chance. I've actually had more contact recently with her husband and daughter (since she's been sicker the past few days), but most of our conversations happen around the puzzle table. Today, I ran into her daughter who was writing in a card. "Looks like you're keeping busy," I said. "Yeah, just writing a note to my parents. Today is their forty-second wedding anniversary." Instant tears filled my eyes, and I couldn't stop thinking about it when I got back to my room. In fact, as I sat on my bed praying for them, my mind went to this bag of nice chocolates I was given that still remained unopened...there was a reason for that. I wrote them a note and took it—along with the chocolates—to her room.

I've had a blast getting to know the art therapist this week. She came by Monday to discuss what I'd be interested in creating and ended up staying an hour or two. We talked about everything from the uniqueness of Pizza King pizza to, "Whatever happened to that thick Elmer's paste we used in elementary school?" It was fun to share some memories and laughs. She also came up with a great idea for me to try! Seeing the prints on my wall, she said I could do something similar. Today, she used the hallway puzzle table as a place for any of us on the floor to do art. One other patient was out there with me. I've only had a couple brief interactions with him, but we definitely had more time to converse while he painted with acrylics and I worked with metallic watercolors. The art therapist thought it would be good to practice the background of my print today. What a great idea, as it took me several tries to get the look I was hoping for.

My nurse the past couple of days is the same nurse who initiated our fifth floor stay last year. Today, we had to have spent three total hours (not exaggerating) between meds, shots, and treatment in conversation with one another. It was always super heartfelt stuff too. She even opened up about her years of infertility and six miscarriages. As she was sharing, there's no way she could miss the tears that were blurring my eyesight. "I am so sorry...I really can't imagine how painful that must be." I now know how to specifically be praying for her.

I've also been extremely blessed by the company that's visited from the "outside world." Last Friday, a couple small group of friends came and even surprised me with a T-shirt they had made. So very thoughtful. Yesterday and today, I enjoyed visits from my in-laws and another dear friend from church. It's certainly a blessing to have such quality interaction.

"Praise be to the God and Father of our Lord Jesus Christ, the Father of compassion and the God of all comfort, who comforts us in all our troubles, so that we can comfort those in any trouble with the comfort we ourselves receive from God. For just as we share abundantly in the sufferings of Christ, so also our comfort abounds through Christ. If we are distressed, it is for your comfort and salvation; if we are comforted, it is for your comfort, which produces in you patient endurance of the same sufferings we suffer. And our hope for you is firm, because we know that just as you share in our sufferings, so also you share in our comfort."

(2 Cor. 1:3-7 NIV)

For ten days, I sat at the very bottom of my white blood cell counts. It began to seem as if they'd grown used to it down there and were refusing to recover. There was a day when I was doing my normal laps in the hallway and the pharmacist asked a casual, "Hey, what's up?" He laughed when I answered, "Not my white cells," and I joined him in chuckling behind my surgical mask. Hey, sometimes it's just helpful to be lighthearted about things you can't control. It was maybe a day or two after this when the number budged! My white cells finally crawled out of the "0.2" or "<0.2" pit they'd been hiding in and reached an encouraging "0.3." Sure, it wasn't a significant shift, but it was a change nonetheless. So you can only imagine my shock the following day when this happened...

WHAT?!

October 11, 2018

The nurse popped into the room this morning and asked, "Has anyone told you what your white blood cell counts are today?"

Me: "No."

Nurse: "Want to guess?"

Me: "Seeing as in they were 0.3 yesterday, 0.5?"

Nurse: "Higher!"

Me: "0.8?!" (I asked in disbelief.)

Nurse: "1.0! And what about your ANC?"

Me: "Wait, I have an ANC? I dunno...0.1?"

Nurse: "0.8!"

Me: "This is absolutely amazing! I didn't expect this! Then again, lots of people have been praying for those white counts to go up."

Nurse: "Everybody must have been praying last night!"

Still reeling from this astounding news (and praising God for the work HE is doing), the on-call doctor walked in.

Doc: "How do you feel about getting out of here?"

Me: "Wait, like going home? Today? Is that even possible?"

Doc: "Your counts are good, you're eating and drinking beautifully, you're walking the halls, and you look great. There's no reason, from my perspective, why you shouldn't go home. Don't get me wrong, there will be frequent back-and-forth appointments here for a while to check your platelets and that sort of thing. But the hospital is a sick place. You don't need to be around that."

She said they were going to have another meeting and she'd give report on what's decided. But man oh man, talk about unexpected news!

Read these fitting words from Psalm 81 today:

"Sing for joy to God our strength;

shout aloud to the God of Jacob!

Begin the music, strike the tambourine,

play the melodious harp and lyre."

(Ps. 81:1–2 NIV84).

Singing, shouting, and making music in my heart to the Lord.

After those brief but mind-blowing dialogues with the nurse and doctor, the ball started rolling...quickly. I stepped out into the hallway for the first time since the news went "public" of my soon departure and looked up to see several nurses and techs wearing long faces. "We're going to miss you." (Cue the tears.) "I'm going to miss you, too." The closest analogy I have to the experience is summer camp. Let's call it *Camp Get Well* for fun. My cabin held several other campers (nine other beds were consistently filled this stay) with various counselors checking in on us, rooting for us, and investing their time for our betterment. In a short amount of time, a unique bond occurred that naturally creates an ache when it's time to say, *Goodbye.*

Keep in touch! Don't forget to write.

Our pharmacist was next to stop by my room that morning. He went over medications and made sure prescriptions were sent to the pharmacy for me to take home that day. A nurse informed me that she *pulled a few strings* so I could get my catheter out sooner than later. In the midst of all this, the art therapist found out I was leaving. She made it a point to come with all the art supplies needed to finish the project we'd started. Another highlight of the morning was a surprise visit from two of my cousins! And God continued to prove He was in all of the details, because my parents were actually headed toward Indy as well, not knowing I was going to need a way home.

Timing couldn't have been more impeccable when transportation arrived, as I had just finished my art project. Wheeling me down to the basement, they parked my bed in the same room where I started three weeks prior. The doctor was still tied down in surgery, which was fine by me. With as busy as the first half of the day had been, I needed the time to rest my mind and body. As I listened to the Lord in the quiet moments before the nurse came by to prep things, I heard the tune and words to an old hymn:

> A mighty fortress is our God,
> A bulwark never failing.[5]

I was so impressed with the doctor, the student shadowing him, and the nurse for spending all of ten minutes with me; they were extremely personable and compassionate. In fact, when the doctor asked me what I was most looking forward to about going home and I said, "Surprising my two girls" (who didn't know I was headed that way), all three of them let out a simultaneous *"Awww."* It was unexpectedly sweet that they would seem to care.

Not surprisingly, running to God as my mighty fortress was exactly what I needed to hear, hum, meditate on, and *do* as the doctor talked through every detail of the procedure to the observing student. It was the only place I could go to escape the bothersome language surrounding the line pulling. Phrases like, "Pushing on the skin you can feel the catheter," and "You have to give a harder tug for the first part to come out" are breeding grounds for fainting, had the Lord not been my hiding place.

---

[5] Martin Luther (1483-1546), "A Mighty Fortress," Public Domain.

In no time, I was back up to Room 5274. After some more tearing down and packing up my belongings, my nurse came in to go over discharge instructions and give me one last Neupogen shot in my tummy. With my parents' help, a cart was loaded with my stuff to pack in the back of their car my dad was in the midst of pulling up for us. When a woman from transportation arrived with my wheelchair, I asked the nurses and techs if it was okay to get a picture with them. They had no hesitations and even let me take one when I wasn't wearing my mask! Then, they formed a tunnel for me to wheel through...cheering me on my way out, into the once-forbidden hallways and beyond.

It was a picturesque fall day—the kind with rich blue skies and white puffy clouds—as my parents and I departed the hospital en route to Muncie. When we rounded the corner to my house, Brian was standing in the driveway—man, it was good to see him! Reuniting with the girls, however, was going to have to wait a little longer. Wendy had spiked a high fever the previous night, so it would be forty-eight to seventy-two hours after it broke before my weakened immune system could be around her. While I didn't necessarily prefer the delay, I also saw it as God's kindness in easing me back into what was once "normal." I also wasted no time in facing the hair loss reality; after only twenty-four hours of being home, I asked Brian to shave my head...once again. It didn't seem worth holding on to the false hope any longer that I may not lose my locks this time around. The noticeable increase in hair loss over a short stretch of time made it obvious: *Okay, this is happening.*

My newly bald head (graced with a chemo cap) was ready to greet Clara when she walked in the house with Brian and Bapa after her Saturday morning soccer game. Her reaction was typical of her: *"Mommy!* How are you home? *Wait,* does Wendy know?" A couple of days later, it was

Wendy's turn. She walked into the family room, crying after having just taken a fall in the garage. "Are you okay, Wendy?" She jumped into my arms and her tears of sorrow were replaced with ones of joy. I think it goes without saying...she was A-okay.

CHAPTER 12

UNRAVELING

H ome is such an interesting taste of reality after a long hospital stay, as I've come to learn. Just like the other two times I'd made this transition, it became apparent ever so quickly that while I was the healthiest among the sick, I was far from well. It's funny what being in your native environment will tell you that a foreign place won't. Taking it a day at a time was going to be a must, and trusting God for strength from one moment to the next wasn't up for negotiation.

Sandwiched in between my reunions with the girls was a hospital visit to address the diarrhea and fever I couldn't seem to shake. It went something like this...

Sunday Morning Clinic

October 15, 2018

It was a ghost town as we walked through the long second floor waiting room to Infusion Suite B. Had it not been for a large poster that says, "We're open! Walk back to the nurse's station," I may have questioned whether or not we were in the right place. Sure enough, it was. A nurse was there to greet us and get me checked in, weighed, and settled in an exam room. When she mentioned the doctor wanted a stool sample, I said I could take care of that right away. *(Wink)* When it was time for vitals and blood draws, the Lord extended His kindness and grace to me once again—another good vein was found (and stuck) without a hassle.

And then we did what we've grown to do best...we waited. The on-call doctor was making rounds and wouldn't be down to see me for a good hour and a half to two hours. Time to make ourselves at home. I bundled up in blankets and visited Psalm 84. What I thought would be a short visit ended up consuming the majority of our stay. A brief backstory. Before we had left for the hospital that morning, I heard the Lord speak these words to me: "They are weak, but He is strong." (Yes, a line from the familiar children's classic, "Jesus Loves Me.") A perfect reminder for me as I finished getting ready to leave, feeling especially limp and lacking. "Your grace is sufficient for me, Father. Your power is made perfect in my weakness" (2 Cor. 12:9, my paraphrase).

Back to Psalm 84. This is not an unfamiliar psalm; in fact, I've circled and underlined most of its words and verses from previous reads. But when I got to verse 5 this time, these words jumped out at me: "'Blessed are those whose strength is in you" (Ps. 84:5 NIV). Oh, how I love that God's Word is living and active! At this point, I was stuck (in a good way) and began ingesting as much as I could from this psalm—looking it up in various versions and reading more about it through commentaries and sermon notes.

In the midst of it all, I dozed off and woke up when the nurse walked in my room with the latest report. The doctor saw my labs and ordered a bag of IV fluids (for dehydration) and magnesium (since it's low). She had to stick me again to start the IV but was able to hit the same vein as beautifully as she did earlier. Praise. It was a two-hour drip, so we were in it for the long(er) haul. The doctor made her way to my room for a quick exam and further updates— my blood counts looked good, so there really weren't any further concerns once these infusions were done. She did order a nose swab (and apologized profusely in advance—for those of you who've had them before, you know) to make sure I'm not fighting a virus. The stool sample tested positive for C. diff, so the doctor sent in for a fourteen-day antibiotic to fight it.

A little after 2:00, we were back on the road headed toward Muncie.

It wasn't the first time I'd had C. diff (you may recall that Fourth of July story from my first hospital stay), but to have it at home?! As my mind recalled the extensive precautions taken by anyone entering my hospital room so as not to contract the infectious spores—be fully robed, wear surgical gloves, wash hands with soap and water (antibacterial stuff wouldn't kill it), bleach anything with which I have contact—it seemed nearly *impossible* not to spread. Coming home from my first transplant, my main concern was that I may "catch" something (especially with the colds people around me were actively fighting). This time, I was more concerned with me passing along something to *them!*

But praise God...it didn't happen!

As is my usual reaction time, it was a couple of weeks into being back home that my emotions finally caught up with me. *Ugh!* I really don't want to be walking down this same old, ugly road as before. To give you a taste of what my soul was feeling...

A Lament

October 20, 2018

O Lord, my heart cries out to You:

"Where are we going with all this?

Where are You taking me?

How much longer before You reveal Your plan?"

Please, Father, let not the process

be the plan.

You've parted seas for me to walk on dry ground;

don't destroy me now.

Silence the Enemy who

wants to claim victory,

who wishes to threaten me with his lies.

Lead me out of this valley

where death's shadows dance

to a place of abundance.

"Restore, O God!" My soul cries, "Restore!"

Rebuild my life upon the ruins

that Your unmatched Name

be lifted higher.

Where else can I run

but to You, my Mighty Fortress?

October 28, 2018

While my body works to regain a sense of normalcy, so does my heart. The frequent appointments don't allow my mind much breathing room to think far beyond the disease. But that's where I long to be...far beyond. Past the threats of GVHD, failed engraftment, relapse, or any number of illnesses that want to feed on a weakened immune system. Being home doesn't change (perhaps only amplifies) the fact that I need to remain hidden in the shadow of the Lord's wings so that I don't "fear the terror of night, nor the arrow that flies by day, nor the pestilence that stalks in the darkness, nor the plague that destroys at midday" (Ps. 91:5–6 NIV).

Two weeks ago, I mentioned being recaptivated with Psalm 84, and it's a place God continues to take me. In fact, I need to just commit it to memory. I want my soul to yearn and faint for the Lord, as the psalmist's does.

Sometimes I think I'm there; other times I find myself running to a different shelter for false security. Or I realize that I've spent more time asking Him for what I want (healing) than praising Him for who He is and basking in that reality. I want to say with confidence, "Better is one day in your courts than a thousand elsewhere" (Ps. 84:10 NIV). My head knows it's true, but my heart doesn't always show it believes.

A New Thing!

November 6, 2018

As I went through the motions of getting ready for church on Sunday morning, I found myself on the verge of discouragement. I began to question whether we are even moving in a forward direction, or if this whole year has just been one giant leap back to the starting line. I knew it wasn't true, but based on what I could see (even what I literally see in the mirror as I picked out a scarf to cover my bald head), things looked all too familiar.

Then again, that's not the nature of faith. Faith isn't concerned with what I can see. Rather, it gives us "assurance about what we do not see" (Heb. 11:1 NIV).

Little did I know as we made our way to church that God was getting ready to disarm any hint of discouragement that had crept its way in through the cracks. I honestly couldn't tell you tunes or titles, but as the congregation joined voices in melodious worship that morning, three different songs included the word "new." The first time I heard it, my ears perked up. Second time, I took note. Third time, tears welled up in my eyes. I get it, God! You're doing something new! As similar as my life "looks" to last fall, this is different... this is new.

Before making my way to the car after the service, I ran into a friend who had another timely word (though neither of us were aware in the moment of its full significance). She shared that whenever she prays for me, she sees this picture of a river flowing through a desert. Yes, it's a dry wasteland, but God is bringing refreshment in it.

When I got home, the message continued to ring loud and clear. (Oh, how I appreciate when the Lord so graciously repeats Himself!) And while I didn't think I needed more confirmation, the Father decided He wanted this gift wrapped in pretty paper and topped with a vibrant bow—He left no chance for further questioning. That evening, I started a new devotional, and the first reading was from Isaiah 43:18–19 (NIV84):

"Forget the former things;
do not dwell on the past.
See, I am doing a new thing!
Now it springs up; do you not perceive it?
I am making a way in the desert
and streams in the wasteland."

This is why they call it the Living Bible—because it speaks; rather, HE speaks through it. I've read these verses many times (even underlined them in my Bible), but this time...this time...it was as if the Lord looked me in the eyes and spoke the words directly to me. He combined the messages I had heard that morning into one lovely package. To be able to have such a personal relationship with the Creator of the entire universe always leaves me reeling in awe and wonder.

Brian and I were both hit with some sort of stomach bug, but mine continued to linger. Fearing it was a C. diff rebound (not what I wanted to hear having just finished the fourteen-day treatment), the doctor had me schedule a visit. That early November appointment proved encouraging for so many reasons: My veins continued this new trend of being easy to find; my previous week's bone marrow biopsy (tenth and counting) showed no detectable leukemia and that I was 100% donor; my blood work and chemistry looked good (despite several consecutive days of diarrhea intermittent with vomiting, I wasn't dehydrated); and my stool sample tested *negative* for C. diff.

I also had some concerns about residual lumps I felt in my breasts. Was this normal? Radiation was such a foreign concept to me and my blood cancer that I wasn't sure what to expect...should those lumps be gone? And my oncologist didn't know either. Having a follow-up appointment with the local radiologist put some of my fears to rest. She didn't think it was concerning, though she also lacked the knowledge of my "normal" when it came to all of this. Her advice was simple, yet genius: Wait a month and compare to today. If no changes, no worries. If there are, then you know.

Despite some residual rumblings in my tummy, I headed for home in good spirits that day. It was my thirty-sixth birthday, and a dear friend of mine was on her way to my house with ingredients to make some homemade soup. Upon word of her arrival, I made my way toward the already-opened garage to greet her. That's when I got one of the biggest surprises of my life! There stood not just *one* good friend, but *six* of my closest college friends (several who had flown in from various parts of the country) holding onto balloons and sporting polka-dotted party hats— one of them being my sister-in-law who *also* turned thirty-six that day. Talk about a birthday to remember!

Thanksgiving Eve
November 21, 2018

On this eve of Thanksgiving,
there's much for which to be thankful
As always.
I've never had a shortage

of blessings to list
    Past or present.
God's grace so astounding
poured out for me
    Without limit.
Second and third chances
of extending life in this
    Earthly tent.
Surrounded by an incredible
support system of
    Friends and family.
O, to compose a new song
to sing unto the Lord
    Giving thanks.
He is worthy—always worthy—
for He is good, and His love
    Endures forever.

Parallel and Posture

November 28, 2018

I'm so thankful we serve a God who doesn't waste anything. In fact, this is one of the most rewarding (not to mention unique) aspects of the Christian faith! God can create beauty from ashes, grow spiritual fruit in the most unlikely environments, and offer joy amidst sobering circumstances. The trials we endure in this life aren't for naught. We can forget that "suffering" takes on various forms, and that the appearance of ease isn't always an accurate gauge of difficulty. What is it about waiting seasons, for instance, that is so doggone hard?

I want to do; God says to be.

I want to speak out; God says to remain quiet.

I want to be seen; God says to remain hidden.

I want to run; God says to walk.

It's a lot like resistance training, I guess. There's not much that "feels good" (or natural) when your muscles are working against an unmovable force, yet there is a joy and expectancy knowing the result will be an increase in strength, power, and endurance.

O, that I may not lose sight of the inherent value of waiting.

O, that I may not envy the culture around me that is abuzz with activity.

O, that I may wait well—praising, magnifying, and trusting the King of my heart.

There's a medication they started me on (Maybe a month or so ago?) that's newly approved by the FDA. It's not readily available, which means most places (including local pharmacies) don't carry it. We can, however, order it through the pharmacy there at Simon Cancer, which we have done. In theory, this should be no problem since we're there for frequent appointments. But at our last visit, they were out of stock and couldn't get an order in until after Thanksgiving. While it wasn't ideal, we figured Brian could drive down after work Friday to pick it up. When I called them that day, it still wasn't in and their pharmacy closed at 2:00 p.m. They apologized for the inconvenience, but said it would for sure be in on Monday. When Monday rolled around, my parents actually decided to drive to Indy with me and make the most of the time. And make the most of it we did! We had good conversation on the way there, and enjoyed browsing the hospital gift shop (even bought a Tony Evans book there that I'm really enjoying, so far) until 11:00 (when the shipment was said to arrive).

When I rounded the corner to speak with the pharmacist (again), I wasn't exactly surprised when he said the med was a no-show. He apologized profusely, feeling sorry we had come all the way from Muncie to hear (once again) they didn't have what I needed. Sure, it wasn't what we had hoped or planned for, but we also trust that God knows what He's doing...He knows what I need...and maybe (just maybe) there was some sort of strange blessing in all of this. My liver scores were elevated at my last appointment, so perhaps this extended time I've been without that particular medication is giving my liver a helpful break. I don't claim to have the answers, but I trust the Lord. We did all we could from a human standpoint, and that's all we were called to do. In fact, as we drove away, I had a very strong conviction that this was our last "extra" attempt at getting this medicine. What I mean by that is I'm not going to make another special trip just for that. At this point, we will just wait to get it at my next appointment (a week from today). I felt an extreme peace about the decision, knowing it was from the Lord.

As I was getting ready yesterday morning, I received a phone call from the pharmacy at Simon Cancer. The woman on the other end said they were shipping my medication to me since I lived in Muncie. After validating my home address and phone number, she said UPS would be delivering it to my door tomorrow (today). Since I have to sign for it (and they aren't aware of time of shipment), she advised I (or someone) be home. You got it! This is when I'm most thankful I have nowhere I "have" to be. Homebound I'll be.

(Ha! Wouldn't you know...just arrived. Signed and delivered.)

I hung up the phone in absolute amazement of the Lord. And within the next few moments, I sensed God was saying my "what's next" in life will parallel the mailed medication. It was after I surrendered it ("I'm not making another special trip for this medicine.") that it was literally brought to me. *In the same way, Darla, surrender your "purpose" to me. Continue to posture yourself in a ready position (Bible, prayer, etc.), expectant to hear from me. When the time is right, I will deliver the package right to your door. Be ready to sign.*

Once the eight-day stomach bug had finally passed, I thought we were in the clear. And we were...for a few weeks, at least. At the beginning of December, the chronic abdominal aches and diarrhea resumed, only this time, it was that much more pervasive. I compared it to having a newborn baby without any of the perks—waking me up to four times in the night because...well...nature calls, and keeping me mostly homebound.

Forget Not

December 5, 2018

After contacting my nurse, she ordered a C. diff test, so I headed to our local hospital yesterday morning to the outpatient lab to pick up all the goodies needed to collect my output. I drove back home, did my thing, and then headed back to drop off my lovely sample.

Can we take a moment to appreciate those who do this kind of work? I mean, I can barely handle the sight and smell of my own you-know-what...but a stranger's? A sick stranger's?

(Cue the slow clap.)

We already had an appointment scheduled for this morning in Indy, so we knew beyond the C. diff test (which, by the way, we found out tested negative), there was nothing else to be done but wait until they saw us today. The encouraging news is that my usual blood work looks great! White blood count, hemoglobin, and platelets are in a good spot. And despite all the diarrhea, my electrolytes were also fine (so no IV fluids were needed). My liver scores, on the other hand, had skyrocketed! This, coupled with the symptoms I'm having, appears to point to graft versus host disease. To put it in (hopefully) understandable terms, the doctor assumes that the new cells are viewing my GI tract as foreign, and therefore attacking it. The potential blessing in all this is that at least the donated cells are different enough that they aren't recognizing the environment. From a leukemia standpoint, this could turn out to be an answer to prayer, since the new cells should (we hope) also view the cancer as foreign and attack it; thus, a better chance for a longer term remission.

The urgency now is in getting this possible GVHD under control (because it can also be fatal if it's left to progress). The pharmacist reviewed with us the various steroids they are starting me on (for a time) to temper these raging cells while my nurse contacted the GI department there at University to get me in as an "emergency" colonoscopy. On our drive back home to Muncie, I received a call from their office and plan to be back in Indy Friday at 9:30 for the procedure. They will also biopsy the colon, which (according to the doctor) is much less intrusive than biopsying the liver. If the colon is inconclusive, then they would go for the liver...but I'm praying that there's no need for Plan B.

So, new adventures abound! Well, I should say "new" to us. Not so much to the One who already wrote the story. And what a comfort to know He will navigate us through this. We trust Him...sincerely.

As I was getting ready this morning before leaving for the appointment, the Lord brought Psalm 103:2 to my mind. Seemed fitting then, but maybe even more now.

"Praise the Lord, O my soul,
and forget not all his benefits."

(Ps. 103:2 NIV84)

Besides childbirth and wisdom teeth extractions, one of the "war stories" people enjoy sharing most is the dreaded colonoscopy prep. Because I didn't expect to have the experience for many years to come, I can't say I paid all that much attention to people's previous warnings. I'm not sure if it was due to prayers, expectations, the fact that I'd been dealing with stomach cramps and "the runs" for so long, or all of the above...but the whole thing was pretty anticlimactic. (To those of you who have yet to go through it, you're welcome. It isn't so bad.)

Colonoscopy
December 7, 2018

Unlike the various horror stories I've heard regarding the prep, I can't say my experience was all that eventful. In fact, it was a whole lot better than I anticipated. Yesterday, I was restricted to a clear liquid diet, which wasn't much of a sacrifice given the recent state of my tummy. It also happened to be one of the most worshipful and encouraging days I've had recently. Beginning with these promises from Psalm 125:1-2 (NIV84):

"Those who trust in the Lord are like Mount Zion,
    which cannot be shaken but endures forever.
As the mountains surround Jerusalem,
    so the Lord surrounds his people
    both now and forevermore."

While doing a bit of tidying and disinfecting in the house, I listened to the playlist to which many of you contributed for my hospital stay. Oh, what a blessing those songs were to me...again. Tune after tune added rich layers of reminder to the kind of God who is on our side. Master over all. My inheritance. Seated in the heavenlies. My hiding place. Everything I need. My hope. (To name a few.) And the supernatural response to such a steady dose of truth? Complete peace and joy.

A couple of hours before it was time to start drinking the prescribed NuLYTELY solution, I added the Crystal Light packets (a helpful suggestion by the prep nurse) along with four liters of lukewarm water. Shake. Shake. Shake. Then into the refrigerator to chill. I also marked a glass jar—eight-ounce measurement—to make pouring accurate and seamless with each new drink. Beginning at 6:00 p.m., I drank eight ounces of the concoction every ten minutes. (This is when being a frequent user of the "snooze" button came in handy. From experience, I knew that once my alarm went off to take another drink, hitting the "snooze" button on my phone would automatically put me at ten minutes later. *Perfect-o!*) A few drinks in, I realized ten minutes didn't feel like a whole lot of time between cups. Trying to down the solution quickly wasn't as effortless as I thought it might be because it was thicker and saltier than your average drink (almost leaving a coating or film on the inside of your mouth). So I just kept praying with each new sip (or gulp) I took, "God, please help me get this down and keep it down." And I thanked Him for His grace each time He delivered.

An hour and eight cups later, I was done with the first half! Not to be touched again until 4:00 a.m. At this point, I kept waiting for the show to begin, but it was pretty insignificant. I guess when you've had chronic diarrhea for long enough, there's nothing new or exciting that's really going to happen. (And quite honestly, I wonder if there was anything much left in the system.) I stayed up long enough to take the two Gas-X tablets at 9:00 p.m. and two more at 10:00 p.m. (along with my regular nightly meds) and went straight to bed. When my alarm went off, I headed downstairs for the second half. I was fully expecting this round to be harder and began by praying for grace and endurance. I was shocked with how quick and easy it felt. Before I knew it, I was pouring the last eight ounces into my cup. And done! It was a little after five at this point, so I lay down on the couch briefly before heading upstairs and getting ready. There was some more output throughout the morning, but again, nothing like I thought it would be. What a blessing. God's goodness and grace continue to abound and astound.

We left the house at eight o'clock this morning to get checked in at 9:30. I slept most of the way there (Don't worry...Brian was driving. Ha!), and even dozed off some more while we waited in the curtained off room before I was wheeled back for the procedure. The doctors and nurses who helped us out were an answer to our prayers—kind, competent, and accommodating. Even the IV was started without a problem!

Once I was in the procedure room, chest nodes were stuck, an oxygen tube was placed, and the anesthesiologist spoke these reassuring words: "Here comes the medicine that's going to make you sleepy." The doctor performing the colonoscopy told me to take two deep breaths, and I don't remember anything else until I woke up already wheeled into my recovery room. Now, that's what I call sedation! Thank you, God! Yet another answer to prayer.

When the doctor came back to review with us the initial report from my colonoscopy, he handed us a packet with the same information (complete with pictures taken at various parts in my colon.) He said that there were patches of severe inflammation (characterized by erosions, friability, and shallow ulcerations) found in the entire colon. Meaning, this is probably either graft versus host disease (as suspected, especially because of the high liver scores as well), or some sort of infection (like CMV). Biopsies were taken and sent off, so we will have further (and more conclusive) information next week.

I can't even tell you what an unforeseen blessing these past couple of days have been. Do I like having to go through yet another medical procedure? Well, no. Who does? But it's times like this that I'm better able to recognize something that's always been true...how dependent I am upon God. Once again, He supplied me with sufficient grace and proved perfect His power in my weakness.

(Un)Becoming

"The Lord has done great things for us,

and we are filled with joy."

(Ps. 126:3 NIV84)

While we waited for the official results of the test, God was graciously preparing my heart.

Contentment

December 11, 2018

I woke up yesterday morning in an undeniable and inescapable state of contentment. From an external standpoint, I had no foreseeable "reason" why this feeling was so present and permeating. It was a Monday (need I say more). The night's sleep had proven less than restful. And the only items on my mental "to-do" list for the day were shopping and wrapping (which just so happen to be two of my least enjoyable past times.) But through what could only be accomplished and understood in the supernatural realm, I couldn't wait to get up. I was bubbling over with joy and oozing with peace. In fact, I cannot remember a time when I've experienced this in greater measure.

There is no doubt about it: This was yet another extension of God's grace to me.

I sent a morning email to the family, doing my best to express what I was just explaining to you. I woke up with this amazing sense of contentment. Just thankful that God is in every detail of all of our lives. I was thinking too of the famous line my sister also referred to recently that Joseph said to his brothers. What was intended for harm ended up for his good. I can't help but believe that through all these arrows that the enemy throws our way, God is only getting more glory and fame. It's like Satan himself is helping to stack the deck for God to do immeasurably more. There is an overwhelming sense of peace knowing the Lord is in every turn, even the ones that look unfavorable from our hindered sight. And to know that even death is not a defeat in Christ, I have been set up for an ultimate victory! Oh, what a mighty God we serve! I'm so grateful He came down as a baby so many years ago that we may have this hope and assurance.

Even though I wasn't physically feeling up to joining some other ladies in prayer at the church last night, there was a sense that I should go. So I did. Just as we were about to leave, I received an email alerting me to an update on my online health portal. I logged on to find this message:

Darla,

The biopsies obtained from your colon showed changes of GVHD. Additional tests for infection are pending. Please follow up with your oncologist.

Colon, random, biopsy: Graft versus host disease, grade 4.

Immunostains for cytomegalovirus and adenovirus pending; the results will be reported in an addendum.

I read it aloud to the three other women there, and without request or words, they each got out of their seats...walked over...laid hands on me, and started praying. We wept together, but it wasn't in defeat. There is this sense that God is getting ready to show what only He can do. Grade 4 GVHD is the worst you can get (involves the most organs and has the worst prognosis). Of course. But instead of scaring me, it excites me. While I'm thankful for what the medical world has offered us, it is nothing in comparison to what God can do. Let it be done, God! May YOU receive all the glory and all the honor and all the praise! You are adding fuel to the fire. May the heat of the flames permeate the hearts of the unbelieving. Let the doctor and the medical team get a taste of the God we serve.

Almighty!

All powerful!

Unstoppable!

Oh, how kind the Father is to have prepared me yesterday morning with such contentment and peace. He knew that's what I would need ahead of the news, and it has only continued today.

Who knew that God could use my untrained eye as a gift? He certainly knows how to work all things together for my good, as you'll soon find out from my next journal entry.

A God-Sized Update

December 12, 2018

First off...thank you.

Your prayers!

Oh, how much tireless fighting you have done on our behalf! Pouring out our requests at the feet of Jesus. Pleading with the Father on our behalf. The persistence and joy in which you have done this is quite astounding. You probably aren't even aware that I have been a student of yours, taking notes as I learn from your example. The way you have come alongside us (and remained with us)—out of a willing heart, not a burdensome obligation—is worthy of emulating. Truly, you have enlightened me, challenged me, and broadened my awareness of the vitality of doing life in community.

On that note, God has continued to hold me—cocooned within some sort of impenetrable shield. Unhindered from worry, fear, or potential next steps. Completely at peace. Again, a beautiful testimony to God's hearing and answering the cries of His saints.

Today's visit with my doctor was nothing short of miraculous. The joy that filled the exam room was contagious and palpable. It was much more than some sort of fluffy "think positive thoughts" that allowed us to share unforced smiles and sincere laughter. There was very little talk about specifics, but rather a doctor's pleased report with the direction of things. He had no concerns—either about now or the future of this disease—even stating that he's "optimistic" of our future. "That's wonderful to hear, Doctor," I said. "So are we." He also explained that while the colonoscopy reported the condition of our colon as a "grade 4" this does not equally translate to the severity of GVHD. He said that we are probably dealing with a grade 2 graft versus host. The fact that we could sit in peace in the (false) knowledge of "4" only makes this "2" feel like that much more of a gift! How can God be so good and merciful to us? We continue the course of these high doses of steroids...weaning slowly to the hopeful point of being off (and staying off) of them at some point.

"In that day I will restore
    David's fallen tent.
I will repair its broken places,
    restore its ruins,
    and build it as it used to be."

(AM. 9:11 NIV84)

Now that a diagnosis was in place, it was time to tame my raging colon and unhappy liver with a little thing they call *prednisone*. Though the nurse did her part to prep me for the steroid's likely adverse side effects (things like mood changes, insomnia, etc.), I couldn't fully appreciate her warnings until said side effects (and more) became a reality. Looking back, I realize how tame her language was, 'cause let's be honest—that stuff is an absolute *beast!* Sure, it eventually put an end to my stomach cramps and chronic diarrhea, but the trade-off was...well...near psychosis. They started me on a pretty high dosage at first (98 mg), which surely didn't help. I knew it was bad when I was sitting on the family room floor at 2:00 a.m.

sorting (and sharpening) colored pencils—all while starting a load of the girls' laundry and preparing to make omelettes for the family when they were eventually up. *Yikes.*

Thy Kingdom Come

January 1, 2019

I honestly didn't foresee how hard of a battle prednisone would be.

Perhaps more than any other stage in this year and a half cancer journey, I feel like a stranger in my own body (which says a lot, given the various physical changes I've gone through). To put it in perspective, in my first week of being on the intensely heavy dose of the steroid, I put on as much weight (minus one pound) as my entire pregnancy with Wendy.

It doesn't help that I'm still lacking in the hair department.

Moon face...*check!*

Constant swelling...*check!*

Insomnia...*check!*

Sweat...*check!*

Mood swings...*check!*

Chronic manic state...*check!*

Joint pain...*check!*

Unsettled exhaustion...*check!*

A few weeks ago, I would say I still experienced a tinge of insecurity wearing a mask around strangers (in public places). Now, I would choose that any day over having familiar people look upon my suddenly unfamiliar face. Hiding behind the mask is a gift (Did I just say that?), offering me a moment to forget what I look like unveiled—as if I'm healing from a botched wisdom teeth extraction. I catch friends and family gazing at me differently...in silence. My assumption is they're trying to figure out why my look has changed (quite literally overnight), most likely clueless of the infamous (and very real) predni-sone "moon face" side effect. Makes me want to cower in the corner and return to real life once I'm done with these steroids. In a season when I didn't think I could possibly bend any lower, I've been called to a continual "lower still" state. A couple of weeks ago—as I attempted to adjust to all these changes that came upon me at once—I wondered if this battle is worth it. *Can I just be done, God?* Yet ever since, He has spoken a continual message of this one specific portion of the Lord's Prayer:

"Thy kingdom come,
Thy will be done in earth,
as it is in heaven."

(MATT. 6:10 KJV)

I cannot claim to know all that God is trying to teach me with this repeated message. If nothing else, it's become a daily prayer of mine. But my initial sense is that the Lord is speaking to me about bringing heaven to earth while I'm still here, instead of focusing too much on finishing the race. That until my heavenly home is a reality, the whole point of my present life is to bring HIM glory and reflect who HE is. Funny story about reflecting.

There was a recent evening I retreated to the couch and cried out to God through weeping, "I absolutely hate this moon face." And no sooner had I admitted it to Him that my peripheral vision caught something nearly blinding that was piercing through the window that night. I pulled the drapes aside and saw this big, beautiful ball of light. Yes, the moon. And I knew in that moment what God was saying: *Darla, a moon shines bright because it reflects the sun. And look how beautiful it is when it does. Allow yourself to be a reflection of me.*

I still can't say I like it...or would choose it. But like the old hymn, "When

We See Christ," which reminds me, none of these hardships in life will matter once we gain a sight of the Savior.

Once again, in the midst of the hard, God was blessing.

Printed

January 8, 2019

This past November 8th, I received an incredible birthday gift (one day early):

Good afternoon,

Earlier this year you submitted a story, poem, or piece of artwork inspired by your transplant experience. The Be The Match Patient Support Center has published your submission in a book with almost 150 stories, poems, and art from other transplant recipients and caregivers.

Thank you for sharing your story!

The hardcover book, Blood and Marrow Transplant Journeys: Ordinary people with extraordinary stories, is being printed. We expect it will be available by the end of the year. I'll contact you again with instructions on how you can order a free copy.

The above text was delivered to my Gmail inbox from a supervisor who works for Be The Match (the national marrow donor program from where I received my first transplant stem cells). Also included was a link for an online version where I was able to search for (And find!) my poem.

When I woke up this morning and went downstairs, I saw a mysterious package sitting on the kitchen counter addressed to *Darla Peters*. I crashed early last night, so Brian must have brought the box inside while I was snoozing. Honestly, I had no clue what it would be. Not only was I unable to recollect any recent order I may have made, but I was especially thrown off by the big orange "FRAGILE" sticker gracing its side. What could this possibly be?

Enough suspense.

I opened it, and there was my free hard copy of the book—*Blood Marrow Transplant Journeys: Ordinary people with extraordinary stories*. I'd forgotten all about this! First, an early birthday gift...now, a late Christmas present.

Sure enough, there on page 87 was the poem I had written and submitted, titled "Rebirth."

Unraveled

January 30, 2019

If I were asked to summarize these past few weeks in one word, I would say, "unraveled."

My sparse-to-none communication with the outside world has come (ironically) amidst a season of frequent, transformational whispers from the Lord. While I've had a strong desire (and made several attempts) to share updates, my good intentions have been thwarted. Purposely so, I'm convinced. Even now as I thumb through pages and pages of hand-scribbled journal entries from these past weeks, the vastness of His messages makes it difficult to adequately convey.

And that's okay.

Closer still, the Lord has called me. Hidden further in the shadow of His wings.

It all began with a stretch of uncharacteristically apathetic days. "I don't care" was the theme that darkened the walls of my mind. And while I tried hard to convince my heart that it was true—that sitting in a pit of detachment and indifference was preferable—I finally admitted, "I hate this. This isn't who God created me to be." I was now ready to listen.

As I accepted His invitation to reach out and pull the short bit of string that dangled outside the jumbled ball of yarn the Father began unraveling.

It's funny now as I recognize the parallels with the verses on which I was just meditating this morning. David pens in Psalm 25:

"*Show me* the right path, O Lord;
　　point out the road for me to follow.
Lead me by your truth and *teach me*,
　　for you are the God who saves me.
All day long I put my hope in you."

(Ps. 25:4–5 NIV, EMPHASIS MINE)

Indeed:

He *showed me*...a fear-inducing lie I'd been believing nearly all my life, and spoke the specific truth needed to dispel it.

He *pointed out*...the self-effort and self-righteousness of which I was blinded and needed to repent.

He *led me*...to a place of healthy brokenness and surrender.

And He *is teaching me*...of my utter depravity except for the grace of God, and what it looks like (as I mentioned in a recent post) for HIS kingdom and HIS will to be lived out in my earthly tent.

Man, God is good! If for nothing else other than the spiritual/emotional healing God has done (and continues to do), this journey has been worth every moment. The physical aspect feels far less significant at this point.

(Un)Becoming.

Unraveling

This was the word the Lord gave me one recent morning I awoke, and it couldn't more perfectly describe what the Father has been doing. In a season which has otherwise been very ugly and unflattering (encouraged by the prednisone), the Potter has been diligently shaping and molding this clay into the work of art He intended it to be.

From a medical standpoint, things seem to be moving in the right direction (except for my platelets taking an unexplainable recent dip). The symptoms of my graft versus host disease have waned, and the weaning of the prednisone is (beginning today) down to half a pill (8 mg) a day. I was under the assumption that if "all is well" when I go to my appointment a week from today, prednisone would become a thing of the past. However, in communication with my nurse about some other mediation questions, I found out (today, in fact, via email) that I will continue the beastly steroid for another month or so. My first reaction was one of disappointment—I'm really ready to have my face back (among other things). Yet I will choose to trust that, as John Newton famously put it:

> "Through many dangers,
> toils and snares
> I have already come
> T'was grace that brought me safe thus far
> And grace will lead me home."[6]

I so often want to throw off the yoke (as if that would be better) and "freely" run ahead of the Lord to the "next thing" (whatever that is). Please pray for continued perseverance and a willingness to position myself closely to the Father so that I may discern His voice and follow His leading.

---

[6] John Newton (1725–1807), "Amazing Grace (How Sweet the Sound), 1779, Public Domain.

(Un)Becoming

Just Ask

February 5, 2019

In my last post, I mentioned how I was in recent communication with my nurse about medications. Two of the drugs I currently take were prescribed specifically for use during the time I'm on steroids, so I wondered if they were even necessary to refill (falsely assuming my steroid days were nearly over). Once I found out I had another month or so left on prednisone, the answer became clear.

Translation: Yes, refill both meds.

Because one of the drugs is uncommon (and most pharmacies don't carry it), we were advised to have it filled at the University Hospital in Indy. The only trouble with this plan is it's not exactly convenient to drive over an hour (one way) to pick it up. Hoping to eliminate some of the hassles we experienced previously with a similar situation, I decided to make some calls—first to University and then to our local pharmacy at Walgreens. God was gracious in granting my request to speak with understanding, compliant individuals (I'd had the opposite experience last time I attempted this). Before I knew it, the pharmacist from Walgreens was calling me back with the good news that they could get me the medicine the next day.

Jehovah Jireh. My Provider.

The man went on.... In a very kind (as well as hesitant) way, he "warned" me how much this was going to cost. Even with insurance coverage and a "$1,500 coupon" (Not sure what that was, but we'll take it!), we would still have a 1,700-some-dollar copay. I responded first with appreciation in letting me know, and went on to explain that we were prepared for this kind of news. A similar shock occurred at the beginning of last year upon refilling a prescription; our deductible restarting in January means high costs at this time of year.

Praise God for the several months of free (essentially) medications we'd had up to this point.

So last Thursday afternoon while I was out and about with the girls, we pulled into Walgreens to pick up my prescription. As I pulled the car close to the drive thru pickup window, I heard the Lord say, *Just ask.* And oddly enough, I knew what He was talking about. "Okay, God...well...if there's any way that this medicine can cost less than they said, I pray it would be done." After walking through the normal back-and-forth (name, address, etc.), the pharmacist said how much I owed, though quite honestly, it was a bit muffled and hard to decipher through that intercom system. (Anyone with me on that?) But it certainly didn't sound anything like $1,700 to me...because it wasn't.

Forty dollars.

Let me say that again—FORTY DOLLARS!

I drove away cracking up and crying at the same time. The girls were wondering what had come over me and I said, "Jesus! He did this!" (and went on to explain what the Lord had done). We proceeded to have a little church service in the car, praising the Lord for who He is. Then I called Brian at work (which I rarely do), and he answered with, "Is everything okay?" I was nearly shouting on the other end: "YES! Everything is MORE than OKAY! Listen to what the Lord just did!"

The day just kept getting better. I received a phone call from my nurse later that afternoon, who let me know that the results of my peripheral blood draw to check donor status were in. I'm still 100% donor! In the midst of rejoicing over that news, I shared with her over the phone about our other God-ordained miracle.

Phew! Astounding.

I'm done reliving the excitement of it all...for now *(wink)*.

It's so easy to grow accustomed to accepting things at face value, but

(Un)Becoming

sometimes God has a greater work He wants to do to further display His glory. We just need to ask.

> "Let the people...sing for joy;
>> let them shout from the mountaintops.
> Let them give glory to the Lord
>> and proclaim his praise..."

(Isa. 42:11–12 NIV)

CHAPTER 13

Unfolding

After a stretch where the Lord was so obviously speaking, things became relatively quiet. The thread I had reached out in faith to pull had either unraveled the entire ball of yarn, or caught a snag that required more faith to get past than I had in the moment. For now, I could rest in the beautiful truths the Lord taught me in that season and carry them with me into the next.

By mid-March, I started noticing a slight pain in the upper part of my left ankle. I tried to ignore it, but over a short amount of time, there came swelling, redness, warmth, and radiating pain that had me asking Brian one night, "So, I already took two Extra Strength Tylenol...can I take an oxycodone on top of it?" To answer my own question, no, I couldn't. And no, I didn't. *But* when I reach the point where medication—*especially* a narcotic—sounds appealing, you know I'm hurting! Remembering the cellulitis I had in my right ankle February the previous year; I began to wonder if that might just be what was going on...again.

Sure enough, it was.

An antibiotic was prescribed, and I was on the path to recovery.

Unbeknownst to me (and to the nurse who prescribed the antibiotic), I was allergic to the medication I was taking to heal the cellulitis. When I developed a mysterious rash—on my arms, back, and (mostly) upper legs—they wanted me to come in to do a "skin biopsy" to test for GVHD. Even though I went in knowing about the biopsy, I had a very different picture of how it would play itself out. As soon as words like "chunk," "stitches," and "removing the suture in seven to ten days" were being spoken, it became apparent that I had overly softened things in my mind. This was going to be more of a "procedure" than I had anticipated. Yet God proved to be my help once again as I sang in the shadow of His wing. I had just read that psalm this morning:

"Because you are my help,
  I sing in the shadow of your wings"

(Ps. 63:7 NIV)

It was a total "aha" moment as I was there humming a tune to myself that God put on my heart during the procedure. *That's it!* The psalm was a beautifully concise expression of who God is during each of these unpleasant experiences (my help), where He has me in the midst of them (the shadow of His wings), and what He has me doing while I'm there (singing).

Since I sort of gave it away already, you won't be shocked to find out it *wasn't* graft versus host disease, rather, it was an allergic reaction to Keflex (the cellulitis medication). So much praise!

A week later, I came down with the flu (twice in two years), as did Brian. More rashes soon followed, though these proved more mysterious and less definable as before. They initially diagnosed me with skin GVHD, but over time—since the rashes were morphing and migrating—didn't exactly know what they were. Maybe heat rash? Contact dermatitis? Though the flu had passed, the coughing hadn't. And similar to my previous year's post-flu cough, it was the kind that sent me into absolute "fits."

May 9, 2019

I've lost count, but I believe I've officially reached four weeks of this cold-like *yuck*. I first went to urgent care one evening and got treated for a sinus infection, but seven days into the antibiotic I realized I wasn't improving. Visiting my primary care doctor, she determined that I have seasonal allergies. (New stem cells, new developments.) I've been following her advice for a week, and at least I'm feeling improvement as far as facial pressure goes.

I had a regularly scheduled appointment with my doctor yesterday. After hearing my wheezy cough and of the green phlegm I've been consistently bringing up with it, he suggested I get nose swabbed for viruses. Not that there's anything to do, per se, if I have one. It's just that we won't have to—as he put it—chase after anything more. Good plan. He was pleased with blood work, and the rash—though still present—hasn't worsened. Because he asks me during every visit now if I have "any new lumps or bumps," I *actually* did a bit of homework this time. There is a curious bump on the top of left foot. I'm honestly not concerned about it, but at least wanted a chance for him to see and sort of "document" it. After examining, he said we'd keep an eye on it.

Last night, after another uncontrollable fit of hacking, something got pulled. I couldn't tell if it was in my back, side, rib, or all of the above. Wherever it was, it hurt so tremendously that I actually yelled out a desperate "Ouuuuuch!" I had just walked into the girls' room to help Wendy pick out an outfit for school the next day when it struck. I felt immobilized. In a moment, I could no longer walk, move, breathe, or cough (of course) without triggering severe pain. Using Brian as a crutch, I hobbled over to our room to take two ibuprofen and then downstairs to wrap a heating pad around my entire torso. I felt miserable and had flashbacks to the beginning of my cancer story. I texted some friends to pray. By the time I went to bed, the pain had gone from an 8...to a 5...to a 3...to a 2. And when I woke up, it was nearly gone. What remains now is only the tenderness my ribs felt prior to this incidence due to all the coughing.

Praise God for His healing power.

As much as I'm "over" being sick, God reminded me that had I not experienced "one thing after the next" on this physical journey, there wouldn't be the same story to tell of His grace, His power, and His love.

The month of May has always been one of my favorites. The heavier, more consistent rains of April have mostly passed, and the signs of life are written on every flower newly budded and tree boasting full foliage. You can't miss the message God's creation speaks of restoration and redemption this time of year. Yes, so many parallels to the life in Christ. Yet this spring was different. *Stopping to smell the roses* was no longer the picture of peace and tranquility it once was.

Holding the Umbrella
May 20, 2019

At the beginning of last week, I realized how the dragging on of this cough has served a purpose perhaps I didn't expect. It's brought close to the surface a feeling that's surely been there the whole time, hovering near the ocean floor in hopes of going unnoticed. Now that it can no longer hold its breath, it's come up for air.

I'm really "over" being sick.

"I want to throw off the shackles and run free!" I expressed to Brian. "I don't want to live the rest of my life under the—as I called it—'oppressive umbrella' of leukemia, GVHD, and every other oddity that seems to comes with it all." It sounds so delightful to wake up one day realizing this whole thing has just been some silly dream. Or to turn the page of the book, read *The End*, close it, put it on the shelf, and walk away—never to pick it up or crack it open again.

But the reality is there isn't an obvious finality to this—at least not in my limited range of sight. Apart from several more years of clean biopsies (not to mention no further recurrences of tumorous AML), or some sort of God-ordained miraculous occurrence, this isn't "going away" anytime soon... maybe ever. Another relapse is a likely potential and graft versus host disease is chronic; meaning, it can worsen and/or pop up in various forms until I breathe my last. And the "go-to" for taming GVHD is the beast named prednisone, which needs not my further commentary.

And yet...God keeps bringing me back to the word, *Praise*.

Last Friday morning, as I was getting ready to help chaperone Wendy's field trip, I obeyed the Lord's nudging to begin audibly declaring who He is. The list was lengthy, but far from comprehensive. And when I spoke out, "You are the Alpha and Omega," tears started streaming down my face. Yes, He is the beginning of time and the end of time. But more than that for me, He is the beginning of my leukemia and He is the end of my leukemia. Like two solid bookends on either side of me, I am hemmed in on every side by His unconditional love and unending grace.

Then God, in His spectacular omniscience, brought it all back to the word of choice (umbrella) I had used earlier in the week. He showed me standing under that umbrella, but it wasn't oppressive (as I'd called it before) and I wasn't alone. Jesus was with me, holding the umbrella over us both and wrapping His free arm around me, keeping me close. The storm was still raging, but that was secondary to the peace and protection I had found in Him.

The harder parts of these past couple years haven't always been easy to predict. Take church, for example. I never expected it to be one of the more difficult places along this journey. It makes no sense! On any given Sunday, we have the privilege of gathering with people we love, united in worshiping the same God we love. How can that be anything but joyous? But something about it has felt like sandpaper to my heart, more wounding than healing.

As I quietly sat among the congregation yesterday morning, I began having a private conversation with the Lord. I asked Him to help me understand what was behind all of this. *Why is this so hard?* And He gave me clarity, for which I'm so grateful. Here's what He revealed: Our church serves as a reminder—more than any other place—of how my life has changed. Friendships. Small groups. Ministry.

I don't want to face "what once was." There's pain and grief in that. I don't want this constant reminder of who I was then and who I am now, and how that's affected the way people interact with me (or don't interact with me). I want to feel "normal"—like two years ago "normal."

The topic of yesterday's sermon was the cost of being a Christ follower. In Matthew 10, before Jesus sends out the twelve apostles, He gives them the scoop on what it looks like to genuinely be His. Among the Lord's instructions were these words: "If you refuse to take up your cross and follow me, you are not worthy of being mine. If you cling to your life, you will lose it; but if you give up your life for me, you will find it" (Matt. 10:38–39 NLT).

There is a daily denying and dying of self that is required in following His lead—a letting go of the tight grip on this life and clinging to Him instead. In asking God if there was something in my life I still needed to deny, I heard His answer in Paul's words to the Philippian church: "*Forgetting* what is *behind* and *straining* toward what is *ahead*... (Phil. 3:13 NIV, emphasis mine). In that moment, I knew what He was asking of me. *Darla, deny yourself of "what once was."*

It's as if I'd attached the wrong verb to the wrong adverb. Instead of *forgetting* what was behind me, I've found myself *straining* toward it at times. I guess I sort of understand what the Israelites were feeling as they navigated their way through an ambiguous wilderness: *Can we go back to Egypt now?* Maybe the Lord is taking me on this *biiiiig loop,* and at some point, I'm going to find myself back at the beginning. Wouldn't that be lovely?

But it *wouldn't* be lovely. To (re)gain health but to lose Christ? There is no comparison. If I went back to my "Egypt," the difference would be striking. In fact, it wouldn't feel like "home" at all; rather, like a foreign country to a touring visitor. My relationship with the heavenly Father has been refined through this fiery furnace. There's nothing in "Egypt" worth what I've gained since leaving.

I'm so thankful for the Lord's timing in all of that, because when I was at the zoo with Wendy for her end of kindergarten field trip, things were not good. Making my way through the park, my breathing was incredibly restricted, so much so that I contemplated letting someone know in case it worsened or I blacked out. I honestly wasn't sure what to expect, as nothing like this had ever come upon me. Brian and my family back home were praying, as was I. I kept the picture of Jesus and me under the umbrella on the forefront of my mind...trusting that He was going to protect me through this storm.

And He did.

It's notable that apparently (as I didn't know before this), my brother suffers a great deal with his allergies in the months of May and June, so much so that he purposely avoids being outside during that stretch of spring. His symptoms are different than mine, though he did have asthma as a kid. All this to say it wouldn't be surprising if all of this were new allergies brought on by my brother's stem cells. I also seemed to grow his hair this time around— quite different from the fine, silky, nothing but straight locks I once had. The struggle to figure out coarse, dry, curly hair had me in quite a quandary. In fact, the next time I saw him at a family gathering, I looked at him and said (in a teasing, yet truthful way), "Man, Daniel! I never knew how hard you had it!"

Walking in someone else's shoes (somewhat literally in my case) breeds a greater depth of compassion and grace.

After hearing *another* "pop" during *another* coughing fit, I called my local clinic to see if there was an opening with my doctor that day. There wasn't, but the nurse practitioner was available. *Done!* It's not just the coughing that's troublesome, but the good deal of pain in my ribs from the constant trauma brought on by it. When the NP listened to my lungs, she heard wheezing, so I had blood drawn and chest x-ray taken. There was no pneumonia found (Praise!) or other infection (Praise!), which meant it was most likely asthma or allergies. They suggested having a pulmonary function test to confirm, but my oncologist advised we hold off until a year after transplant (when I will have to run the gamut of tests anyhow).

By early June, my cough was virtually absent, my ribs were tender free, and no wheezing was detected when the doctor listened to my lungs. Things seemed to be moving in the right direction...

Until the end of June when another concern arose.

My Growing Foot Friend (or Foe)

June 26, 2019

A couple of months ago (Maybe more?), I discovered the tiniest bump on the top of my left foot. It was so small, in fact, that the word "bump" seemed too extreme of a title. Still, I felt it necessary to bring to (the doctor's) attention. "Let's just keep an eye on it," were his words of wisdom.

Weeks went by without any noticeable change...until shortly after my last appointment. Maybe it was my imagination, but it looked like the thing had grown. I wasn't certain enough to make a call. Who knows? It could have been the lighting. Too much sodium, perhaps?

But when we were on vacation last week (such a blessed time away with extended family), it became undeniable. The bump now lived up to its name and was a good two to three times its original size. On our drive home, I also discovered that my littlest two toes on the same foot were tingly/numb; I'm guessing the lump is putting pressure on nearby nerves. Since being home, the area has developed a bit of an "ache" as well...especially when I'm sleeping (as I favor my left side).

Needless to say, a call was made and an appointment was scheduled.

Brian and I—along with the girls—made our way to Indy this morning. Because I was added to my doctor's schedule last minute, I predicted a much longer wait; somehow, the opposite played out. We were especially thankful for that, given Clara's and Wendy's added presence.

The good news is my blood work looks great!

The uncertain news is the lump was suspicious to my doctor's examining eye (which wasn't a surprise given its increased size). Because mere sight and touch aren't sufficient in accurate diagnoses, I'm waiting to hear back from General Surgery as to a day/time for a biopsy.

I'm thankful for God's continued peace. I was telling Brian on our car ride home that I don't feel worried...I don't feel scared. Praise the Lord for that! What I am tempted to feel, however, is more of an annoyance. The toddler in me wants to throw myself to the ground, kicking and screaming through selfish sobs, "*I doooooon't waaaaaaannnnaa!*" In the past couple of weeks, I've felt as close to "normal" as I have in a long time. My hair is growing back, my moon face has mostly waned (Seriously, that prednisone!), and my cough is nearly nonexistent. On vacation, I could eat at a restaurant, put my feet in the lake, and hike the "rugged" trail at the Indiana Dunes. It sounds nice to settle in to this cozy place and make a permanent home here. *Comfort* can be such a luring lowercase god.

For all we know, this could be nothing more than a harmless cyst! (Praying to that end.) But because we've walked a similar road before—in breast lump form—it's easier to assume this leads to the same destination (myeloid sarcoma). I liken it to a long road trip. The first time you drive it, the ignorance of the various twists and turns make it impossible to dread upfront. But the second time you hop in the car to make the same voyage, you find yourself having to guard against the anticipation of the parts that make it difficult. Otherwise, *dread* will replace *delight*.

Just this morning, I was appreciating anew the truths that King David penned at the beginning of Psalm 144:

"Praise be to the Lord my rock,

who trains my hands for war,

my fingers for battle.

He is my loving God and my fortress,

my stronghold and my deliverer,

my shield, in whom I take refuge..."

(Ps. 144:1-2 NIV)

As expected, I received a call from General Surgery to schedule an appointment for my biopsy. What wasn't anticipated, however, was learning that July 16th was the surgeon's earliest available opening.

Hold that thought.

I explained to the woman on the other end of the phone that I needed to check in with my doctor before proceeding. Either I had misread (my doctor's) urgency in the matter, or this was as "ASAP" as they came. Leaving a voicemail for my nurse, I trusted she would set things straight—for them, for me, maybe both?

Several hours later, the office coordinator called me back. Bless this woman for all the behind the scenes work she did! She spoke of contacting several departments that didn't work out—one that was booked through September and another that didn't perform biopsies (plastic surgery, apparently)—until she finally landed on Dermatology.

Oh, and get this! They could get me in the next day at 3:00 p.m.

Done!

God is so incredibly fun, isn't He?

Unfolding

June 27, 2019

After my parents left the house with the girls in tow this morning, I lay on the living room floor in a prostrate position. *Discouragement* and *dread* were knocking on the door of my heart; I could hear their taunts but refused to let them in. Admitting my fragility, I wept before the Lord—again, declaring my willingness to follow Him *"even if,"* but also pleading with Him for a favorable biopsy. Per usual, He then called me to praise in various forms: listening to worship songs, revisiting Psalm 103 (and reading it aloud), and then going to the piano to play/sing. It was when I sat before the ivory keys that the Lord gave me a promise to hold on to today—something I (and others) had specifically asked Him for. It came through the lyrics from the Vertical Worship song "Shelter," which offered timely reminders of God's promises to keep me safe and never forsake me.

Other sources continued to confirm that this was, indeed, His message to me. *He is with me* through it all.

The directions my doctor's office coordinator gave me over the phone yesterday were spot-on. We had no issues finding the Dermatology department, and check-in was a breeze—especially considering I was a first-time patient. *Thank you, God.*

When my name was called, Brian stayed in the lobby and I followed the nurse to the exam room. While there was a lot of waiting once I got back there, I actually appreciated the time. It gave me a chance to pray more, praise more, and sing the lyrics to that Vertical Worship song on repeat. In fact, the Lord had me in such a place of peace and rest that I nodded off to sleep for a moment between the numbing and the biopsy.

The dermatologist—well past the age of conventional retirement (at least in looks)—and a young student doctor walked into the room. They made great first impressions with their smiles, handshakes, and mutual desire to know my backstory before proceeding. It wasn't a typical case for them, and they wanted to do it well. In examining my foot, neither could determine what it was. It felt firm, not malleable like a cyst...and if it were a cyst, the location certainly threw them off.

When the student doctor began cutting the area open, I mostly turned my head away and spoke with the dermatologist. But from time to time, I actually would catch a quick glance. That in and of itself speaks of the healing God has done in my fear of medical things (though I still don't like them). Her first cut wasn't deep enough, and with one more dig, she squeezed out a ganglion cyst! She and the doctor were both in shock. And I...I couldn't contain my joyful laughter and a, "Praise the Lord!"

They still sent the tissue off to pathology, for which I'm thankful. But the chances that this is cancerous are "slim to none," according to the specialist.

"Praise the Lord, O my soul" (Psalm 103:1 NIV84).

A few days later, I got a call that I thought was going to be Dermatology giving me the "official" update...it wasn't. Instead, it was from my oncologist's office; he had seen the sample that was sent to pathology and wasn't convinced the doctor had gone deep enough to get the actual nodule. Because of this, he wanted me to come in so he could take a look at my foot. Under normal circumstances, this would rattle me, but I felt confident in what I saw and what the dermatologist had initially reported. I appreciated his desire for accuracy and thoroughness, but when I explained all that I saw and heard the day of the biopsy (seeing the ganglion cyst sac pop out and hearing the dermatologist assure me that chances it would prove cancerous were slim to none), the doctor was satisfied. No need to come in sooner than my already scheduled appointment.

The following afternoon, I received a call from Dermatology to hear the wonderful news that the biopsy indeed came back as "completely normal."

Normal.
That was a word I hadn't heard in a while.
And you know what?
Sometimes it isn't bad bein' a regular ole (Darla) Jo.

CHAPTER 14

UNFINISHED

M edically speaking, things seem to be in a stable place; it's the longest stretch we've had since diagnosis without any sort of new medical anomaly rising to the surface. *Such* a gift! On the last day of July (2019), my third (And final!) round of those five pediatric immunizations was *completed!* What a significant milestone, especially given the fact that this is further along than we got post-(first) transplant. When the breast lump proved to be leukemic last summer, all treatments and medications were immediately terminated. Two out of three isn't bad (2018); three out of three is better (2019).

It was also decided at one of my more recent appointments that the small amount of immunosuppressant medication I was still taking (0.5 mg Tacrolimus every other day) could be stopped, along with my daily dose of fluconazole. As of my last visit, the Bactrim I was taking three days a week was also discontinued, which means I'm currently left with only one medication—a far cry from where we started! Acyclovir twice a day...that's it! Even this shouldn't be a forever thing; the goal is for me to be fully weaned when the time is right.

Now that it's been a year since transplant, my doctor doesn't need to check in on me quite so frequently. The space between my last appointment and next is a whole *three* months, which—I gotta say—takes some getting used to. This past December, they drew extra labs to check my thyroid function—all was well! And though some of my other numbers from that appointment were in the red, the nurse explained that my blood work was quite "normal" given how far along I am post-transplant. Because I'm feeling so well compared to where I've been, it's easy for me to forget my body is still healing. When I really stop to think about it, it makes sense that it would take time to completely recover after having been "reset" twice in two years. I also had a DEXA Scan to determine my bone density; not surprisingly, with the various treatments I've had (including the high doses of steroids) and being that I'm post-menopausal (triggered from the transplant chemo concoctions) I'm considered osteopenia. And since I've graduated from infancy, the two most recent vaccinations I received were adult-sized (as opposed to the infant dosage I'd had up to this point). Ahh, I'm growing up! Beyond all this, I have the MMR and chickenpox vaccines to anticipate two years post-transplant, Lord willing. Some have asked me when my next bone marrow biopsy will be. When I asked my oncologist the same question, his answer was "Never. The only reason you would need another one is if we suspected a relapse." That was certainly welcomed news.

As I sit here penning the last words of the book, I'm chuckling that my biggest "issue" with writing it in the first place was that I had no concept of the ending. Truth is, I still don't. Due to my limited sight and understanding, this is as far as I can see and know for now...and that's a good thing! Yes, sometimes I find myself still itching for some foreknowledge of the unfolding work that God has yet to do, but then I'm reminded of how gracious He's been *not* to plop the whole weight of it on me all at once. In fact, one of the consistent thoughts I've had in writing and piecing this thing together is: *Wow! Thank you, God that I <u>didn't</u> know what was ahead!* The Lord has also kindly reminded me at several points along the way that in this side of heaven, *no one's* story is finished.

And let's be honest...praise God, there is more to be written!

I mentioned in a previous chapter how tough that prednisone stretch was (for several reasons), and how catching a glimpse of my reflection in the mirror one day that winter—with a moon face and barely enough hair to cover my scalp—I thought: *This is so unbecoming!* A morning shortly after that—somewhere in the transition between sleeping and waking—God planted the same word in my subconscious, but with a new and incredible twist:

(Un)Becoming.

I knew what He was getting at, because it seems to be one of the central messages the Lord's spoken to me throughout this journey. Challenging me to see things from a different angle, through a grace-filtered lens. Reminding me to fix my eyes on Him and on the *unseen* things, rather than the things I can see. Or, as *The Message* translates 2 Corinthians 4:16–18: "So we're not giving up. How could we! Even though on the outside it often looks like things are falling apart on us, on the inside, where God is making new life, not a day goes by without his unfolding grace. These hard times are small potatoes compared to the coming good times, the lavish celebration prepared for us. There's far more here than meets the eye. The things we see now are here today, gone tomorrow. But the things we can't see now will last forever."

And what exactly am I—are *all* those in Christ—*becoming* as we behold Him?

"And we all, with unveiled face, continually seeing as in a mirror the glory of the Lord, are progressively being transformed into His image from [one degree of] glory to [even more] glory, which comes from the Lord, [who is] the Spirit."

(2 Cor. 3:18 AMP)

From glory to glory, His sanctifying work is making me (and those who profess to know and follow Christ) more and more like Himself. What a phenomenal promise to hold on to!

Several months before the word "leukemia" was on our lips, the story of Joseph—one of my all-time favorites—resurfaced. Talk about a guy whose life took a left turn...more than once! Having been sold into slavery by his brothers and thrown into prison by his boss for a crime he didn't commit, I think anyone would understand if he were even a little bit resentful. But instead of seeking revenge on his brothers when they approached him in their time of need, he speaks one of the most beautiful phrases to them in all of Scripture: "You intended to harm me, but God intended it for good..." (Gen. 50:20 NIV).

People are often surprised when I tell them that cancer is one of the best things that's ever happened to me. It does sound a bit unconventional, I suppose. No, I don't bow to leukemia as if this deadly disease deserves my praise. It most certainly *doesn't;* in and of itself, it *is* evil and wretched. Rather, I worship the One to whom even cancer must bow—the same God who is able to make "all things work together for good" (Rom. 8:28 KJV). For HIS glory and my benefit! Like Joseph, cancer's attempts to destroy actually made me *better!* The things that were pruned in me along the way, the people I met, the Gospel that was spread, the Heavenly Father with whom I gained a whole new level of relationship and admiration (to name a few)...it's changed my life in the best possible sense. If chemists are able to concoct what we call "chemo" out of lethal chemicals (bad) in order to kill off cancerous cells (good), how much more can God as Master Creator and sustainer take the ugly stuff of life and make something beautiful?

And that simply leaves me in awe and wonder. I can testify to its truth.

I also recognize that the Lord's work in me wasn't for my benefit alone, but hopefully *yours* as well. In fact, it was this very potential which gave me the extra *nudge* to keep writing in moments motivation proved scarce. While you may not identify with the specifics of "leukemia" and "stem cell transplants," suffering is a common denominator to being human. I'll never forget being up in the wee hours of the morning–woken up by the side effects of steroids–and picking up someone else's story of an obscure illness that led him down his own winding road of healing. As I read, it was as if the Lord was sitting on the couch next to me, reaching into the unmet depths of my soul and whispering, *I see you, Darla, and I understand.*

"All praise to the God and father of our Master, Jesus the Messiah! Father of all mercy! God of all healing counsel! He comes alongside us when we go through hard times, and before you know it, he brings us alongside someone else who is going through hard times so that we can be there for that person just as God was there for us."

(2 COR. 1:3-4 MSG)

There's more road ahead, but the directions are the same as they were at the beginning: *Fix your eyes on Jesus.* Look straight ahead. Gazing behind breeds sorrow, looking to the sides stirs up discontentment, and focusing on the uncharted territory ahead induces fear. Rather, He's been teaching me a better way (one I'm still learning): Beholding *Him* who is the *way* and the *light,* I have peace and all that I need to put one foot in front of the other, trusting Him as He treads new ground on this uncharted territory of life. Letting go of control, and letting Him be Lord of my life. *Darla, leave your boat, and come...follow Me.*

The Becoming